ADOLESCENTS

EXPLORING RESISTANCE TO

TALK ABOUT

AND ENGAGEMENT WITH TEXT

READING

Anne R. Reeves
Susquehanna University
Selinsgrove, Pennsylvania, USA

INTERNATIONAL
Reading Association
800 BARKSDALE ROAD, PO BOX 8139
NEWARK, DE 19714-8139, USA
www.reading.org

The International Reading Association attempts, through its publications, to provide a forum for a wide spectrum of opinions on reading. This policy permits divergent viewpoints without implying the endorsement of the Association.

Director of Publications Joan M. Irwin
Editorial Director, Books and Special Projects Matthew W. Baker
Managing Editor Shannon Benner
Permissions Editor Janet S. Parrack
Acquisitions and Communications Coordinator Corinne M. Mooney
Associate Editor, Books and Special Projects Sara J. Murphy
Assistant Editor Charlene M. Nichols
Administrative Assistant Michele Jester
Senior Editorial Assistant Tyanna L. Collins
Production Department Manager Iona Muscella
Supervisor, Electronic Publishing Anette Schütz
Senior Electronic Publishing Specialist Cheryl J. Strum
Electronic Publishing Specialist R. Lynn Harrison
Proofreader Elizabeth C. Hunt

Project Editor Charlene M. Nichols

Cover Design Linda Steere; photo by Artville

Web addresses in this book were correct as of the publication date but may have become inactive or otherwise modified since that time. If you notice a deactivated or changed Web address, please e-mail books@reading.org with the words "Website Update" in the subject line. In your message, specify the Web link, the book title, and the page number on which the link appears.

Library of Congress Cataloging-in-Publication Data
Reeves, Anne R.
  Adolescents talk about reading : exploring resistance to and engagement with text / Anne R. Reeves.
      p. cm.
  Includes bibliographical references and index.
  ISBN 0-87207-536-2
1. Teenagers--Books and reading. 2. High school students --Books and reading. 3. Reading (Secondary) 4. Reading interests. 5. Teenagers--United States--Interviews. 6. High school students--United States--Interviews. I. International Reading Association. II. Title.
  Z1037.A1R44 2004
  028.5'5--dc22
                                                                    2003025354

Contents

Preface

When I began teaching adolescents, I (like many novice teachers, I suspect) was brought face to face with my students' disinclination to study material that was distant from their personal experiences. One seventh-grade student spoke for many when she asked, "Why do we have to learn all this stuff about the Romans? Why can't we learn about something interesting—like shopping?"

As I gained some experience, I spent a good deal of energy trying to show young people that literature and history—and all school subjects—are valuable as well as intriguing. And I found that it is often possible to tell the stories of literature and history in ways that stimulate young imaginations. But even when this succeeded, it became obvious that another, more worrisome and pervasive resistance underlay the students' resistance to content—resistance to the act of reading.

This was harder for me to understand because I have been a voracious reader since childhood. I grew up in a family of voracious readers. Reading provided a great deal of information, and the act of reading felt good. Reading could gratify hungers, ease out knots in the mind, and simultaneously soothe and stimulate. Yet many of my students experienced reading as a burden, an unwelcome and unrewarding labor. Naïve as it sounds, I was surprised at the degree and frequency of their reluctance to read.

Curiosity overtook surprise, however, and after six years of classroom teaching, I decided to attend graduate school to explore the phenomenon of adolescents' reading. Specifically, I wanted to know what reading meant to them and how they used it. I wanted to hear adolescents talk naturally, extensively, and in their own words about reading. It was obvious to me that they were responding to various texts and to the act of reading in ways that made perfect sense to them, and yet these were not ways that I could predict or even fully understand without more information.

The research that I did from 1994 to 2000 for my doctorate in the English and Education program at the University of Michigan, Michigan, USA, gave rise to this book. I spent one year observing in classrooms and talking with teachers and students at a middle school and then moved to the high school in the same district, where I spent almost five years observing, interviewing, and listening. During this time, I recorded the reading stories of the five high school students whose case studies are presented in this book.

My purpose in writing this book is to give others access to the reading stories told by the adolescents I interviewed. These stories may be of interest to anyone concerned about literacy, but I hoped as I wrote the book that teachers, especially, would find it useful. I found these young people's stories to be extremely helpful in interpreting retrospectively the reading behavior of my own previous secondary school students, and I hope that other educators will find that knowing the students in this book will help them be better teachers. What was most helpful to me is that these stories illuminate the students' purposes for reading as well as their reasons for rejecting many assigned texts. Purposes can have many layers, from the superficial to the deeply buried, and I found that digging deeper to get behind the quick labels such as "fun" and "boring" that students were prone to using revealed a bedrock of personal motives.

Chapter 1 tells the story of my own reading life and describes what happens when a teacher who loves to read tries to work with students who, by and large, do not. Chapter 2 prepares for the students' stories through description of the research setting, procedure, and theoretical support. The five case studies follow in chapters 3 through 7. The order in which these students are presented to the reader is not immutable or inevitable; they could be in another order, but I chose this sequence because it makes it relatively easy for the reader to understand the problems with secondary reading, to see how listening carefully to what students say can clarify and explain both problems and reading successes, and to see some ways these problems can be addressed. Finally, chapter 8 closes the book with a retrospective and discussion of the implications for teaching.

I hope that this book will help other teachers see beneath the surface of their students' resistance to reading. I also hope this book will help other teachers see beneath the surface of their students' engagement with texts they love. Understanding why adolescents resist or engage in reading can make teaching more rewarding and successful.

Chapter 1

Investigating Adolescent Readers

During the summer that my daughters were 12 and 14, a German boy about their age came to stay with my family for a week. We took him sightseeing in San Francisco, California, USA, on one long, jam-packed day. We came home exhausted, and as soon as we walked in the door the girls and I automatically, without thinking or saying anything about our intentions, headed for our favorite reading spots and our current books. Stretched out in the hammock, I suddenly noticed that our visitor was pacing around the house, checking out first one and then another one of us, finding us all withdrawn into private worlds. Seeing the three of us through his eyes was a little startling—how very odd we must look to someone who apparently did not assume that reading was the natural thing to do after a long outing. (He had not brought any German books with him and I never saw him look at print, so I could not know how he used reading.) I had not realized that my daughters and I each had a habit of recovering from an exhausting experience by reading a book. But reading seemed such a reasonable thing to do that *not* reading was puzzling— we did not know another way to restore our mental energies. Our guest settled down when I suggested he watch television, and we all spent a peaceful hour.

Embedded in this incident are some points about reading that teachers should keep in mind. One is that for some people, but only some people, reading is an intrinsically delightful activity, similar to listening to music or having a pleasant dream. Text opens the imagination, simultaneously soothing and stimulating the mind. In a text-filled culture, a great distance opens between people who find reading restorative and almost as natural as eating and those who find it to be tedious labor. These groups puzzle—and sometimes alienate—each other with their different assumptions about what reading is and why it is done.

I also bring up this incident because its telling reveals something of the way I approach both the research and the reporting of this study. My interest is in the varieties of reading experience, especially when they collide with schools' attempts to make reading a uniform practice (see Cook-Gumpertz, 1986; Evans, 1993; Moje, Dillon, & O'Brien, 2000, for other comments on this collision). My way of investigating these varieties of reading experience is to ask individual readers what goes on in their minds as they engage in reading, struggle to engage in it, or decide not to engage in it. Speculating about why the German boy was not reading illuminated some of my own reasons for reading: Reading provides a way for me to be by myself and to process stimuli on my terms, at my pace, with my images and thoughts and emotions, selecting and lingering over the parts of the text that I find interesting or pleasing. Looking at my two daughters, one reading a novel and the other reading a heavily illustrated book about the art in King Tutankhamen's tomb, I wondered what their experiences meant to them. I also thought about the bind I felt caught in as an English and social studies teacher, implicitly charged, I felt, with turning all my students into readers when they were telling me, with their behavior more than with their words, that they were not and did not want to try to become what English teachers call *real readers*.

Observing Adolescent Readers

I was inspired to become an English teacher largely because I loved reading and writing and language. I already had worked with two very different kinds of readers: elementary school students in a Junior Great Books group and middle school students in a reading clinic. Students in the Junior Great Books program already were good readers; the point of the program was to engage in interpretive reading and discussion to heighten their enjoyment and appreciation of the stories. Students in the reading clinic, on the other hand, were not reading at grade level; the goal for them was to improve reading comprehension so that they could manage the reading demands of school comfortably. Working with both groups of young people impressed upon me the complexity of reading and confronted me with the great distance between the beginning reader who is struggling with see-and-say decoding, and the imaginative, experienced reader who can move immediately to thinking about intertextual themes and cultural context. The students who struggled to read forced me to see how many steps are involved in making meaning from marks on the page because their reading could, and often did, break down at any one of those steps. Before meeting these students, I was unaware of the complexity of the reading process because the individual steps happened in my own mind instantaneously and effortlessly, as they seemed to do in the minds of the Junior Great Books students as well.

I also had to see that what we did not know about reading was at least as great as what we did know. As a teacher in the reading clinic, I often consulted with the specialists who worked with dyslexic or learning disabled children. These consultations made it clear that the specialists did not have any sure treatments for these students or explanations for their difficulties. We really had very little idea about why reading was so difficult for them, and we could not necessarily attribute these problems to the students' environments. Students in the reading clinic often came from families who valued literacy. Their homes may well have had books, other family members may have loved to read, and the children probably had been read to at a young age. Students who struggled with reading came from all kinds of homes; they were not classifiable by race, sex, socioeconomic status, or intelligence. I had to see that as much as I—and my own children—love reading, it is difficult, uncomfortable work for many people, and no one really knows why.

Teaching English and social studies as a classroom teacher, I worked with enthusiastic readers, resistant readers, and every kind in between. It was in the classroom that I really began to question what was going on in the minds of these students, especially those who resisted reading. I always had found reading so rewarding, so indispensable to getting along in life—how else did one learn all the things one needed to know to make sense of the world?—that I persisted in thinking that if students would just give it a serious try, if they would just put in the time to get past the struggles with phonics and vocabulary and slow decoding that made reading such hard work, they would love the stories and information that reading would bring them.

But I was wrong. They clearly were not all going to become enthusiastic readers, even those who obviously were capable enough when they put their minds to a reading task. Some of them were not even going to become capable readers, necessarily, if they already had passed through 10 years of schooling without becoming comfortable with the printed word. I kept asking myself, What is really going on here? More specifically, What goes on inside students' minds when they are required to sit through English classes, reading, writing, speaking, and listening, concentrating on their language and on others' language? What goes on inside students' minds in their other classes when they are required to use print to learn about science, math, and history? As a teacher, I did not have the time for long conversations with individual students about their reading and learning, and I did not know enough to interpret the evidence I did have about the sources of their resistance. I hope that teachers who read the stories of the students in this book will find connections between them and their own students so that they can see more clearly than I could then into the forces behind reading resistance and engagement.

No one in my teacher education program had prepared me for resistant readers. Whether it was assumed, as Clutter does (Clutter & Cope, 1998), that reading with competence and pleasure was a baseline to be taken for granted or that the problem was not discussed because no one knew what to do about it, I did not know. Perhaps these English teachers were not fully aware of how pervasive reading problems are because, like me, they had immersed themselves in reading all their lives and, like me, assumed that other people enjoy reading more than they actually do. Whatever the reason for official silence on this problem, I still had to face it. When I assigned reading as homework, at least one third of the students—sometimes much more—did not do it. If we read aloud a story together in class, a number of students, varying from one time to the next, seemed restless and inattentive, even those who had demonstrated at other times that they could read at grade level. What was going on in the minds of these students? Clearly, it was different than what went on in my mind when I read. I was baffled.

Reading is a complex phenomenon: It is a cognitive activity, a social practice, a personal experience, and a means of communication. It is impossible to separate the act of reading from the content and the context of the text being read. When educators require students to read, they are requiring students not only to practice a skill but also to focus their minds on the subject of the required text they are reading. Thus reading exemplifies the conflict that many adolescents feel between doing and knowing what they want to do and know and doing and knowing what school requires them to do and know.

This conflict was impressed upon me at one point when I was teaching seventh grade. One night, I watched a television program about a small group of people native to the Amazonian rain forest. In this tribe, young boys went on hunting expeditions with the men and began to use bows and arrows to kill birds and other small prey. Watching them learning how to hunt—alert and eager, taking in every word and gesture of their elders—I was struck by how removed boys in the U.S. education system are from this natural setting. Instead of asking children to find food for the community in the forest, we require children to sit at desks and look at books all day. Not only is the content of the education and acculturation in the rain forest tribe completely different from ours, the method is completely different as well. Instead of working productively alongside men, boys in the United States are required to spend a good deal of time sitting quietly and listening to educators—most of whom are women—talk. I was particularly aware of the discrepancy between these two ways of raising children because a large number of the boys in my seventh-grade classes were obsessed with hunting and war. They spent hours poring over gun magazines, and they argued constantly with their mothers over their desire to go out and shoot songbirds with BB guns. Playing paintball also was a dream to be discussed endlessly among themselves and argued further with their parents. All their story-writing assignments were filled with imaginary hunting and war scenes. As their English teacher, I felt a deep conflict between the expectations of their parents and the administration that I would somehow civilize them by making them enjoy reading and writing about civilized things, and the evidence before me in the form of these boys' complete focus on living warriors' lives.

As I watched the men of the Amazon teach their sons how to track and kill game, I also remembered a journal entry one of my students had written. In it, he described helping his father, a contractor, build a deck for a customer. My student, a person who generally held back from engagement in schoolwork and whose required journal entries usually were not only of minimum length but of minimum content (e.g., "On Saturday I played baseball, but my team lost. On Sunday I went to my friend's house to watch a video"), expressed great satisfaction in the work he had done with his father. He explained how good it felt to be able to look at the deck after it was finished and know that he had helped make something real and useful. This was the first time he ever had elaborated on any of his activities, much less his thoughts or feelings about them. Doing real work alongside adults is what many adolescents long to do. To them, school is only pretend work.

I thought about some of my students who would have enjoyed the rain forest life, learning by doing with their elders something that seemed a natural interest for them. I wished we could be teaching them something they were so eager to learn. However, teaching the prevailing culture is what teachers do, regardless of how the students feel about it. A big part of an educator's job is to persuade young people that they do want to take part in their culture, to play by the rules and enjoy the rewards for doing so. But in the United States, the culturally accepted stories about what is valuable and how it should be attained do not always make sense to adolescents, and I felt confronted by evidence of their alternative values every day.

It is a child's job to make sense of life's experiences and to fit into the surrounding culture. Teachers are charged with the job of helping young people with these two responsibilities. What are the children or their teachers to do when the children's experiences, especially of their own talents and desires, create conflict with their culture? What if, for example, the skill and practice of reading, so valued by contemporary culture, is achingly dull and burdensome to a young person coming of age in that culture? This question, staring me in the face every day, inspired this study.

The Researcher as Reader

Because this is a qualitative study exploring adolescents' personal relations to literacy, the data on which the study is based comes primarily from students' own explications of those relations. As the interviewer who conducted and transcribed those interviews, making all the decisions and interpretations inherent in that process, my own personal relations to literacy are inevitably part of this study.

In fairness to the reader, as well as to the people whose stories I present, my own reading history must be included.

Like many English teachers, I live with happy memories of new worlds discovered in books of childhood. Like young readers everywhere, I grew into a realization that these worlds are a source of information about what we call *the human condition*—not just my life, but everyone's. Other lives informed mine. Fiction was my favorite source of this kind of information because it told me what I really wanted to know about how people thought, felt, talked, and acted—in short, how they lived. I read, or tried to read, everything in the house, but one of the books I loved and read over and over was an old, thick book of fairy stories. Somehow I knew that the magic was not real in any literal way and existed only in the world of these stories, but I also knew that the human characters represented real people like me, and I often imagined, when I was walking or playing alone, what it would be like if a wizened old man with bright eyes should appear suddenly and ask me a deceptively simple question, or how I would respond if a frog or a beast needed my kindness. One particularly compelling scene was a little too frightening to enjoy imagining: the unwary villager in the woods at nightfall hears some beautiful music, and following the sound to a clearing, encounters fairies dancing in a circle. Once lured inside that circle, the mortal human either danced until death overtook him, or, if he escaped alive, lost his wits. In still other versions of this story, the person was doomed to a lifetime of longing for the enchantment of the fairies' music, and without it he or she could never be happy again.

I knew that circle. Or rather, I believed that such a thing could happen to a person, even if I also believed that fairies were real only in stories. Stories themselves were a magic circle, and once inside, it was impossible to get out unchanged. I knew how difficult it was to put down my book and rejoin the ordinary world. Stories made me want to be in a place where Dr. Doolittle could exist, where wishes would be granted if you passed the test. But being captive in that circle was not always pleasant; sometimes the dance was exhausting. When I read *Little Women* (Alcott, 1868), I cried over Beth's death for two days, feeling headachy and weary and unable to find reality as real as the world of the story.

Forty years later, in my first graduate school class, a seminar in Marxism and Romanticism, the professor, Marjorie Levinson, told us to "step into and out of the charmed circle of the text" so as to give ourselves over to the poem the writer had created, but then, also, to ask what the poet was doing in writing this poem, how he was using poetry to ask his own questions or solve his own problems, and how it was part of living his life. Having spent a lifetime practicing negotiation of this charmed circle, I could do it with less psychic disruption now than earlier, but the professor's description of this negotiation started me thinking about three important things I had learned about reading over the years.

First, the metaphor of the charmed circle provides insight into a reader's relation to the text that we need to share with our students. It is one of many facts about reading that we should teach secondary students: We can give ourselves over to the text entirely by remaining in that imagined world, protecting it from the assault of actuality, enjoying the experience as a virtual participant, not wishing for a distanced analysis of it. Or we can remain outside, reading with an intellectual and perhaps a degree of aesthetic engagement but not an emotional or spiritual one. Moving across the boundaries between the world of the text and the actual world, as my professor asked her students to do, is not a universal reading experience. Depending on the circumstances, readers may resist either analysis or immersion.

Second, *reading* is a word that took on meaning when I began reading, so that early in my life it meant a person making meaning from printed symbols on a page. Thinking about my professor's request to explore the charmed circle, I could see that I had been gradually learning to apply this principle to all kinds of metaphorical reading. We try to read everything around us, and the charmed circle image describes our reading of not just books but everything that people create. On one hand, it is productive to respond to the creation as its creator meant us to do; it also is illuminating to step further back and examine the creator and the creation together and ask about their relation to each other and to the culture and human existence as a whole. In this way we can read art, inventions, theories, institutions, and human practices of all kinds, including raising and teaching our children and even including reading itself.

Third, when my professor spoke of the purposes to which the poet put his writing, how writing the poem helped him examine questions and live his life, I finally realized that that is what we all do with reading. I thought I read for enjoyment, but beneath that word lies a vast storehouse of needs, convictions, conflicts, and desires. I thought I read to learn interesting things, but again, that definition hides a great deal of information about how I function both privately and publicly. One reason my students were so resistant to school texts could be that school texts did not help them live their lives. The irony is that adults teach these texts precisely because they believe that the texts will help students in the future, but many students do not understand their purpose.

I began to see that reading was much more complex than my own personal experiences had led me to believe. I was not aware at the time of the research supporting Gough and Hillinger's (1980) description of reading as an unnatural act (see Stanovich's, 1986, article for references supporting this characterization), but, similar to many other teachers who take easily to reading, I had to adjust my understanding of what reading was like for the large numbers of people to whom it does not come easily.

Beyond these tactical questions, I worried about more theoretical ones: Should the purpose of an English class be to help students handle language more fluently and competently? Or should I conceive of the primary purpose of English class in terms of exploring the themes and concepts—questions of self and society, good and evil, what we can know, how we can act—that literature explores? Is it legitimate for English class to become more like a philosophy or psychology class and less like a language class? Because I cannot deny that students who handle written language well have an advantage in the world beyond school, am I being fair to students who do not handle the written language so well if I encourage them to compensate by focusing on learning to think and speak persuasively and by expressing themselves in images, music, or dance? Because contemporary western culture is offering more alternatives to reading, should teachers be promoting other forms of communication such as spoken language, visual images, and music? In short, what role should reading play in English class? What role should reading play in any class?

These questions are versions of a debate between a developmental model of teaching English that "celebrate[s] the personal experiences of students and the expressive nature of language" (Hynds, 1997, p. 5) and a more formal, academic study of English that values knowing the right texts and having the right skills. The latter viewpoint has been reinforced by Hirsch's (1987) "cultural literacy" argument that "what counts in the sphere of public discourse is simply being able to use the language of culture in order to communicate any point effectively" (p. 103). It has been supported more recently by a nationwide emphasis on standards and the standardized tests that go with them.

This debate provided the cold comfort that the questions I was asking about the goals of English class had no settled answers. But I was convinced that what goes on in individual students' minds as they confront reading should be a significant part of the data used to guide my teaching practice. However, most of the studies about individual secondary students' reading were written from a teacher's viewpoint. Rosenblatt's (1978) transactional theory of the work that readers do when they engage a text was more helpful. She emphasizes the importance of what readers bring to the text— those experiences and needs that profoundly affect the meaning they will make from it. Once readers (with their experiences and needs) begin to make meaning of the text, they create what Rosenblatt calls the poem. This reading, or meaning making, is not a fixed object but an event, an "experience shaped by the reader under the guidance of the text" (p. 12). Rosenblatt's reader response theory acknowledges readers' agency and goes a long way toward explaining differences in responses to the same text. My question then was, What needs and experiences are young readers bringing to the texts schools require them to read? Are they able to create a poem from these encounters? If so, what is the nature of that poem?

Another debate that interested me was about the texts that secondary students should be reading. It was sometimes embedded in the larger debate between the child-centered progressives and the traditional-culture conservatives: Should students be allowed to read young adult fiction or even popular fiction in school? Or should school time be reserved for the classics, the treasures of Western civilization? What was suitable only for leisure reading, and what standards made it so? As a reader and an educated member of society, I had benefited from reading those books that libraries classify as "literature" (separate from "fiction"), but as a teacher, I valued those texts from which students could make something meaningful, and I was not confident that it would be possible to teach youth the full power and wisdom of many classics, or even enough of that power and wisdom to make these texts the best choices for teaching students how to be successful members of their society. I was concerned about the distaste for literature that our curriculum seemed to be generating in many young people. Furthermore, I remembered being enlightened, moved, and educated by young adult fiction when I was a teenager. Therefore, I admired the work of writers such as Sarland (1991) who carefully examined some students' responses to both required school literature and books the young people chose to read. He describes how and why the readers he talked with "find themselves" (p. 79) in certain texts (the ones they choose) but not others (usually the required canon). He concludes with the provocative thought that

> Perhaps, as English teachers, we should see our role not as telling them what they should know and what they shouldn't know, but instead as helping them to understand what they do know and enabling them to learn what they want to know. (p. 133)

These debates and theories formed the beginning of the conceptual framework of this study. I was looking for ways to understand why and how reading worked or did not work for my own students, and from this beginning the fundamental questions of this study took shape: Why do so many adolescents resist reading? Why do some books engage some teenage readers but not others? What can teachers learn from listening to students talk about their reading?

Reading This Study

Because reading is a largely invisible activity, it is difficult to know what is going on in a reader's mind as he or she looks at text, which is why answers to these questions are so elusive. The obvious way to get as close as I could to the source of information about adolescents and their reading was to talk with them, repeatedly and probingly, in a series of interviews that provide the basis for this study (see chapter 2 for information on methodology). Five students' reading stories are presented as case studies. Each student reads some things with pleasure and satisfaction but finds school-assigned reading boring and pointless. Readers disagree about what is interesting and boring, even when they are in the same class, have the same teacher, and are reading the same books. Conversations with these students provide insight into the reasons for their different responses and offer teachers ideas for maximizing the chances that a student will connect with a particular text.

The goal of the interviews was to learn what it is about each student that generates a connection with a text or resistance to it. All the students can and do read when they find something that interests them. Their responses depend on the match between what they are looking for and what the text offers, although they rarely are aware of just what it is that makes the match rewarding. They speak of books being "interesting" or "boring" as if these qualities reside in the books themselves, but what becomes obvious in the course of the interviews and subsequent analysis is that the reader's connection with a book or resistance to it comes from psychological and cultural factors that constitute the student's purposes for reading. These purposes may be so deeply embedded in the adolescent's mind and environment that he or she is largely unaware of them. They are taken for granted. They seem inevitable, and to a certain extent they are, because they have to do with that relentless transformation of the present into the future, the movement from adolescence to adulthood.

As students engage in the work of growing up, they look for ways to negotiate the process of becoming a successful man or a woman in their society. Their reading choices reflect their understanding of what manhood or womanhood consists of in their culture. Reading choices also reflect their individual desires and their conflicts with societal norms. They use fiction and nonfiction as sources of information, inspiration, comfort, and challenge as they make their way through adolescence toward adulthood. They resist those texts that tell them something they do not want to hear, and they resist texts that take them away from the experiences they seek. Naturally enough, they also resist texts that they do not understand. Contrary to some popular belief about adolescents seeking only thrills, these interviews show students' purposefulness in their reading choices. Different students find satisfaction in many kinds of texts, but when they do choose popular culture texts, such as readings about vampires, sex, violence, or romantic fantasies, they are doing so for reasons based on their psychological and social development, not, as so many adults assume, because they are rebellious or thoughtless. On the contrary, these interviews reveal

each student's serious focus on integrating desires and responsibilities and on finding a way to be a happy, productive member of
the community.

Chapter 2

Investigating the Reading Process

Qualitative research has been well defended in the past 20 years as a legitimate source of useful and reliable information. But as Denzin (1994) reminds us, "In the social sciences there is only interpretation. Nothing speaks for itself" (p. 500). When an educational researcher employs qualitative methods, as I do in this book, he or she not only relies on interpretation but also must be scrupulously careful about representing the people in the study responsibly, giving particular attention to those participants who are not yet adults. While this study does not precisely fit the category of teacher research because I was not teaching the students whose stories are presented here, I have been a secondary teacher and am currently a teacher educator, and the data for this study was primarily collected within a school. Teacher research has been described as "a way of thinking about issues of power and representation and storytelling and much more" (Fleischer, 1995, p. 4), a characterization that I apply unhesitatingly to my research. Another question often raised about this kind of study is what use can be made of the findings—how reliably can they be applied to other situations beyond the research site? Howe and Eisenhart (1990) answer this by saying that "successes and failures can only be judged relative to given purposes" (p. 3). The purposes of this study are to uncover sources of resistance and engagement with reading and to explore ways of using that information to make teaching practices more rewarding and effective for all concerned. Those who are involved with adolescents' reading and those who make these teaching explorations will judge the study's usefulness.

What Is Reading? Theoretical Questions

When students first made it clear to me that the experience of reading took many forms, I had to realize that my own reading did not match a universal norm. Nobody's did, because, of course, there is no universal norm. When I began to read about reading, I discovered an enormous field of theory, research, personal accounts, and some speculation. It is much too large a topic to cover completely here, but I do want to give some idea of the kinds of thinking people have been doing about what reading entails. All of what follows can illuminate the individual stories that the five students tell by shaking up assumptions about and scrutinizing the particulars of what happens when a person reads. I found these ideas helpful in uncovering my own buried assumptions and beliefs about reading.

Discussions of reading repeatedly emphasize that decoding the symbols of a text is not reading, although, of course, decoding is a necessary part of the process. The critical feature of reading is making meaning from the text. This is what makes reading so important and at the same time so controversial. Theorists get into serious ideological disputes when they ask whose meaning is acceptable or which meaning is privileged. More ideological disputes arise when they ask about the nature of the "self" that makes meaning. Furthermore, in recent years theorists, researchers, and educators have expanded their understanding of what a text is and, therefore, of what reading a text means, so that now films, images, music, mathematics, social interactions, and social structures of all kinds are included in their definition of texts to be "read." Any sign system can be the source of a text. Indeed, any artifact, object, or event can be "read" or examined for its history or other information.

This expanded understanding of what we do when we read has resulted in a widespread use of the term *literacies* (e.g., Gee, 1989; Phelps, 1998) and an increased appreciation for the kinds of knowledge that people have as well as the kinds of interpretation and meaning making that they do on a daily basis, even when they are not proficient readers and writers of alphabetic texts or are not using alphabetic symbols at all. Alphabetic literacy is further contextualized by symbolic interactionists and social constructionists who emphasize the importance of the social purposes for reading, in all senses of the term, and the social contexts and interactions that reading entails (see Moje et al., 2000, for a helpful discussion of the theoretical positions taken by symbolic interactionists and social constructionists). Street (1984, 1986), for example, discusses two models of literacy: *autonomous literacy*, a name for what people learn from writing essays in school, a literacy whose benefits are perceived as economic success and intellectual development, and *ideological literacy*, which describes literacy practices embedded in ideological, and therefore cultural and social, practices. Ideological literacy includes oral as well as written language and is used to interrogate power relationships rather than reinforce existing means of social control. Street (1986) argues that the autonomous literacy model erroneously ignores the social contexts in which literacy is used; in fact, all literacy is ideological because it is all "encapsulated within cultural wholes and within structures of power" (p. 2). Heath's work (1980) makes clear the social uses and methods of reading practiced by members of a community within their community. She emphasizes that examining actual reading practices in daily life reveals how much people's learning to read and write depends on what they need to use in their jobs, communities, and families.

If we focus on alphabetic literacy, we can distinguish different ways to read alphabetic texts. Rosenblatt (1978) describes aesthetic and efferent reading, the first being reading of literature for aesthetic, artistic experience, and the second describing reading for information. Langer (1957) makes a related distinction between the communicative function and formulative function of texts (see Sumara, 1996, pp. 22–23, for a brief summary and discussion of Langer's terms). One of the difficulties many people have in school is that the difference between reading for an artistic experience and reading for information is rarely explicitly addressed. Learning to read in school involves various kinds of comprehension tests, and these can lead students to believe that their job in reading is to figure out what the text says by finding the facts, whether in a science textbook or a novel. This basic form of comprehension is still a form of decoding, albeit a more sophisticated kind of decoding than the discovery that words are represented by printed symbols. Most students are not explicitly taught, and consequently do not understand, that learning what the text "says" is not all there is to learning to read. Their belief that the text is a clear, omniscient container of meaning, produced by the expert and anonymous "they," is consistent with both their elementary school training and the

New Criticism belief that the text is an object holding a particular meaning (Eagleton, 1983). This view has a long history (Tompkins, 1980). In recent decades, however, reader response theories have gone far toward displacing text-based beliefs about reading.

Reader response theories are important to my study because as the name indicates, they put the reader and the reader's social and psychological context in the spotlight. This group of theories is not a unified or internally consistent dogma but rather a loose collection of theoretical ideas that cover a range of positions, each putting different aspects of the reader's experience and relation to the text in the center of the examination field. Rosenblatt (1978), one of the earliest writers to remind us that the reader as well as the writer does creative work, describes the text as serving as a blueprint to keep the reader from leaving the text too far behind but emphasizes that the reader makes a personal reading using all the experiences and influences that he or she brings to the reading of the text. The writer and reader work together. Like Rosenblatt, Holland (1975) and Coen (1994) look to the mental phenomena readers generate and experience as they respond to text. Holland focuses on the particular psychological makeup of the reader who brings personal fears, desires, and defenses to the text, and Coen (1994) looks at ways that people deal with unacceptable rage and fear as readers and writers. Coen and Holland, interested in both literary criticism and psychoanalysis, accept the importance of unconscious forces in reading and writing. Holland believes that each person has what he calls an "identity theme" (1975, p. 60), a characteristic way of seeing and interpreting experiences that shapes a person's reading of a text, while Coen concludes that readers can "seek comfort and connection with the author as other, for whatever needs of another we may have....we collude with the author in her or his poetic transformations of badness into poetry" (p. 183).

Iser (1993) asks why people create literature, what they use it for, and how they use it. His (1974) account of reading compares looking at text to looking at stars in the sky: One person sees a dipper, another a plough. Thus a given text has far more potential than any one individual is likely to realize. Particularly useful to me in my study is Iser's (1971) insight into the gaps or indeterminacies in the text that each reader fills in a personal way, thereby creating an individual reading from a text made up of certain fixed and observable elements. All texts have gaps because it is impossible to communicate everything. A good way to see these gaps clearly is to listen to ordinary speech and pay attention to the number of times the listener infers meaning or fills in missing bits. Inferring, guessing, and figuring out what is meant are constant features of conversation and reading.

Because I was searching for explanations of the work that readers do, I was interested in the ideas of Bleich and Fish, both of whom moved much further away from the text and toward the meaning-making the reader does. Bleich (1978) argues that because words are symbols in our minds for experiences, reading is a process of creating a symbolic mental world; therefore, the only text is the one in our minds, and interpreting what we read is interpreting our own symbols. Hence, reading is properly thought of as resymbolization, an operation within the reader's mind by and on the reader's own faculties. Fish (1980), too, argues that there is no text but in the reader's mind; texts are, in effect, written by readers because textual features (e.g., line endings) that may appear to be forms in the text for readers to work with are in fact the product of the reader's interpretations. For Fish and Bleich, the text, in the usual sense of the word, does not exist.

The difficulty with dispensing with the text is that we are left with only the meaning the reader makes rather than a meaning negotiated between reader and author. This leaves open the possibility of absurdly idiosyncratic readings. Whereas Rosenblatt, Holland, and Iser agree that the text provides a stimulus to which readers respond differently—or with which they work differently—both Fish (1980) and Bleich (1986b) depend on the community of readers, large or small, to prevent readers from ranging too widely in their interpretations. In theories that move so far in the direction of the reader that the text disappears entirely, other readers, rather than author's words (i.e., the text), serve to keep the results of reading comprehensible and communicable.

Culler (1975), a structuralist whose work supports the reader response critics in their shift of emphasis away from the text, draws attention to the conventions of literature and criticism that underlie both reading and writing. Individual readers are not the focus of Culler's argument, as they are for Rosenblatt, Holland, and Iser; rather, the community's shared agreements about literary forms are the basis for making meaning from text. Readers with what Culler calls *literary competence* create the text through their understanding of social and literary traditions. Knowledge of the language alone is not sufficient for making meaning; one must know how others have read and written.

Culler (1980b), however, harshly criticizes Holland's (1975) psychological work with readers' identity themes. As a structuralist, Culler is interested in explaining facts about literary form and meaning rather than in individual differences among readers, arguing that we should be "study[ing] reading rather than readers" (1980, p. 56). Culler ignores the pedagogical implications of Holland's study, showing no interest in the steps by which student readers gain competence, but argues instead that we professionals should focus on making public our own skilled interpretive processes. While I agree that writing about what good readers do is essential, I reject the notion that what goes on in individual student-readers' minds is unrelated to a general account of what reading consists of. But as a structuralist, Culler is interested in the similarities of reading experience (among experts), whereas I am interested in the differences (among both experts and beginners), in part because I believe that these differences are inevitable and valuable, as are other varieties of human experience, and in part because I believe that not understanding these differences accounts for many of the problems of instruction in secondary schools. I believe that it is possible to use these differences as a source of instructional success, but first we must examine and appreciate them.

Furthermore, although in my study I do not attempt to find the psychological identity themes that Holland (1975) found in each of his readers, I do assume that each of these students is an individual only partly—sometimes slightly—influenced by classroom context. Formulating or recognizing a person's identity theme is difficult. Holland, in addition to being possessed of an acutely analytical intelligence, has been well trained in psychoanalytic theory. He does not attempt to explain how others (e.g., teachers or students) might go about working out their identity themes, nor does he imply that it is necessary to do so. He uses what he believes to be his college-student readers' identity themes to make his point that readers respond to texts the way they respond to everything else—by conferring meaning according to who they are. Although Thomson (1987) implies in his discussion of student readers that they can be taught to find their identity themes, I believe that they can and should benefit from psychoanalytic theory in a more general way, namely to see that their own and others' readings have a private, personal aspect "but still reach agreements about a 'reality' that we know only as a public consensus among private persons" (Holland, 1975, p. 250).

Moje et al. (2000) make an excellent argument for understanding that learners in school are people with multiple and changing subject positions "shaped by relations within and across contexts" (p. 166). The interviews I conducted strongly support that view, revealing students' concern with present and future roles and identities, inevitably influenced by the past. Although for all of us identities are multiple and changing, each of us functions as a system of agency, coherent in the sense that we have reasons for behaving as we do. It is the logic of each person's behavior that I use the case studies to examine. Like Holland, I seek the individual's psychological reactions and responses to texts, but unlike Holland, I am primarily interested in the pedagogical implications for adolescents. Their responses signal successes and failures of reading in school. These hot spots of engagement and tension and cold spots of indifference would remain invisible if all reading theorists avoided studying individual readers and if we did not recognize the complexity of the person who is either reading or refusing to read.

Some theorists who are not usually included in the reader response category nonetheless further reader response efforts to examine readers' active engagement with or creation of the text. Feminist (e.g., Fetterley, 1979), gay and lesbian (e.g., Rich, 1979), African American (e.g., Morrison, 1993), and postcolonial criticism (e.g., Bhabba, 1994) all describe ways of reading from a position outside the dominant cultural discourse. These critics work against the grain, reading subtexts and examining assumptions invisible to mainstream readers and writers. Theirs is a highly active reading that goes beyond bringing a text to life; their goal is to interrogate and challenge texts that seem to insist on being read from the center of a cultural nexus. Such transgressive readings are invaluable models for understanding the source of adolescents' alienation from school readings. Students who do not read from a middle class, college-bound cultural center are likely to feel confused or bored by texts written by highly literate adult authors for highly literate adult readers, especially when those texts require extensive knowledge far outside the students' life experience and when the characters inhabit a fictional universe in which contemporary adolescents can find no home. Corcoran (1992) and Giroux (1983) are among the critical theorists who argue that teachers should encourage students to read resistantly by explicitly teaching them to recognize and reject textual ideology, even though that may mean forgoing a full emotional and aesthetic engagement with the literature.

In this way, critical theories, such as Street's (1984, 1986) autonomous and ideological literacy models, overlap reader response theories. Street, like Giroux (1983) and Gee (1989), does not attend to the moments of connection between reader and text, but instead draws attention to the broader social context and the politics and power policies therein. This view of literacy shares with reader response an interest in ways that texts are received and used by reader-agents, in contrast to text- and author-based views that focus on text as agent.

Reader response theorists do not, in general, write about the cultural power struggles that occupy critical theorists such as Street and Giroux. The contrast between these points of interest—one group directing their attention to the reader's mental activities, the other to the culture surrounding and affecting the reader—highlights a feature of reading research that makes it both fruitful and difficult: Although reading superficially appears to be a simple activity requiring only that a person look at a text, more careful analysis reveals a deeply complex activity that involves not just a person's eyes (or fingers, in reading Braille) and forebrain, but the whole personality and a storehouse of knowledge and experience. Further, although some readers experience reading as a personal, individual activity, it always is embedded in a culture and, therefore, has significant—even life-changing—effects on those who do and on those who do not practice it (see Moje, 2000, Purcell-Gates, 1995, and Stuckey, 1990, for studies of people on the margins of literate culture).

This complexity gives reading researchers, theorists, and teachers a wide choice of where to focus their attention. One clear model is described by Bell (1993), who conceived of four common-places of literacy: the Text, the User of the text (reader or writer), the Society surrounding the user, and the Process or interaction between Text and User. Bell does not distinguish between reading and writing and so does not enter the debate whether the reader or the writer is more important in determining what meaning results from reading. But even with this conflation, these four commonplaces provide generous opportunities for the researcher's, teacher's, or theorist's choices. Bell is interested in the interactions of pairs of these commonplaces; she cites Heath (1983) as documenting the influence of Society on the Process of reading, and Freire as an example of a theorist who is most interested in the action of the User on the surrounding Society.

Mapping out one's own understanding of the relationships between these four elements can be illuminating. In this study, the center of my attention was the User, engaging in Process, responding to various Texts within a context determined by Society. Sometimes the student was a Non-User, not engaging in Process, refusing Texts, but still—always—within a social context. I concentrated on following each student's lead into her or his own understanding of what was at work in encounters with text. In subsequent analysis, I tried to keep the student's personal vision in mind while I stepped back to include other cultural and psychological forces to which the student may not have drawn attention. Another way to describe my focus is to say that the best match between my interests and a theoretical mode of investigation is a phenomenological and psychological approach, using Iser's, Holland's, Bleich's, and Coen's insights into the way that readers' personalities, needs, desires, interests, cultural positions, and gender, together, determine their reactions to texts and the judgments they make about a story or a character. Social forces were hard at work on the adolescents I studied, as when a student would say that friends had told her that she should stick with a book because it got better further on, or when someone found popular culture to be an irresistible alternative to schoolwork. The English teachers in this school did not make an explicit, ideological point of creating a community of readers, but the five readers' stories presented in this book are studded with evidence of other people's influence on readers' reading.

 ## Defining Terms

The construct of adolescent that emerges from my reading of these interviews is a hybrid of theories, because, as Miller (1989) observes, each theoretical school focuses on a different quality of adolescent experience, rather than offering a full picture. In different theories, that focus is on biological changes, social environments, cognitive development, emotional growth, or interactions among two or more of these. One feature of adolescence that stood out for me as I talked with these students was their work of identity formation. This concern with identity worked on several fronts: gender (the teenagers in these case studies reveal a deep and abiding concern with what it means to be a man or a woman in their culture), cognition (some had made decisions about how they best learn and think, while others were struggling to understand themselves in this regard), and interests and talents (these were quite clear to all the interviewees). Affecting all these aspects of identity was concern with social relationships on all levels and of all kinds: friends, family, teachers, other students, employers, members of the students' churches—virtually every relationship absorbed at least some attention.

Recently, the intersection of identity formation and literacy has received significant attention from researchers that provides insight into these young people's concerns and behavior. Identity is not seen as a single, inflexible, essential state of being, nor is it the purpose of adolescence to develop such a state. Rather, as they grow up, people develop and experiment with various identities that they express in various contexts. The potential difficulty with the idea of multiple, shifting, contextual identities is that if it is carried to an extreme, we wind up with social and psychic chaos. Moje (2002) argues for the concept of hybrid identity as a way to recognize that people can see themselves, be seen by others, behave, dress, feel, and think in numerous ways but still be coherent persons. Hagood (2002) examines the ways that texts structure readers' identities and contrasts that power of the text with the power of the reader as active subject who resists being constructed in an undesired way. In my study, I saw students in both these situations: being brought into the world of the text against their will when that world caused psychic pain, and also exerting themselves as subjects who controlled their experiences by refusing to read what threatened them. At other times, students eagerly sought out texts that supported identities they enjoyed.

The students in this study, being in middle or late adolescence, have made some decisions about the roles and positions that they see as being available to them, but in their ongoing negotiations of these possibilities, they show marked awareness of the differences between the roles that school imposes and those that are available to adults in the larger culture around them. As adolescents on the threshold of adulthood, they are heavily engaged in developing their future selves.

Overview of This Study

The heart of this research is a set of case studies, verbal portraits of five young adults and their relations to reading and, to a lesser extent, writing. Because reading and writing are not just school activities but ways of taking in the world and communicating with it, much of these students' lives outside school are included. Because reading and writing involve a whole person, overlapping with many other interests and activities and relationships, much of what might at first glance seem to be outside the purview of reading and writing is included as well. Case studies permit a reader to understand what goes on in the minds and lives of individuals who make up a particular population—in this case, high school students—by examining the complexity of those lives.

Each of the case studies grew out of conversations with the student. I did not impose a structure on the interviews because I wanted to see where each student would take our talk about reading and what else would come up in connection with that talk. As a result, each case study is structured a little differently from the others, although in each case I present information about the student's reading history, preferences and dislikes, reading attitudes and beliefs, and the meaning that each student makes from readings that he or she finds important. I also include a discussion of each student's writing because a person's production of text can reveal a great deal about his or her relation to text. Writing can show us what a writer notices and decides to use in writing and what audiences he or she chooses to address. Ultimately, these students' writings show us what meanings they make of their experiences as they transform those experiences into stories they value and carry with them.

What sets these case studies apart from other research that focuses on individual students (e.g., Fry, 1985; Hynds, 1997; Millard, 1997; Moje, 2000; Sarland, 1991; Smith & Wilhelm, 2002) is the depth of examination each student and I conduct on his or her reading situation. Each student has a story to tell but is not always fully aware of the nuances or implications of that story until they are revealed by sustained, probing, interpretive readings. Students' words are quoted at some length so that readers can see what I am responding to as I attempt to probe beneath the surface of immediate reactions and encourage the students to explore their own ideas and feelings. One example of this is our dissection of the meaning of *boring*. In addition to analyzing talk, an essential part of my interpretation is finding a pattern in pieces of evidence (spoken or behavioral)—a pattern that explains engagement or resistance and that may not be immediately visible to the student. The result of this work is a series of fine-grained portraits that reveal, within their cultural settings, the intellectual, social, and psychological uses to which these young people put reading. Just as important, these portraits reveal why much of school reading is not used in this same intellectual, social, and psychological work.

I attempted to make each of the case studies both fair to the student and enlightening for the reader. As a result, each student's story is a full chapter in length and contains complexities and sometimes contradictions.

My researcher identity was that of observer, interviewer, and interpreter. In my conversations with students and teachers and other school personnel, I wanted to be friendly but to maintain a degree of distance so that I could avoid becoming overly enmeshed in the ups and downs of students' and teachers' lives. Above all, I wanted to be an interested, sympathetic, and clear-minded listener. This mode of inquiry, known as interpretive research, has as its goal what Alvermann (1999) describes as "understand[ing] from the point of view of the researched what (and how) meaning is attached to specific phenomena" (p. 139). Interpretive researchers are expected to be in the world of the research subjects and yet outside it, avoiding becoming part of the world they study and yet imagining what being in it means for others.

In some ways, this felt very natural to me; I always was extremely interested in everyone I spoke to and valued the interpretations they made of the experiences they had. On occasion, it was difficult to maintain distance, for example, when Sting's family moved in the middle of his sophomore year. He was distressed, and I ached to see repetition of his pattern of leaving friends, sacrificing schoolwork for the cause of making new ones, falling further behind, and getting more discouraged. There were moments of celebration, too, when Duke showed up at school full of energy and had a great time reading a play in English class and when Valisha officially cleared all the hurdles to graduation. At these and other times, I could offer sympathy or congratulations but had to maintain some reserve.

Interpreting the data for a qualitative study such as this one means trying to put all the pieces of evidence together into a coherent whole. Evidence is primarily students' words, and because I am interpreting them according to the way I read not only the words but also the person and the situation, my interpretation is never a fact. Qualitative research is not replicable, like laboratory research, so my goal is to report what I heard, saw, and thought, and invite the reader to draw his or her own conclusions. I expect that readers will sometimes—maybe often—come to different conclusions about what a student was thinking or feeling. That is wonderful; it would not happen if readers were not doing their own readings of these students, and my primary goal in writing about this research is to connect readers with these students.

I do need to make it clear that in keeping with the interpretive mode of inquiry that I was engaged in, I was not looking for nor did I find a system of categories into which I could put students. It would perhaps be convenient to say that each student is representative of a certain kind of challenge and opportunity for teachers, but such categorization would be Procrustean. I chose instead to preserve as much as possible the natural, individual character of each student's reading story. In this way, I hope to focus the reader's attention on the whole person that each student is and to emphasize that it is this whole person, complete with invisible background and immediate concerns, who is doing the reading.

Students in this study repeatedly referred to the conflict they felt with both the institution of school and the assignments of particular teachers who promote its goals and cultural values. This conflict revolved around reading, both as a process that students did not want to engage in (because they generally believed that they already could read well enough and did not want to be bored further) and as a practice applied to particular texts (the literature taught in English classes and the textbooks used in other disciplines). This conflict may be overt or subliminal, expressed or withheld, but too often both teachers and students are frustrated, bored, angry, or resentful when reading is the work to be done. My interest was in getting beneath the surface of this conflict to exam-

ine its origins. Thus, the case studies begin with individual responses to classroom work because it is at this student-to-teacher
and student-to-text level that conflict is kindled, felt, and expressed.
But cultural influences from outside the school are an extremely
important part of the conflict as well. That culture is brought into
school via students' clothes, magazines, food, ideas, memories, and
desires, and students clearly are making decisions about which
cultural influences are most appealing, interesting, and important
to them. Nothing highlights differences between the school's goals
and the choices available outside school more than students' reading choices. For the purposes of stimulating both public discussion
and more effective teaching practices, I aim to understand and ex-
pose the dissatisfaction that underlies resistant behavior of individual students whose reading is not working for them in school.

The School and the People in It

The site of this study is Oak Creek High School (pseudonym) located outside a small Midwestern city in a suburban, working class
neighborhood. Oak Creek High School is within 25 miles of a major metropolitan area in one direction and within 12 miles of a large
public university in the other. The student body of Oak Creek High
School is racially and socially diverse: Just over half the students
are African American; slightly fewer than half are white, and there
are a small number of Hispanics and Asian Americans. When a
Middle Eastern family moves into the area, the student body may
include one or two Middle Eastern students. As the school counselor said, "It just depends on who's living here." The school's total
enrollment is about 600. Most of the students come from working
class backgrounds and conclude their education with high school,
but some students are from middle class families and extend their
education beyond high school. A few come from families under severe economic stress, and a few come from families with enough
money to travel to the Caribbean during spring break. The dropout
rate is high; the counselor told me that about 200 students enter
ninth grade each fall, but only about 100 graduate four years later.
Not all 100 "missing" students drop out of school altogether. Some
of them move (and, of course, other students move into the area as
well). A sizeable percentage does not pass all the required fresh-
man classes, so they remain first-year students longer than one

year. Several high school teachers explained to me that the middle school from which most students come passes them on to the next grade even when they do not pass their classes; therefore, students are not prepared for a different system at the high school, a system that requires passing grades for promotion. Even though students are informed repeatedly that they will not move on if they do not earn a D or better, many students do not seem to take passing classes seriously until they have failed one or more of them.

About 60% of the graduating seniors end up going to college, but sometimes not until several years after graduation from high school, and then they often attend a community college. One teacher told me,

> A lot of them get where we want them to go, but they don't take the most direct route. They have their own ways of getting there. They'll come back to visit after five years and say, "I'm over at the community college now," or "I'm going to open my own business soon." They don't usually take the university route.

The students at this school sometimes refer resentfully to what they see as the school's unearned reputation as having serious problems with drugs and high rates of various social problems such as crime and teenage pregnancy. According to the staff, many of the students who drop out are caught up in these problems, but the students who actually attend school are not any more involved in risky or illegal activities than students in much more affluent communities. The exception to this might be that Oak Creek has a higher rate of student pregnancies than schools in more affluent communities. After the school day ended, I often saw small children appear with their grandmothers or caregivers to meet their teenage parents. But when I walked around the school and I observed classes or students in the cafeteria or the library, I did not see any evidence of drugs or criminal behavior. I did see careful monitoring of the hallways by adults equipped with two-way radios who checked students' destinations and sometimes escorted them to class. I did not see student resistance or active resentment of these monitors; the monitors seemed to be accepted as a necessary part of school life.

Although this constant monitoring might seem excessively heavy, the authoritarian control of students' whereabouts was mixed with a great deal of friendly, personal give-and-take. The staff seemed to know most of the students, and as far as I could see, the hall monitors did, in fact, know everyone. They had connections in the community outside the school, as well, and I frequently heard a student say, for example, that a teacher lived down the street or that an aide was a relative. The attendance officer lived in the neighborhood and sent his own children to the school. One of the students presented as a case study, Rosa, belonged to the same church as the library aide. This caused Rosa some minor trouble when the woman wanted to censor some of the books Rosa planned to check out, but Rosa avoided the problem by waiting until someone else was at the check-out desk when she wanted to get a book on abortion or on some other topic that did not meet with church approval. In general, however, this overlap between community and school worked very well to promote a sense of belonging and being cared about. One of the teachers said that the fact that some of the students came from disadvantaged homes meant that the teachers could develop bonds with them by filling in some of what was missing in their lives—everything from hugs and jokes to meals and rides to school.

Students Talk About Reading

Because I am interested in finding out what goes on in reluctant readers' minds when they are faced with a reading task, I wanted students to tell me in their own words about their reading. The selection of the five case study students and my understanding of their relation to reading is grounded in a preliminary set of interviews with 25 students. I first wanted to get a broad picture of the range of reading stories they had to tell. This was important for my own education in how the students at this school talked, thought, and felt about reading (see chapter 8 for a summary of the information that emerged from these 25 interviews).

Students who were 18 years old signed their own permission forms, but younger students had to get their parents to sign a permission form and then had to bring it to school and give it to me. The interviews were semistructured in that I had a list of questions I asked each student in some way and at some time during the interview (see Appendix A). I did, however, follow the students' leads for the particular course each interview took, as students brought up various and multiple associations with reading not directly addressed by my questions. These associations reinforced my observation that reading is a whole-person activity and that reasons for doing it or not doing it are consistent with an individual's social and personal network of interests, needs, and talents.

In addition to the open-ended interviews, which yielded a sprawling, interrupted, and sometimes disjointed narrative of the student's involvement with literacy, I asked four of the case study students to read passages from school texts and from other leisure-reading texts of their choice and to explain what was going on in their minds as their reading progressed. (I did not ask Valisha to read aloud; she had said vehemently that she disliked reading that way because it made her feel incompetent.) I discuss the students' reading aloud in the individual case study presentations.

I interviewed all these students at school individually and privately for an hour each. (Some of the follow-up interviews with the students presented as case studies went on longer than an hour.) I brought food for the students to the interviews—whatever they asked for, usually chips and soda, but sometimes sandwiches or chocolate or, on one occasion, fruit salad. I did not ask the students specifically why they had volunteered to be interviewed, but the offer of free food clearly attracted some, while others obviously were interested in talking about reading. The students in the latter group usually were students who read well, liked most reading, and were interested in talking about reading, a phenomenon that reminds me how little opportunity many students get to talk about reading on their terms. They did not want to talk about school texts but about the books they enjoyed. They also enjoyed talking about how much they had read over their short lives—reading constantly in elementary school, developing favorites among authors and titles, sometimes sharing an interest in reading with a relative (usually their mothers) or a good friend. They did, however, have some kinds of reading they did not like, which I will discuss in later chapters. Two seniors saw themselves as "literary men" who wanted to become writers and who took their literary educations seriously. They, too, had favorite genres, authors, and titles, but they were more willing than most of the others to tackle the canonical authors in English class—not that they necessarily enjoyed these books; they just recognized that these texts are culturally and artistically important.

I did not include students who were diagnosed as learning disabled because my intention was to examine the reading habits and attitudes of students who make up the general population rather than a specialized portion of it. As I expected, those students who have severe difficulties with reading generally were not interested in talking about it, even when food was offered, and did not volunteer to be interviewed. The exception was one senior who is profoundly dyslexic. He raised his hand when I was passing out permission forms, and then he came up to me after class to say that he had an unusual reading story that I might find interesting. When we sat down for the interview, he somewhat nervously asked me what kind of a reading test I was going to give, and when I told him that I did not have a test but wanted a conversation, he looked quite relieved. Apparently he had heard me say *reading*, and then his past experience with strangers who come into classrooms to talk about reading took over, so he assumed that a test was the next order of business. Once that was cleared up, he talked freely about his disability, his family's support of him, his love of gardening, his plans to become a landscape contractor, and of the severe headaches, stomachaches, and neck pains that trying to read induced in him. I was glad to have talked with him because he reminded me, again, that although for me reading is a physically comfortable and comforting enterprise, it literally makes some people ill.

In deciding which students I would present as case studies, I looked for students who would be in some ways typical of the interviewees, but who in other ways were particularly well suited to the purposes of this study. I made a conscious choice to include both male and female participants, as well as both African American and white students, because I believe that being a reader or not is not a function of race or gender. I also was looking for people who would be willing to make the journey into their own experiences and desires and talk about what they found there. The final group of five is composed of one African American male, two white males, one African American female, and one white female.

Chapter 3 focuses on Sting, a ninth-grade white male who is in many respects a good reader but is failing most of his classes. Sting is deeply absorbed in professional wrestling and rap music. He uses these interests to connect socially with other boys as well as to express both what he experienced when he lived in a big city and what he fantasized about the man he would become. Duke, an African

American male in the 12th grade, is the focus of chapter 4. Duke also is an excellent reader in many respects and is involved in sports and rap music. Duke's story makes very clear his patterns of resistance and engagement with specific required texts and the desires that underlie those patterns. Duke's story is followed in chapter 5 by Rosa's—a white female who is the only enthusiastic reader of the five. But Rosa reads illicit texts—romance novels and mysteries—and does not do well with most required school reading, especially expository texts. Valisha's story is presented in chapter 6; Valisha is an African American female who is the only person of the five to have no happy experiences with reading, and yet she is in the process of finding out what reading can do for a person. On her own, for the first time in her life, she has begun to read books from cover to cover. Chapter 7 focuses on Joel, a white male who is feeling the results of not reading since middle school and wondering why he cannot understand so much of what he is required to read in high school. Joel's story reveals that he does engage with some stories, that he does try to read his assignments in school (although he often forgets homework), and that there is much that teachers can do to help him.

All the students I interviewed had personal stories about reading that would make interesting and instructive case studies. The five I chose are not necessarily more interesting than others, but all told stories that are uniquely individual and yet have features in common with many other adolescents. Each student makes a clear contribution to a picture of adolescent reading. Each, also, was able to think and talk about the phenomenon of reading and was willing to pursue questions that at first appeared unanswerable. Although I feel sure that we could learn much from those less articulate students who seemed to face a blank wall when I asked them about responses to reading, penetrating the mysteries of that blankness would require a different kind of study. Of the five I do present, Joel comes closest to representing these less articulate students. The other four, especially Duke and Rosa, enjoy talking about their experiences and opinions.

I originally intended to interview parents of these five students if I could reach them and if they were willing to talk with me. As it turned out, Sting's mother was the only parent I interviewed. I tried calling Rosa's mother several times but never reached her, and as the student interviews progressed, I collected so much data—far more information about each student than I could include in the case studies—that I decided not to gather more data from parents. Including data from one parent interview but not others is another instance of my sacrificing symmetry of reporting format to preserve the integrity of an individual's story. I include some of the information I learned from meeting with Sting's mother and having three telephone conversations with her because Sting's family life was a significant factor in his current literacy practices. Talking with this mother reminded me that parents' views of their children are cumulative, incorporating all the years and stages of their children's lives. Sting's mother sees him as a good reader and as a smart person capable of getting excellent grades, as he did in elementary school. In contrast, teachers' views of their students are much more likely to be snapshots of students at particular times of their lives. Most of Sting's teachers saw him as smart but disengaged from school; rather than comment on his reading ability, they mentioned what they noticed about him, which was primarily that he did not turn in assignments and concentrated instead on his social life.

I interviewed each of these case study students between three and five times, in addition to informal brief exchanges and classroom observations. I also interviewed and spoke informally with teachers. Teachers are not a focus of the research but are included as part of the context in which students are practicing (or not practicing) literacy. Talks with teachers showed me how they related to reading themselves (the English teachers are enthusiastic readers; most of the others are less so) and how they understood the assignments they were giving to students. Teachers also provided their own views of the individual students. In some cases, they had known a student for a number of years; for example, Valisha's business education teacher had known her and worked with her for her entire high school career. The attendance officer, who also coached the track team, had known Duke for all his high school years. The teachers' appreciation of the students, as well as their occasional frustration with them, helped me develop a fuller picture of the students' relations to and experiences of school as the students talked about their lives inside and outside this institution. Talks with teachers also stimulated my thinking about what could be done to help them, as well as the students, to improve the state of reading in high schools. In chapter 8, I discuss my recommendations in detail.

Reporting

Because the students' experiences and viewpoints are so important to this study, I want to present their words in a way that will be easy for a reader to follow. Therefore, I use the narrative analysis forms explicated by Riessman (1993). Following Gee (1991), she breaks the narrative text into pieces according to linguists' structural analysis of speech. When I laid out one student's words in this fashion, I found that his speech, which had seemed somewhat indirect and cluttered with verbal fillers such as "um" and "you know," suddenly became much clearer, and even beautiful, like a song. When I removed most of the fillers, it was obvious that laying out the students' words in narrative blocks does more justice to the speakers than representing speech in prose sentences. The reader, too, can follow more easily the speaker's thought because the speaker's words are laid out in lines that consist of chunks of meaning. Because it is so important for readers to get to know these students through their words, I want to present those words in a way that facilitates that process.

On many occasions during the interviews, a particular story or topic of conversation was interrupted by digressions. When a story was told piecemeal, I collected the parts from various points in the interview and gathered them together to present in one block. I included explanatory or additional information that I added during transcription in square brackets. Sometimes a student would return to an earlier idea or tell more of a story in different interviews. Again, I gathered together what he or she had to say in one place so that I, and the reader, could see more easily what the student's point was. When the different parts of a story were separated by more than just a prompting question from me, I put an extra space between chunks of speech. As an example of the whole process, here is how I would deal with a student's answer to my question about why she likes reading plays. The student says,

> In the beginning—if you've done a play, like, I've done school plays in seventh grade, and familiarized with my character by reading the beginning, how they have the descriptions, and in this book, they have, like, a filler before and afterwards on what happens and stuff, but I like reading plays a lot because you get to figure it out for yourself, about the characters and everything, and just, like, visualize

how that person is and everything like that. And I'm a visual learner, so I like plays a lot better.

A few minutes later, when the conversation had turned to writing, she remarked, "I'd rather write a play or a script than a short story. I go blank when it comes to short stories."

As is always the case, I had to create the punctuation that I believed most faithfully recorded the student's speech. That decision is built into every act of transcription. But I went further than generating punctuation. This student's passage is not included in the body of the book because she is not one of the five case studies, but if I were to include her words, I would present them in the following format.

> If you've done a play—
> I've done school plays in seventh grade,
> and familiarized with my character by reading the beginning,
> how they have the descriptions,
> and in this book,
> they have like a filler before and afterwards on what happens,
> but I like reading plays a lot
> because you get to figure it out for yourself,
> about the characters and everything,
> and visualize how that person is and everything like that.
> And I'm a visual learner,
> so I like plays a lot better.
>
> I'd rather write a play or a script
> than a short story.
> I go blank when it comes to short stories.

I omitted the first phrase, "In the beginning," because I realize that the student began by talking about character descriptions at the beginning of a script, and then changed her mind and backed up to fill me in on her own experience with plays. Then, she picked up the idea again of reading the beginning of a script once she had laid the groundwork. The opening phrase, "In the beginning," looked confusing to me when I tried including it, and because it doesn't contribute to the student's point about why she prefers reading plays to reading prose, I felt justified in omitting her false start. I also could omit "If you've done a play," because that, too, is superfluous to the making of her point, but in an effort to keep the students' voices as intact as possible (while I also strive for as much clarity as possible) I chose to leave it in. These are the kinds of decisions and compromises I made throughout the writing of these case studies.

In the five case studies that follow, I count on extensive quoting of the students' words to keep the students in the foreground. I present my own analysis and interpretation in prose following each narrative block of student speech (and Riessman's, 1993, and Gee's, 1991, method of narrative analysis helps the reader keep the distinctions between the students' words and the researcher's interpretations quite clear because the two voices are presented on the page in different forms). I hope that the reader will engage actively in his or her own interpretation of the students' words as well.

Chapter 3

Sting: "I Stopped Bein' a Good Little Boy"

Sting was failing his ninth-grade English class. At 14, he rarely read anything, and when he did, his favored texts were wrestling magazines and online conversations in Internet chat rooms. He resisted school reading and writing assignments vigorously unless they happened to connect with his interest in sports, rap music, or science fiction.

What makes this all-too-common story particularly interesting is that Sting was not always resistant or failing: When he was in elementary school, he was a devoted reader and a straight-A student. He used to read, he says, for an hour every night before he fell asleep. He loved adventure stories, especially the Choose Your Own Adventure series and *Jurassic Park* (Crichton, 1999). Furthermore, when he was in the fifth grade, he was reading at a seventh-grade level. The school wanted to double-promote him into seventh grade, but instead his mother chose to have him stay with children his own age. Then, in sixth grade, he stopped reading and failed four of his classes. He says now, shaking his head in a mixture of rue and disbelief, "I got four E's on my report card, and they passed me." He has been in and out of academic failure ever since. He has not been reading since then, either. Why did this happen?

The reasons for the change in his relationships to reading and school are both simple and complicated. The easy explanation is that the internal upheavals caused by the onset of adolescence coincided with external upheavals in Sting's circumstances—his parents separated and his mother moved from place to place with Sting and his younger sister and baby brother. Sting was forced to leave new friends in new schools as soon as he got used to them and begin again in yet another place. "We've moved, like, five times," he says. "And I gotta make friends." These new friends let him know that readers were nerds. The combination of Sting's need to make friends quickly and his adolescent desire for independence from authority led to his rejection of reading, an all-but-complete rejection that meant he stopped reading for pleasure in his spare time and gave up on assigned reading in school. Reading was not cool, and it certainly was not as important as a social life. Sting began spending as much time as he could with other boys, abandoning the imagined worlds of books in favor of the popular worlds of sports, video games, and hanging out.

The more complicated explanation of Sting's conversion from academic success to "getting sidetracked and being the class clown," as he puts it, involves a more detailed analysis of what he has rejected and what he has embraced. It also involves a movement outward to examine broader social phenomena and inward to examine personal psychological phenomena. All these examinations overlap and connect with one another in various ways. In this case study, I will follow the thread of Sting's reading through the labyrinth of social and personal events, broad and narrow, that constitute his adolescence.

The Student We See

Sting was a skinny adolescent boy going through a growth spurt so rapid that it seemed to be on the verge of outstripping his ability to eat enough to keep up with it. When he talked to someone, he sometimes pushed his pale, soft face forward, peering through his thick glasses as if he was outgrowing his prescription as he was outgrowing everything else. Like almost every other boy in his school, he wore big clothes—long, loose shirts over pants so large and baggy that, although he hitched them up every time he stood, they slid immediately down to the precarious position on his hips that signaled to other kids his membership in the adolescent mainstream. Tight clothes, as he disdainfully referred to clothes that fit the way adult clothes do, were worn only by nerds.

Clothes were important to Sting because the social message they carry affects the most important aspect of his school life—having friends. His mother favored the imposition of a dress code because she believed that children of Sting's generation were too concerned with clothes. She compared her experience with Sting's.

It's a social event.
When I was in school,
Levis was the main brand,
and if you didn't have a pair of Levis, they just...
but it didn't interfere as much with our work
as it does now.
You don't have this type of shoe,
that type of shirt,
that type of pants,
if your hair doesn't look this way,
if you don't talk a certain way, you know,
then it's like everybody in the school will shun you.
I was hoping that they would pass that law—

Sting knew that she was referring to a recent attempt to impose uniforms on students in this public school district and disagreed firmly in his usual outspoken way: "I don't want it." His mother continued wistfully, "Uniforms. I want it so bad," but he told her, "No. Hey, I like my K-Mart Janco-lookin'-like pants." (These are pants that he bought at K-Mart "because we can't afford no real clothes...and there was these pants, and everybody thinks they're a pair o' Jancos, which are, like, $50 pants.") A minute later he added, "Think about this. That the way I dress is...it's something like a free speech, or freedom of speech, or som'n like that."

His mother concurred: "To a point. But when you're in school...."

Sting's answer, in contrast to his mother's concern with schoolwork, showed his focus on his social standing: "But nobody's beatin' me down, nobody's doin' nuttin' to me for wearing this," he said, indicating his clothes with a sweep of his hand from shoulder to knee.

Sting's stage of adolescence and his concern with his clothes and social life had everything to do with his relationship to reading, which seemed as precarious as the position of his pants on his slight frame. When I asked him what came into his mind when he heard the word *reading*, his prompt response was, "Read a book that I don't like." He went on to say that the literature anthology they used in his English class was such a book. When the teacher told the class to open their anthologies and read a particular story, he thought, "Oh my God, here it goes again with another stupid...," and to avoid it he said,

> I start talkin' and talkin'
> and we [Sting and the friends he is talking to] ain't gettin' nuttin' done,
> and she starts yellin', and threatens me,
> and I'm sayin', "Ohhh, I'm about ready to tear your head off—"

Occasionally, Sting was sent to the office for arguing with his teacher, but more often he tried to control his tongue: "So I just open up the book and read it as fast as I can." While it is true that Sting and his ninth-grade English teacher were often in open conflict, that was the exception; generally, Sting was friendly to everyone, including teachers, even if his friendliness did not extend to being attentive in class. "The teaching I just ignore," he said. "I hate it when people are trying to teach me something I don't want to learn."

Sting first began to turn away from reading in order to fit in with new friends who themselves had no interest in reading. When he told his story, he did not talk much about becoming bored with the stories he had previously enjoyed or of anything else going wrong with his relationship to books and reading. What he remembered was that he hated feeling friendless in each new place he moved, so he put more time and attention into other people. Consequently, his habit of reading faded into a childhood memory. However, three or four years later, he had become so estranged from reading that he dreaded being assigned a story and turned to his friends in order to avoid being bored, irritated, and, perhaps, confused by reading a story he was not interested in. The young reader that he used to be was hidden deep inside him, but it still made its presence known at unexpected moments.

Sting the Reader: Changing Choices

Mahiri (1994) describes the literacy practices of a group of adolescent boys who were deeply interested in basketball and demonstrated remarkable abilities to use reading, writing, and critical thinking when basketball was involved. They were far less accomplished and interested in school reading and writing, however.

Alvermann (1998) describes schooled literacy as a discourse that alienates children and devalues what they already know, a view shared by Bintz (1993), Moniuszko (1992), and Oldfather (1995). The students I interviewed for this study evinced the same division between school values and their own. All insisted that I understand two facts: (1) that they could read and (2) that they did read when they were interested in the text. The problem with most (and for some students, all) school reading is that it is not interesting. Sting was like all the others in this respect; in the first conversation we had, he said,

> If there's som'n I like to read about,
> I'll read it, if I got an interest in it.
> Like pro wrestling, stuff like that.

In the second interview, he reaffirmed his position.

> If it's something I'm interested in,
> I like reading it.
> I like reading about science stuff,
> or science fiction, or stuff like that,
> like alien guys crashing places and taking over the world....

When I asked him if he liked real-world science, he hesitated slightly before he said, "Some stuff," and then, interestingly, in the next breath jumped immediately to "I like reading the Bible." I later learned that the church he and his family attended (see section on "The Writing We Read" for related discussion) taught a fundamentalist dogma that opposed evolution, causing some conflicts with Sting's longstanding interest in science and explaining both his hesitation after my question and his association between science and reading the Bible.

Sting and his family attended church every Wednesday night. Sting wrote in a journal entry that he hated to miss church, "but I usually don't miss it all the time." He said of the Bible he read that

> it's in the newer versions
> where they ain't got all the "thou"...
> I didn't mind the older language,
> 'cause I like how they said it,
> it was interesting how they did it.

This is typical of the puzzle Sting presented to his teachers: Here was a boy who was failing English but was interested in the archaic language of the King James Bible. Here was a boy who hated reading the literature anthology but could be drawn into its stories in spite of himself. For example, he said about one story,

> In "Little Dog Lost" [McCord, 1967]
> I felt like I was the little boy that lost the dog.
>
> Could I end up like what happened?
> Am I going to mess up the same way he did,
> Could that happen to me?
> I could lose my dog.

The empathy and imagination Sting showed in this remark are discussed further in the next section on reading ability. Note here that in spite of his earlier statement that the stories in the English literature anthology were "stupid," he did speak freely about his identification with a fictional character, responding to literature with imagination and self-reflection. It was impossible to know with certainty at this point in Sting's development whether this kind of response was a remnant of childhood reading that was disappearing forever or an enduring quality of readership that was only temporarily eclipsed by the changes of adolescence.

Although Sting complained about required school reading, he did continue to use printed text as a source of information about his favorite subjects. His preferred reading material was professional wrestling magazines. When I asked him if he would actually sit down and read an entire article in one of the two thick wrestling magazines I had brought to an interview, he said, "I'd read both entire books." He was altogether enamored of professional wrestling, but he also liked football. When his English teacher brought the class into the library to choose a book from the Accelerated Reader collection, the school librarian offered Sting a book about Dan Marino, the former quarterback for the Miami Dolphins professional football team. The Accelerated Reader program is a set of books and related materials available for purchase by schools; each book is labeled for reading level and given a point value based on its length and other measures of difficulty. When students have finished reading one of these books, they take a 20-question test on the computer about the book. If they pass the test, they receive the designated number of points. If they fail the test, they do not receive any points.

Sting was pleased with the Marino book.

> I like it, and it's not too long—
> I think it was, like, 60-som'n pages in it.
> That's not too short.
> I think it's cool, man.
> It tells a lot about how—
> how good he was in college,
> and then how he got drafted and everything in college.
> I found out some sweet stuff,
> like he used to be a baseball player and a football player in college.
> I think it was the Boston Red Sox
> wanted to draft him while he was in college
> for a couple thousand dollars a year,
> and he turned 'em down
> because he liked the sport of professional football.
> He's my favorite player of all time.

In a later interview, Sting told me that he read almost all of the book, but did not finish it because he kept forgetting about it. Then, when he was supposed to take the Accelerated Reader test on the book, he learned that the school did not have access to that particular test. "So I ended up readin' it for nuttin'," he said. When I started to remind him that he had spoken of it with approval earlier, I got only as far as "Except you did say—" before he admitted, "Well, besides I liked it." This juxtaposition—"readin' it for nuttin'" against "I liked it"—illuminates the tensions that pulled Sting in opposite directions. On one hand, he read only because he had to in order to pass his English class and graduate from high school some day. He resented not getting paid in grade credit for the work he had done. On the other hand, he was interested in football, and reading was not onerous for him when he cared about the subject. He did learn some "sweet stuff" about his football hero. But now Sting was far enough away from being the little boy who loved to read that he needed to be reminded that he did, in fact, occasionally enjoy a familiar partnership with print.

Reading Ability

Sting's mother kept his state proficiency test scores, not only in her records but in her memory as well. In our interview, she told me that when he took the tests in first grade, his percentile scores were in the upper 90s in all the tested subjects. "He topped his class," she said. When I listened to Sting read aloud from wrestling magazines, I could see and hear that he read fluently, finding the units of meaning in the sentences and reading by phrases rather than by words. Even more telling, he was able to use context and background knowledge to understand both the main point of a paragraph and individual words that were new to him.

When he read the first part of an opinion column from a wrestling magazine, both he and I got a little lost temporarily: he because some of the vocabulary was new to him, and I because I lacked the background knowledge to make sense of the references being made. We sorted it out together by pooling our resources, and Sting, who had already correctly guessed at the meaning of the words he did not know, understood what was going on before I did.

> "So where was my *TV Guide* cover. Jeez, if Mankind and his dirty Socko can share space with the *TV Guide* logo, then why can't I? Heck, why can't Bill Apter?"
>
> [Sting interrupted his reading to remark, "I have no idea who that is." Then he resumed reading.]
>
> "I wish I could say that Mankind will never grace the cover of this great publication, but due to the theme he will have to do for now. Anyone hungry for ravioli?" (Menkowitz, 1999, p. 51)

At this point I interrupted to say that, so far, this made no sense to me at all. I did not have the slightest idea what the writer was talking about. Sting patiently asked if I knew what *TV Guide* was and then told me that *TV Guide* covers had featured six World Wrestling Federation (WWF) wrestlers. (Note that the WWF is now World Wrestling Entertainment. See Mazer [1998], pp. 15–16, and Ball [1990], pp. 49–50, for more information about the WWF.) Sting also explained that Mankind, a famous wrestler, had made a commercial for Chef Boyardee

> where he was holdin' Mr. Socko
> and he was goin' around eatin' everybody's
> and he yells out,

"Mmmm! Beefy!"

So far, Sting was doing much better with this text than I was. In the next paragraph, however, he met his match in vocabulary.

> "There are those who love to disparage the great legacy of rule-breaking."

He knew that a legacy was, in his words,

> like a hand-down
> from a back-in-the-day form of rule-breaking,
> and it's just going on and staying.
> From generation to generation.

The word *disparage* gave him more trouble; he felt that he knew its meaning on some level, but he could not explain it. When I gave him the choice between defining *disparage* as "talking good about something or talking bad about it," he was confident about saying that it meant "putting it down."

Other words in this article he did not know were *huckster*, *heinous*, *savage*, and *deviant*. Once we had finished talking about these words and it was clear to both Sting and to me that he did understand the paragraph in spite of unfamiliar words, he said, "God, you're just teachin' me stuff that my teacher just couldn't teach me." Sting's remark points out how a curriculum that is removed from students' interests makes the teaching job as difficult as the learning job. I suggested that if his teacher were able to read a wrestling magazine with him, things might be different. I also reminded him that the learning was going both ways because I was finding out as much about wrestling as he was about the new words. During this reading, we talked about background knowledge, and I told him how confused I was without it.

> When I'm listening to this, I'm lost because it keeps referring to people I never heard of and to events that I don't know anything about. So I'm finding it very difficult to actually process the information that you're giving me, and I keep thinking, I'm sure this is how you feel in history class or math class sometimes.

Sting's reply was simply, "So now you got the feeling."

Sting had three weaknesses in reading: vocabulary, background knowledge (related to school texts), and motivation—which is a constellation of experiences, tastes, purposes, and desires. His strengths also were in his experiences, tastes, purposes, and desires—and in the imaginative, responsive quality of his mind. When he was interested in reading a text that he believed would give him information or experiences he valued, his imagination made the reading into a lived discovery.

> I'm visualizing it in my head
> and makin' it sort of come to life.
> It's like a dream
> you know how you see a dream?
> Like when I dream
> I never see myself,
> but I know I'm there.
>
> I didn't mind the Anne Frank one,
> the way it was put,
> it just caught my attention.
> Made me read.
> In the beginning I didn't really want to read it,
> but since I read it before,
> I knew what it was about,
> so I already gained interest in it
> back in fifth grade.
> I thought it was kinda sad...
> because of everything that was goin' on,
> and they had to be locked up.
>
> When I'm pretendin' all this stuff in my head,
> I'm usually in it, too.
> I pictured her—
> I pictured me as one of the characters,
> I just put me in the picture,
> and then it felt like I was in the story already.
> I felt like I was that one dude that she didn't want to talk to,
> but then at the end
> she ended up talkin' to.

Wilhelm (1995, 1996b) argues persuasively that reading is seeing and that good readers live the stories they are reading by imagining themselves watching or participating in the scenes of the book. Readers who do not visualize the events of the book have no way of experiencing or working with the story. Sting (like most people, I suspect) sometimes read with great engagement and mental drama, as when he was reading *Anne Frank: The Diary of a Young Girl* (Frank, 1993), and sometimes with none. His failure to engage with a story, he said, began at the beginning: "If the lead don't attract me, then I don't even pay no attention to the story.... It just don't come visually."

Like any resistant reader, he was discouraged by long books that he thought would be boring, which included just about all books that were not about one of his particular interests. Being assigned a book by a teacher made the whole process worse.

> Accelerated Readers...
> they were all stupid.
> I didn't want to read a long book
> about how Sal got his hair cut in a museum
> while his friend was dying.
> I don't like reading big books.

His own assessment of his reading ability was, I think, realistic. He said flatly, "I can read," and furthermore,

> I can read real fast, too.
> If I needed to,
> like for books or somethin',
> if they're, like, due the next day,
> can read a chapter in about maybe,
> if it's real long,
> probably about half and hour
> but if it's a short five-page,
> I could probably do it in about two minutes.

Sting said that he was never taught to skim a text, that skimming just came naturally to him. It was a skill that he used often in school, and I had a chance to observe it in action during our second interview. I had come to the interview with a cold soft drink, a bag of chips, and two wrestling magazines for Sting. I was interested to note that when he found a small, folded paper in his bag of chips, he immediately unfolded it and began examining it. It bore a picture of Buddha on one side and fine print about winning money on the other. He scrutinized the text without hesitation. When I commented that it looked like a lot of fine print, he said, still scanning the paper, "It just tells where it came from."

Two things are interesting about this small event. First, it shows that Sting read easily. For him, reading was not necessarily conscious work; when his eyes met print, making meaning could be automatic and virtually effortless. Readers who are not so practiced may have to make a conscious decision to read and deliberately decode the print they are encountering. Sting, however, did not hesitate to find out the purpose of the paper in his bag of chips, undaunted by print which was densely packed, fine, and faint. Even his posture reflected this ease; he remained leaning back in his chair, apparently relaxed and comfortable.

The other interesting point about this moment is that Sting was able to give me the gist of the print without reading any of it to me and without using any of the language he was reading. He automatically moved from the level of making meaning from the print to translation of that meaning into terms that told me what I needed to know: "It just tells where it came from."

This event highlights another point of conflict between required school reading and personal taste: When Sting was reading for information, he preferred that a text get to the point as quickly as possible. Unless his imagination was fired by an adventure or an emotional situation, he wanted straight facts. For example, an article in one of the wrestling magazines was written not in sentences but in phrases connected by ellipses: "...a six-foot-two, two-hundred-sixty pound native of Venice Beach, California...started wrestling in 1985 with a man who would later be known as The Ultimate Warrior...the team was called The Bladerunners..." (Sting, 1999). Sting enjoyed this style. He said,

> It's just telling what has happened from...
> like a career overlook...
> it's, like, talking and then fading on to what happens later on.
> It's a lot easier—
> instead of having all the stuff in it that I don't like to read,
> like 'and he was acting partners with...back in 1940...and he was a
> really good...'
> I don't like listening to all of that bull crap.
> I like just hearing the facts.

"Hearing the facts." When he was younger, Sting enjoyed the imaginative world that fiction could provide for him. He especially remembered mystery and adventure stories and brought up the Choose Your Own Adventure series as one of his favorites ("I loved them books," he says). However, at 14, he was focused on the outer world: his friends, his sports heroes, his future. He looked back on his reading years with reluctant nostalgia at the same time that he criticized as inauthentic the kind of stories he once enjoyed. When I asked him if he thought he had missed anything by making the change from reading a lot to not reading much, he said,

> I don't think I've missed anything reading
> because usually it's all fake.
>
> **Anne:** ...and therefore sort of less interesting or less useful...?
> **Sting:** Both.
> They're not useful,
> but they're nice,
> some of 'em are nice to read.
> 'Specially science fiction books.

Sting's reading reflected his maturation: In childhood, he enjoyed imaginative fiction, and whether or not a story was fake was irrelevant. As he has matured, his interest in facts and his desire to make sense of the world has taken precedence. His following answer to yet another of my questions about reading choices showed how he valued what "makes sense" to him:

> It's got to make sense.
> If it interests me,
> like the wrestling books.

The juxtaposition of "making sense" with "interesting" is telling here. A more experienced reader would recognize that texts that make sense are not always interesting, but to a 14-year-old who had separated himself from most reading, the two qualities are conflated in his experience—what does not make sense is automatically boring and what is interesting automatically makes sense. His seamless movement from one term to another also suggests two things: First, imaginative writing was no longer at the forefront of his ideas about good books, and second, he often encountered texts that did not make sense to him.

The Writing We See

The reader Sting was as a child showed up when he found a book about a subject in which he had an interest. The reader he was also showed up in his writing. Although his writing was full of oral constructions and unconventional spellings (some deliberate, such as *cuz* for *because*, which he said he used to keep the writing labor to a minimum), it revealed his experience with the conventions of written English. In his first journal entry for his English class, he wrote, "During the summer I go to [Small City], MI, and me and my friends came up with our own wrestling federation called H.W.f. which Stands 4 Home wrestling federation and I am the Heavyweight champion and the cruiserweight champ also...." The sentence continues for four more lines, all the way to the end of the entry. In fact, the only periods in the entry are those after the initials H.W.f. These periods are worth noting, however, because they reveal Sting's understanding of a writing convention that is not observed by the professional wrestling federations he is using as a model. The federations present themselves without periods (e.g., WWF, PWI, and ECW). Also noteworthy are the commas around MI and the correct spelling of *heavyweight* and *cruiserweight*. In other journal entries, Sting had correctly written *it's* seven times and omitted the apostrophe where there should be one (*its*) only three times. He also wrote *should've* correctly, in contrast to many ear-dependent writers who write *should of*.

All Sting's journal entries were written in a flow of language that sounded like his speech. Virtually all of them consisted of a single run-on sentence because Sting did not use periods at the ends of sentences. He knew that he should put them in, but he believed that he did not know where they should go. In fact, when he read aloud his delivery showed that he "knew" where the sentences ended, but he lacked the confidence to make it official on paper. This is almost certainly the result of his moving from school to school—not only would he have missed certain lessons by not taking part in a school's sequenced program, but he also was too busy making friends to pay much attention to what the teachers were saying.

All Sting's journal entries contained uppercase letters in unexpected places, a writing habit that Sting himself recognized as an error. On the day that he and the other members of his communications class were preparing pieces of writing to submit for the state proficiency test, he stopped working on his final copy early in the class period. Half an hour later, the teacher, working at her desk, looked up to see him drawing instead of writing. Her disappointment was obvious: "Sting, are you drawing on your folder? Honey, I was trusting you to be writing. How much have you written?" She sounded genuinely grieved, and when he held up his paper with two lines of writing on it, she repeated, "Sting, I was trusting you, I thought you were writing the whole time. I gave you two A's for today, and now look what you did to me." She picked up her grade book and erased the A's, replacing them with C's. Sting told her he had been working, but that it was hard. The teacher didn't understand what was hard about it: "The final draft should just flow when you've got the rough copy checked." Sting told her that he kept putting capitals in it. She said that she did not care about capitals, but Sting clearly did. He added, "All over the place." She had calmed down by this time and said equably, "I can handle that." Sting picked up his pen and began writing again.

This episode illustrates another way in which Sting was pulled in opposite directions. He knew that his writing was difficult to read (he mentioned it several times to me) and that his use of capital letters was wrong. He did not want to hand in poorly written work, but he did not know how to do better, so he stopped altogether. His judgment about the right way to write is better established than his ability to produce that kind of writing. In a way, Sting's reading background has made his schoolwork more difficult: If he were unaware of the conventions of "correct" language use, he might be less discouraged about the way his own writing looks on the page, and he might hand in more assignments. Motivation theory, specifically self-efficacy (Bandura, 1982; Schunk, 1991), postulates that when people believe that they are capable of learning in a particular domain they will work harder and longer to accomplish a task. Sting's belief that his handwriting was poor and his punctuation inadequate contributed to his general feeling of discouragement about writing for school assignments, and the low grades he usually received justified that discouragement. On the other hand, however weak his sense of self-efficacy about school assignments may have been, his self-efficacy was strong when it came to writing for his own purposes and for his chosen audiences.

The Writing We Read

As I observed Sting and talked with him, I gathered that he had three main goals in class: (1) to make and keep friendships, (2) avoid work he disliked, and (3) earn a passing grade. Obviously, these are not mutually compatible goals, and often Sting chose to forgo the passing grade in order to socialize and keep work to a minimum. Interestingly enough, he sometimes used writing as a way to meet the first two goals by writing lyrics to rap songs during class. He explained,

> Whenever I can,
> whenever I'm not paying attention in class.
> I have friends in it [the song],
> like J-Rock,
> that's my friend Justin Parker.
> Kind of graphic in language....
> People like it,
> 'cause some people have seen it,
> and I've gained acceptance because I can write good lyrics.
> They compare mine to others,
> and I guess they think that mine's the best—
> even though I know there's a lot better out there....

Sting volunteered to show me some of his songs, digging into his pants pockets to pull out a stack of folded sheets of notebook paper, eight in all, creased and grayed, looking as if they had been carried in a pocket for a long time. (Unlike most students in his school, Sting did not carry any school materials with him. He did not use a backpack; he may have had a pen or pencil in his pocket, but he depended on teachers and friends to supply him with paper and any other materials he would need during the school day. Metaphorically as well as literally, he refused to be burdened any more than absolutely necessary by school.) When I read the words on the paper he handed me, I had trouble hearing in my mind what the song was supposed to sound like. I asked him to read it to me, and his immediate response was a veiled apology for his handwriting: "'Cause you can't read it, can you?" I told him that I could read the words but not find the beat. He readily agreed to read it and then did so quickly with a clear beat. Following is the written song:

Playa's, thugs, n' G's By: G-DawG

I want a Palace for my thugs I hope you
understandin me cause if you aint Im gonna start
planing and plug the fan in let the sweat Dry off
if you a Playa Play for all you got and if you
a thug the start busting some shots cause I just   5
lost my mind when marcus crossed the line, I used
to have Bad LUCK untill I Busted a cap in a white
Duck, now who gonna pop me ghetto aint got you
cause if it Did it would of dropped you. Pop shit cause
Im the second Best Ghetto Nigga putting up with   10

J-Roc: as I walk through that Door Bustin cop's
wit my 44 you get capped in your Back you Hit the   30
floor then i Run out the Door Sooner or later
yo kid turn 4 you now handikapped wit the cap
still in ya back. G-Dawg, J-Roc, Playa, they Girl's Stacked
Playa: and that's the way to stay if you gonna be a Playa...

He made the beat stronger by adding words in three places.
He added "of you" to line 3; added "then" in line 4 to create the
phrase: "if you a Playa then Play for all you got"; added "done" to
line 9 to create the phrase "it would of done dropped you." In line 5,
he dropped "the," clearly meant to be "then," to create the phrase "if
you a thug start bustin some shots." He also omitted curse words
in his reading without losing the beat; he compensated for the absence of these words by changing the emphases in the lines and
holding the previous words longer. He knew exactly where the lines
ended, although he did not mark these places in his writing with
punctuation or line breaks. He did stumble over the word *planning*
(which he had spelled *planing*) but otherwise read fluently, always
with a beat, improvising improvements and accommodations for
his audience (me) as he read. He seemed to enjoy it, as well; he volunteered to read more after pausing in the fifth line.

Sting clearly knew how to use reading and writing for his own
purposes. Although his literacy practices did not generate much
academic credit for him, they rewarded him socially. His literacy
was a clear example of what Street (1984) means by ideological literacy: It is obviously embedded in cultural and social practices. As
numerous researchers in addition to Street have pointed out (e.g.,
Brandt, 1989; Cook-Gumperz, 1986; Gee, 1989; Heath, 1983), people use reading and writing for real-world purposes that may have

nothing in common with school literacy practices. Sting is a living, breathing example of this dichotomy between school and the rest of the world, and to the extent that the dichotomy reflects his alienation from school literacy, it threatens to have serious consequences for his future.

The eight rap songs that Sting carried in his pants pocket were only part of his production; he had even more in his coat pocket and said that he had ambitions to sell them "but I just can't find out how." In a later conversation, he mentioned again that he was trying to get his lyrics sold through a friend who was getting into the music business but who had just moved away. "I gotta ask around...anybody knows where he is," Sting said. He added,

> And I'm trying to get in with the Insane Clown Posse,
> they're like really, really, really explicit rap.
> They made a song,
> it made record of having the most curse words in it.
> They said it 93 times,
> so I went and I thought,
> Hey, I think I can beat that,
> so I went and I made a song
> and I did it to where I said the word
> 126 times.
> Within six minutes.
> Which felt like a good accomplishment to me,
> but you know...

He trailed off, and I said, "Right. You don't get much school credit for stuff like that, do you?" He just shook his head.

Sting was well aware of how little his interests had to do with the interests of school. In a journal entry, he wrote,

> school just Puts you into the world to make tax Dollars so you can make money for the goverment which im Stating that we actually Dont need school unless you want to Pay someone for letting you work in a Restaraunt, factory, or what it may be so i say PeoPle that like school should know their Role and shut their mouth if you smell what the Rock is cooking!

When I asked Sting for the source of this observation, he said,

> My science teacher
> she told us that.

She didn't word it just like that,
she was like,
most of the reasons that you go to school
is to go out in the work area,
and the government wants you to go out in the work area
so you can make money
so you can give them tax.
So they can get what they want.

Sting saw himself as street smart, a person who learned by doing rather than by reading or listening to teachers. He wrote in his journal,

> I think that I wont need any of this crap we have teachers teaching since I know how 2 Read talk I just choose Not to use it in my every Day life and I talk I just Dont talk like a person should to the School's Prespective I learn alot of the Stuff By Being out with friend's and my mom and if i Dont know what a word is we got a Dictionary to look up the words Defanition and i alReady have 2 stay an extra year in <u>Schools</u> county Jail [his emphasis]

As a writer, Sting intuitively understood that teachers did not share his views or his background knowledge. Even though he did not write for a naive audience, and he did not explain terms or references his reader would need to know, he was aware that a reader could not make sense of a text without knowing something about the context. His first journal entry of the year in English class described his desire to be a professional wrestler.

> Im gonna become a professional wrestler when i get out of school cuz wrestling pay's good when you become a wrestling Superstar and no one wuntz me to be a wrestler But my friends so when I become a wrestler and my family or People who dont Believe in me I will have 2 wordz 4 them Because thats the like 7th or 8th most important thing to me is wrestling cuz I can proform it so well as a heel or a good guy I can work the croud cuz During the Summer I go to [Small City], MI, and me and my friendz came up with our own wrestling federation called H.W.f. which Stands 4 Home wrestling federation and I am the Heavyweight champion and the cruiserweight champ also I have about 6 persona's and when I be come a wrestler Im gonna give up money to contractors to build more Home less shelters and animal shelters!

In the upper left corner, the teacher wrote, "Date entries and be neater. I can't read this writing." Many young writers would interpret this comment as a discouraging lack of interest and effort on the reader's part, but Sting recognized that her remark meant that he was not going to get credit for this entry, so, without getting angry, he made a point of talking to her about it.

> I guess what she couldn't understand
> is the wrestling in particular,
> so I started talkin' about wrestling to her,
> and she kind of took on a little bit.
> It's like I used to use the Rock's catch phrases,
> like "smell what the Rock is cookin'"
> after what I'd say,
> and she asked me what that meant,
> and I was, like, that was just
> "if you know what I mean."

This teacher, like most of Sting's teachers, liked him and was willing to listen to him. When Sting wrote later entries in the same idiosyncratic style, she did not criticize their unreadability. In fact, she did not comment on them at all, and when I gained Sting's permission to read them, she suggested that I write responses on them. She was confident that Sting would not know whether or not she had written them, and she made it clear that she did not know what to say to him that would not be critical or discouraging, which she did not want to be. (I did not say anything in response to the teacher's suggestion. I believed that to adopt the teacher's role of writing responses to Sting's journals would be out of keeping with my role as researcher. I did, however, see her request as originating in a desire to provide Sting with supportive responses to his writing.)

Soon after Sting's teacher made this suggestion, I observed her class on a day that the students were writing journal entries in response to the question, What is the purpose of life? Sting wrote at length, bent over his desk and absorbed in his task. When the period was over and other students were leaving, he hung back so he could show the teacher his entry.

> The PorPuse of Life is to Serve god, worship, Praise and Do anything and everything to BRing People in get to know him so they can be Saved and be Not a sinner i aint saying im Perfect cuz im

Not Near it im a sinner but i have Been saved and I know that evolution iz a bunch of crackRock and Shaving creme there's No such thing as evolution God made everything and it is the same from the Day He created All that We know and dont and evolutionist Dont know that Before god flooded the earth there was a ice layer in the Atmosphere of the earth when it DiDn't flood man used to Be 10 11 feet tall and lion's used to eat Plant's so we were made Here to serve god (and if you would like to come to my church it's on Palmer Road by Chickinn it's calle city asmbely* of god come next wednessday Please) (u aint got to though)

*Note: The teacher wrote the word *Assembly* above this word.

This entry was written on a Thursday morning, presumably after church service on Wednesday night, which might have increased Sting's interest in writing it. Note that he did not use obscenities in these journal entries. As much as he liked to say what he thought, he almost never used language that would offend his audience. The word *crap* does appear twice in 14 entries, but considering the rap lyrics he listened to, that does not seem very serious. He may not have thought of that word as an obscenity.

The teacher read the entry while Sting stood by, and after she corrected the spelling of *Assembly*, she talked with him briefly about religion, telling him that she belonged to a Catholic church, which implied that, therefore, she would not be visiting his church. Her manner was very friendly; she seemed pleased with what he had written as well as his interest in showing it to her. She complimented him on "a good writing," and after he left, she remarked to me, "He's got some good philosophy there." Her own interests and background knowledge enabled her to read and understand this entry, whereas she could not read the entry about wrestling. When I compared the two entries, I saw similar writing; the big difference was the subject matter. What the teacher saw in the first entry was unreadable writing, but what she saw in the later entry was a statement of values she respects.

When she wrote, "Date entries and be neater. I can't read this writing" on the first entry, she appeared to be addressing the messiness of the physical writing. Her injunction to date the entries was a marginal attempt to establish some order in a writing that appeared to transgress boundaries to the point of near chaos. What Sting understood in some way, even if she did not, was that she was actually addressing the messiness of his bringing professional wrestling into her classroom and circle of responsibility. The desire for the theatrical display of working class masculinity that professional wrestling evoked in Sting was even more difficult for her to respond to. Encountering this first entry, she felt incapable of comprehending his ideas and dreams for his future because they are so alien to her own. Sting understood that the way to help her "read" it was to bring himself and wrestling into her conscious understanding by speaking with her in person. Instead of rewriting his text, he "rewrote" his text's relation to his reader by providing her with what she needed in order to make her reading of his journal a living experience in her mind. Making the physical writing of the text neater would not accomplish this end.

In another journal entry, in response to the question, What do you always find time for? Sting wrote, "I always find time for wrestling, my family, my friends, try 2 find time for church...." Note that none of these pursuits has anything to do with school, and wrestling was mentioned first. Wrestling is probably not more important than family and friends, but it is not surprising that he would write it first. Wrestling was on his mind a good deal, and he even wrote a book about it. Following is a journal entry in which he talks about his book:

> It's not too big,
> it's a nonfiction tied in with a fiction.
> It's about the wrestling thing that we got,
> it's like what's going to happen in the federation that we got,
> so it's like one of our—
> it's like our story plans.
> How it started is about eighth grade
> I was walkin' down the hall
> and there was this old book,
> a notebook, half the pages were torn out,
> it looked like nobody wanted it.
> I picked it up,
> and for some reason I just started writing about wrestling,
> and kept going on and on.
> And kept on writin'
> and eventually it ran out of paper
> and I couldn't write no more.
> I think I'm on the ninth or tenth chapter.

Just as Sting was eager to read every page of a wrestling magazine, he also was eager to write about wrestling. His fantasy life was filled with images and dramas inspired by the professional performers. He and his friends in the small city where he spent time each summer had their Home Wrestling Federation, and in addition to writing his book, he more recently wrote what he described as "this little contract thing saying who we wanted to be" for a group of school friends with whom he had created a new wrestling group. They were inspired by, and named themselves after, a group of professional wrestlers called Degeneration X, performers who set themselves up as outlaws against the good guys of the wrestling scene.

Wrestling Fantasies: Performing Manhood

Developing his own version of Degeneration X illustrates the way that Sting found in professional wrestling what he cared about most. Wrestling allowed him to act out his fantasies of being an admired, manly performer; the many personas of the players gave him a wide range of identities to try, including rebellious ones; and sharing this fascination with other adolescents generated closeness with them. He explained this last point.

> So now we became a lot better friends—
> instead of just bein' in-school friends
> we go to wrestling parties and stuff all together,
> stay the night at friends',
> sleep over....

His code name, Sting, which he chose for himself for this study, comes from wrestling, too. When I asked him for a code name, the question seemed completely natural to him, unlike many of his peers who seemed bewildered by it. Sting, however, had been living with named alter egos as long as he has been interested in professional wrestling. "Cold Hard Sting, or just Sting if that's too long," he said. Sting it was. I was touched by his consideration of my need to have a code name of easy length. I also was unsurprised by his choice, knowing (because he had taught me) a good deal more about professional wrestling than I ever imagined I would know. I recognized Sting as the stage name of his current favorite among professional wrestlers, a burly Viking-esque showman who, like all successful professional wrestlers, was a performer as well as an athlete. Ball (1990) describes the wrestler Sting in terms of "a new heroic image," projecting the values of "honesty, work, and patriotism" (p. 92). The wrestler's 14-year-old fan, the young Sting of this study, had the code name in his mind long before I asked for it.

Mazer (1998), in her study of professional wrestling, notes that

> Many men...have confessed to an earlier period of hard-core fandom, with wrestling fantasies forming an important bridge from childhood, the illicit pleasures of watching wrestling and of fanzines hidden under the bed an important part of the transition into adolescence.... (p. 21)

In Sting's case, there was no need to hide his interest in professional wrestling. His mother knew about the amateur federation Sting and his friends had created. She did not criticize him for reading wrestling magazines, nor did she try to curtail his interest generally; the only tension that wrestling seemed to generate between the two of them arose when Sting talked about wanting to become a professional wrestler. His mother told him, "I have no problem, but you need a field with a future, if something should happen to you. It's better to have a backup. What if you get seriously hurt?" Sting's response was that he would go to a community college. He certainly could not argue that wrestlers never get hurt; one of his favorite wrestlers, Owen Hart, died from performance injuries in the spring of Sting's ninth-grade year, and another prominent wrestler, Darren "Droz" Drozdov, broke his neck the following autumn and now is paralyzed below the waist.

Sting did not try to hide his interest in wrestling from anyone. Of the 14 journal entries that he had written for his English class, half mentioned wrestling. Wrestling inspired his art projects. He wore a jacket with a picture of Stone Cold Steve Austin on the back, and although school rules prohibited jackets of all kinds in class, Sting wore it anyway. Occasionally, a teacher would tell him he had to put it in his locker, which he did without argument, only to put it on again for the next class.

Whenever I asked about reading, Sting said that he did and would read about wrestling—and not just magazines, which he read whenever he could, often going to drug stores to browse through the periodicals rack. He was eager to read books about wrestlers as well. He asked the school librarian to get some of these books, specifically Mankind's autobiography, although he doubted that she actually would do so. He also expressed hope that Owen Hart would be the subject of a book that he would somehow have access to. A friend of Sting's had a book about a wrestler, and Sting had looked at it long enough to read a few pages. He said he would like to read the rest of it.

Sting's story illustrates the way that the interests of the school institution diverge from the interests of individuals, especially as they approach adulthood. In elementary school, many children can and do read books of their own choosing, and most of those choices are easily approved by teachers and librarians. Adults are happy to see children enjoying books and children are happy to read them. In adolescence, however, several things happen that limit reading: Many young people, like Sting, become more interested in actual experience than in vicarious, fictional experience and want to spend their time not only engaging in sports, video games, and group activities but also forming close ties with peers (Csikszentmihalyi & Larson, 1984; Hersch, 1998). Another common event that alienates adolescents from school reading is that in middle school and high school, the reading curriculum becomes much more focused on literature written by adults for adults, leaving little room for students to read about the subjects in which they are truly interested. The subjects they are interested in and the dramas they enjoy experiencing through text usually have a great deal to do with the psychological work of becoming an adult. Sting's interest in professional wrestling is part of his working out what it means to be a man.

As we examine the question of why a smart, friendly boy such as Sting would be so resistant to cooperating with the demands of school in general and reading assignments in particular, we need to understand that his natural focus is on growing up according to his way of thinking about what that means. Early in my discussions with him about his change from reader to nonreader, he said, "I guess I just stopped being a good little boy and doing what adults wanted me to." At another point, he explained the change when he said,

> I go to different places,
> and you got a good grade,
> it wasn't cool,
> and I got glasses,
> and it changed my whole life around.

Understanding that he had turned away from being a nerd who wore glasses, from being a good little boy earning good grades, and turned instead toward his peers, wrestling, and rap music meant understanding that, as Hersch (1998) puts it, "the negative is positive" (p. 81). Although he still was a kind-hearted, sensitive soul who helped his mother ("He's my right hand in anything and everything," she said), went to church, read the Bible, took care of his younger siblings, and felt sorry for homeless people and animals, he also was drawn to tough-talking wrestlers and their display of prowess.

> Chris Jericho,
> he just came to the WWF,
>
> I like him,
> he's a good wrestler.
> He talks a bunch o' junk,
> but he can back it up.
> He'll talk about him beatin' you down,
> and winnin',
> and he'll end up doin' it.

Mazer's (1998) insights into the aggression of professional wrestling help us understand its appeal to Sting.

> Its display of violence is less a contest than a ritualized encounter between opponents, replayed repeatedly over time for an exceptionally engaged audience. The colorful characters presented and the stories told both in the wrestling ring and in the television programming that contextualizes matches are simultaneously archetypal and topical, open to straightforward readings but in that very openness resistant to simple readings of dominant cultural values...professional wrestling's presentations of virtue and vice are more ambiguous than might be apparent at first glance, the event more carnival than Mass. Rather than simply reflecting and reinforcing moral clichés, professional wrestling puts contradictory ideas into play, as with its audience it replays, reconfigures, and celebrates a range of performative possibilities. (p. 3)

Sting's reactions to these "presentations of virtue and vice" were evolving, changing rapidly as he became more aware of the performances and more involved in the "performative possibilities" in his own homemade wrestling groups. When he was 14$\frac{1}{2}$ years old, at the time of our first interview, he was teaching his

6-year-old brother "what's a bad guy and a good guy, 'cause he's sort of saying that Hulk Hogan is a good guy, and he's not." Sting was still angry about Hulk Hogan because Hogan had once been his hero, but then

> Hulk Hogan.
> That's a bad-guy name.
> 'Cause he went with the money to go and....
> He's not the "drink your milk, eat your vitamins and say your
>   prayers"
> kind of guy any more.
> Even though he still does wear the cross.
> That's when I really looked up to him
> and then he went,
> he said,
> "All you little Hulksters,"
> he said som'n really bad,
> it made me really mad—
> "Eff you, you little Hulksters!"
> And he ripped his shirt,
> and there was a NWU,
> a black and white shirt under it
> which was a new group that was full of bad guys.
>
> and they [interviewers] asked Hulk Hogan why he went bad,
> and he was like,
> "Hey, little kiddies, it was all for the money!"

This "betrayal" by Hogan occurred when Sting was too young to appreciate the ritualistic, performative nature of wrestling dramas. As he got older, he enjoyed immensely the good guys who were not pure goody-goodies; they broke rules and talked tough too. As Sting explained it to me,

> The rule-breakers are the bad guys,
> the good rule-breakers are the good guys,
> and the good guys are pure goody guys.

Mazer (1998) also points out that wrestling is "constructed around the display of the male body and a tradition of cooperative rather than competitive exchanges of apparent power between men" (p. 4). This is interesting in light of the psychological work

Sting was doing as an adolescent: He was deeply concerned with gaining acceptance by his peers at the same time that he was establishing independence from traditional authority figures. The long-standing, ubiquitous question of whether professional wrestling is "fake" actually is a layered question with layered answers: Sting, like many other fans, knew that when he watched arguments and fights between professional wrestlers he was watching a performance, but he knew that the excitement of performed rivalry is founded on a deeper agreement between the performers to enact both competition and solidarity. It is just this agreement to perform that he wrote for himself and his friends both at school and in his summer vacation town. His book told the stories that he and his friends agreed to act out. He prided himself on having numerous personas and knowing how to "work the crowd" (as he wrote in a school journal entry). He enjoyed believing in the story (whether it was a story he was watching or one he was telling) and simultaneously understanding how to perform that story. Professional wrestling provides milestones that mark Sting's maturation, showing us that he had grown from a young boy who admired Hulk Hogan to an adolescent who joined with his peers to imitate the outlaws of Degeneration X. An important aspect of this growth is that the Hogan fan believed in what he saw, while the adolescent was aware not only of the wrestler's performance but also of his own.

When I spoke with Sting and his mother in their home, Sting turned on the television when our conversation was interrupted by a phone call for his mother. He and I watched the professional wrestlers shout angrily at one another. He pointed out Mankind, a wrestler who had been injured recently, and explained to me what was going on.

> Him and The Rock got together, right?
> And they were wrestling—
> The Rock is a real egotistical guy?
> And Mankind gave him his autobiography,
> signed to The Rock,
> and The Rock threw it out.
> And he got really mad,
> went up to him and just swang everywhere he could.
> He's really like that,
> they've recorded him in real life....

He told me this story straightforwardly, as if he were talking about friends instead of performers, but after his mother had finished her call and we had resumed the interview, he said,

> Awright.
> So wrestling is fake, too.
> Up to a point.
> It's like people watching soap operas.
> It's like a man's soap opera.

Thus, Sting revealed his simultaneous involvement in the stories acted out in the ring and his growing understanding of how they work. They are a text he was still learning to read—and write.

What Has Sting Taught Us?

Sting was reading and writing himself into texts of professional wrestling, imagining his future self, and thereby beginning to create a future self. This reading and writing has almost nothing to do with the reading, writing, and creation of future selves sanctioned by the school. Sting kept his texts visible by creating them in school; he presented them to teachers when he wrote about wrestling in his journal or read a wrestling magazine during the weekly Sustained Silent Reading periods. As we have seen, however, even when he followed the rules by writing a response to a journal question, these texts make him almost invisible to his teacher. To her, he was an insubstantial, bewildering (and messy) presence on the page he had written, not a flesh-and-blood, comprehensible voice, until he wrote of religion or some other subject that had a solid and meaningful reality for her. She could not read his writing, but the solution to this problem lay not in dating the entry but in her learning to "read" the writer.

Sting is intelligent and sensitive to the feelings of people around him, so he understood this solution, even if he pragmatically put it in terms of what he needed to do to get a better writing grade. His interest in friends may have contributed heavily to his academic downfall, but it is part of his makeup, which helped him get along with the adults in a school environment that otherwise could be quite hostile to him. He was, however, constantly reminded that his interests and his opinions were unwelcome. Most teachers, he said, were offended when he spoke freely, whether he was joking around or expressing a serious belief. He vacillated between deciding to cooperate with school—"I don't feel like failin' any more than I have, stating my opinion just doesn't get me far"—and wanting to drop out of school altogether. He knew that dropping out was unrealistic now because his mother had told him that she would not let him live at home unless he was going to school. He believed she was serious about this, but he was getting progressively more discouraged, and said, "I just want to get out of school. I'd like to drop out, but I can't."

Sting is what Eckert (1989) describes as a Burnout, a member of a part of working class culture characterized by "an activation of working class norms within the school situation" (p. 172). An important characteristic of Burnout culture is that its members adopt adult privileges, such as smoking and partying, much earlier than the middle class Jocks of Eckert's study. Although Sting saw smoking and drug use as a waste of time and detrimental to his wrestling performance, he was eager to leave the constrictions and demands of school. School culture is based on the assumption that adults know what is best for students, but Sting had begun making decisions for himself.

Eckert attributes the Burnouts' early independence to the relative absence of adult supervision in working class children's lives. Older children take care of younger ones while parents work, and children grow up within a network of older teens. Sting's early years did not follow this pattern; in fact, his mother said that they were together all the time when he was young. She did, however, connect his lack of interest in reading to taking on family responsibilities.

> It's been a real rocky time,
> there's been a lot of stress,
> he helps me a whole lot.
> He's my right hand in anything and everything,
> takes care of his brother and sister,
> he has a lot more responsibility than a 15-year-old should have,
> which I think may have contributed to not wanting to read.

Sting's analysis of what happened to his reading was similar but not identical. In Sting's mind, moving from place to place and getting glasses were what changed his life. I speculate that his need to make friends quickly as soon as he entered a new class led him to socialize during class time, which was detrimental to his schooling and encouraged him to socialize with the boys who were most available for friendship (i.e., those least academically engaged). Proving that he was not a nerd in spite of his glasses also pushed him in this direction. In this way, Sting's repeatedly changing schools necessitated his making friends with young Burnouts.

But his mother's version of the story, in which his reading suffered because he had to grow up quickly and be a semiadult support for her, makes sense as well. Sting always had been a wonderfully imaginative person who, as a child, easily engaged in imaginative story worlds. His mother remembered that he invented wildly adventurous bedtime stories to tell his sister and that, in the car, he would talk and talk, telling stories. ("I miss that part," she said wistfully.) Sting's emergence into an adolescence filled with responsibilities (including preparing for future responsibilities) changed his relation to those fictional, imaginative worlds. He began to see them as fake and childish, even though he could still feel their pull sometimes. What was more important to him now than escape into books was real-world information. He valued texts that get to the point quickly. When he read, he could still be caught up in the enjoyment of another world, but he was primarily looking for information about how to be a man in the adult culture of his future. Sports in general and wrestling in particular provide this; it is easy to see how well professional wrestling meets the needs of a boy who responds to fantasy in spite of himself but who also is searching for information about manhood.

Sting wanted his reading to be purposeful and to make sense. When he failed to cooperate with a teacher's reading assignments, it was because the teacher's and the text's purposes were not his. His purposes had changed since his elementary school days, of course, and will continue to change as he matures. In high school, his literacy (like everything else) was pressed into service to support his natural job of growing up in a community of peers. Because school did not seem to contribute much to his growth as he saw it, he was in a fragile state academically. In reading, he was losing ground. He had lost a habit of thinking of reading as something to do when he had free time. (Even when he was reading a book about his favorite football player, he never finished it because he kept forgetting about it.)

The mismatch between Sting's interests and purposes and those of the school could well have lifelong effects. One obvious and serious consequence is that he might not get a high school diploma. He was discouraged, convinced that he was not going to pass his classes in spite of his efforts, and longed to drop out. Another serious consequence of Sting's misfit with school was that he had come to believe that he did not like to read and that reading is not useful. He said,

> I ain't got to read to be smart.
> I don't think I'm gonna learn from no book.
> I learn it by doing it myself,
> by mistakes.

He did say that he would read what he was interested in, but his first association with the word *reading* was having to read a book he did not like. School reading had created this association.

And school reading could go far to undo the damage. Educators might not be able to return Sting to an easy, comfortable relationship to reading as long as his energies are focused where they are, but we can minimize the damage being done every day to his beliefs about reading. We can recognize that the reader within Sting (and others like him) is endangered by the changes brought about by growing up in the time, place, and way that he has been growing up. Some people's commitment to reading is robust enough to withstand years of boredom with institutionally required texts, but others, such as Sting, who seem to derive almost no nourishment whatsoever from English class, need access to what they can absorb. During this period of his adolescence, Sting the reader is similar to someone on a restricted diet. That diet comprises a few elements of popular culture that are as unpalatable to Sting's teachers (though they are good hearted and well intentioned) as the school's literary offerings are to Sting and his friends. The school risks suppressing Sting's reading and writing energies completely when it tries to redirect them toward academic goals that make no sense to him.

In the case studies that follow, I will examine ways to help students connect with some school texts. In this study of Sting, however, I want to focus on the importance of our recognizing that students exercise agency in deciding when, why, and to what extent to cooperate with school. I urge teachers to understand how the whole school project looks to young people such as Sting, and I urge them to see the legitimacy of his viewpoint. He feels alienated not only because he believes that popular culture rather than academic culture fulfulls his needs but also because he meets with failure and adult disapproval too often in his school day.

I am not arguing that we teach only popular culture texts in school—far from it. But I am arguing that we need to be more flexible in recognizing that students have their own purposes in reading and writing. Rarely is a student such as Sting allowed the privilege of reading a wrestler's autobiography for school credit because most educators and stakeholders in public education think he should be reading something better, but our wish to prepare him for a life in the middle class mainstream renders the reader he actually is invisible to us. Instead of seeing this reader, we see the absence of the kind of reader we wish all our students to be. When we see Sting rejecting long Accelerated Reader books, or when we see wrestling phrases in the paper he has written, we say, "I can't read this." However, we are not reading Sting, the reader. Because we have the responsibility of preparing students for adulthood, we believe that our booklists are more valuable to Sting than his chosen texts. We need to understand that for a student such as Sting, one of our goals should be to keep the reader in him alive through adolescence, even when that goal requires compromises in our commitment to teaching school texts. The contribution we can make to Sting's future lies not in the particular texts we admire and promote but in protecting the reader within him. As an adult, Sting may never credit his high school teachers with saving that reader, but we will have succeeded with Sting if, in his adult life, he can enjoy the benefits of reading easily and comfortably for whatever purposes he chooses.

Chapter 4

Duke: Competing Visions of Manhood

"Duke is learning to be a man," his algebra teacher told me. "But not a *responsible* man." This teacher was a practical, no-nonsense woman who had been teaching high school long enough to feel confident in her judgments of teenagers. As she spoke, she watched Duke's back, across the room, as he leaned out the doorway into the hall. A loose-limbed, good-looking, 17-year-old senior, Duke had interrupted his after-school makeup work to talk to his girlfriend, who had been waiting for him. "If it weren't Vanessa, it would be somebody else," the teacher continued. "His brother was the same way. Smart, real smart, but skipped school all the time and just barely graduated. Too social, both of them."

Duke was old enough to feel the urgent pull of a future in which he saw himself becoming a rap-music producer. He was young enough, however, to be taken over frequently by the desires of the moment, such as cutting school and neglecting homework. None of his plans or desires led him to concentrate on school, and he was failing all his classes except one. In his last semester of high school, Duke continued to believe, in spite of his failing grades, that he would be able to graduate. His teachers and counselor were less confident, although every one of them agreed that he was intelligent and capable. The one thing that everyone concerned understood was that absences and failure to turn in the assigned work kept him from passing.

It is true that these "absences and failures" reflected a turning away from school responsibilities, but it is important to remember that they also reflected his passionate interest in life outside school—particularly in music, of which he said, "That's my whole career, right there, that's what I wanna do." The kind of reading assigned in school was decidedly not part of what he wanted to do. Even reading music was not part of Duke's plan because he played by ear.

> Readin' the music always bored me,
> I wanted to be more on my own.
> I like playin' freestyle...
> I love doin' that.

Duke rejected printed musical texts because he wanted to express his own musical ideas rather than interpret someone else's. He loved to improvise. And as will be demonstrated in this case study, his relation to literary texts paralleled his relation to musical ones; his desire for self-expression and self-assertion led him to reject both kinds of text in favor of creating his own.

Another expression of Duke's drive for independence was his determined commitment to earning money as a clerk in a pet store. He worked 36 to 40 hours a week, and the story he told about this job reveals the pull of opposing forces Duke was experiencing.

> I did have good grades for a while,
> before I had the job...
> [I started] February third,
> absences started comin' in quick.
>
> I work 40 hours...
> I mean, it's not really—
> it's like 36 hours.
> It's illegal, you're not supposed to.
> I'm into it—I guess.

The pet store job provided an income that was important to Duke, making possible the purchase of the necessities of adult life.

> I'm tryin' to raise up for after school,
> after high school.
> I'm tryin' to get a car right now, too, so...
> more money possible.
>
> I'm tryin' to be more independent,
> I wanna get more studio equipment
> 'cause that's my whole career, right there,
> that's what I wanna do.

The job consumed Duke's energy, however, and he had almost none left for school. At some points he was frank about this; at others he was characteristically confident that he could do what he wanted even to the point of ignoring his body's demand for sleep.

> That's why I come into school late,
> 'cause I'm tired,
> I've just been stayin' home, and sleepin',
> I wake up, school's already out (laughs).
> I slept all day Monday
> till, like, 2:30,
> and I got up and got washed and dressed
> and went to work.
> Slept all day Tuesday,
> I ain't come to school then,
> I got up and went to work.
>
> When I get home, that's when I work.
> I get home, like 10:30, 11 o'clock.
> Then I do all the schoolwork I can before I—
> I always fall asleep!
> If I was doin' som'n else I could stay up,
> but just 'cause it's schoolwork I fall asleep.
> Let's say I was makin' music—
> I could do that all night.
> Or playin' basketball or som'n.
> I be in the book, just fallin' over it,
> (Mimes falling asleep over an open book)
> And the next thing I know
> my dad's wakin' me up for school,
> and I feel like I slept five minutes.
>
> I have, like, 25 absences in first hour,
> English Twelve...
> I just couldn't get up,
> I was asleep.

Duke admitted here that his need for sleep kept him home from school, but he did not admit that the hours he worked at his job directly interfered with his schoolwork. And perhaps the job did not make much difference—perhaps he would not be doing homework in any case because Duke believed that he could pass all his classes without doing any work outside school. At another point in the interview he said,

> When I come to school I do my work.
> But once I get home,
> I hardly ever do homework.
> I mean, I can count on my fingers this year how many times I did
>   homework.
> I will wait till the next day in school
> and do my homework.
> If I got som'n to turn in first hour,
> I'll do it in first hour and turn it in.
> Second hour, I'll try to do it in first hour.

> I'm just so happy to get good on the test,
> I don't know how that come that way,
> I do real good on tests regardless of whether I study.

Duke's academic problems were immediately due, as his algebra teacher said, to his absences. She attributed those absences to his social life, but when we look beyond attendance records, we find that Duke simply saw his real-life interests (friends, music, his job, and his future) as more important—and more engaging—than school responsibilities. The fact that he seriously disliked school reading contributed heavily to his disinclination to do homework and to his sense that school was just a series of artificial hurdles to clear. Because he failed English the previous year, at the time of the interview he was taking three English classes (and two math classes and an economics class). He had to pass all six classes in order to receive a high school diploma, but he was not doing any of the assigned reading. This neglect, combined with his many absences, made it almost impossible for his teachers to justify giving him enough credit to pass their classes. Every week he got a little further behind and lost more control over the situation.

Duke freely admitted that he skipped classes often and that achieving the necessary credits to graduate would be very difficult. However, he continued to miss classes even when the end of 12th grade was three months away. He continued to avoid reading assignments, trying instead (with only partial success) to make up extra credit in his English classes by writing his own stories, which he would rather do than read. He began writing stories when he had an inspiration, but he did not finish them. If he had a page or two, he would hand in what he had, hoping for some credit. He knew that he was intelligent and that his parents and teachers believed that he was capable of academic success, and yet he continued to choose to follow his own interests instead of cooperating with the school's graduation requirements. Even when his parents and the school administration put him on a contract that limited the number of hours he could work and required him to get teachers' signatures after every class period, Duke began skipping school again after just a week.

Why was such a smart, creative person choosing what seemed to be a self-destructive path? Why were reading and schoolwork so distasteful that avoiding them seemed worth the high cost? These are questions Duke's teachers asked, but it is important to note that they are questions that reflect a school-centered view of adolescent success. Duke was a young man who lived in several very different worlds, some of his own imaginative making and some existing in real time and space—but all making claims on him. School is only one of those worlds, and he was extremely eager to leave it behind. In some ways, he already had left it behind. Duke's loss of interest in school was closely tied to his loss of interest in reading. If we follow the path of his reading through his development from childhood to the present we can clearly see how and why he has come to be a person who can read but will not. And we also can see that his resistance centered on a particular kind of reading that Duke would not do—a kind of reading required by school and valued by English teachers but not, in any sense, inclusive of all the possibilities open to readers.

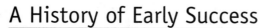 A History of Early Success

Like many underachievers in high school, Duke was a strong and happy reader in elementary school. He had solid support from home and family; he learned the alphabet from his older brother before he started school.

> He had me keep sayin' the alphabet at first,
> I'd always forget a letter, I was real young.
> This was when I was 3.
>
> He taught me the basics,
> Like numbers and letters.

His earliest reading memories are of working with his mother, who taught him to write his name and to express his feelings for her.

> My mom would set me down and she'd have me write.
> When I started writin' is when I started readin'.
> Both at the same time.
> She showed me how to write my name,
> so she would put the pencil in my hand and write with me.
> Then I'd follow and I'd write it out,
> "I love Mom."
> So then she says, "That says, 'I love Mom.'"
> So then I know how to say "I love Mom,"
> and to say my name, *Duke*—
> I used to write that all the time,
> *Duke Duke Duke Duke*, any time I've got the space.

Early reading for Duke meant personal time with his mother and the thrill of learning how to assert the fact of his existence to the rest of the world. Duke remembered it happily, not as work at all. His blurring of the distinction between *say* and *write* suggests more than a convention of dialect. It implies that writing was easy for him, just another way of "saying." When I asked him how he felt about these tutorials, he answered,

> I loved playin' it.
> It taught me how to read out, "hat," "cat."
> This guy who just died recently,
> he used to always come over to my aunt's house,
> and we had family get-togethers,
> and he'd say, "You have a book?"
> And I'd be like, "Yeah, I have a book,"
> 'cause I had these little skinny children's books,
> and he's like, "Will you read me a story?"
> And I'll be happy, I'll read him a story,
> and he all happy,
> he made me feel good to be able to read.
> I was, like, 5 or 6 through 'bout 10.
>
> I was the best reader in school,
> you get a prize or som'n if you could read—
> I loved those prizes!

I used to read little books,
like if you take this decision—
[Choose Your Own Adventure]
I loved them. I loved them.
I know they attract me.
I used to love readin' 'em, all the time.
I tried to get a whole bunch of them books,
'cause I liked to see how my end would be.
I was like, "I know I can get som'n nice."

Many children love the Choose Your Own Adventure series. But it is interesting that this is the only title that Duke remembered from his childhood. And it is through his comments about these stories that we get a glimpse of two themes that will dominate his later relation to reading: (1) exploring possibilities rather than being locked into the author's resolution, and, more particularly, (2) asserting active control over the story to make it into the story that he wants it to be. (Of course the authors determine the outcomes to the stories in this series, but as a child, Duke felt in control because he made different decisions at various points in the story.) These themes become more obvious in middle school, when, like so many other young adolescents, Duke's pleasure in reading began to fade.

Old Assignments, New Independence

Middle school years are times of great discoveries for many children. Whole new worlds open up as young adolescents discover talents in themselves and their friends. New heroes eclipse old ones; social life with peers becomes even more important than it has been, and identities evolve. For Duke, these new worlds came together in his discovery of rapping, which he referred to as his poetry.

I liked to write stories [in elementary school]…
I got kinda bored with that.

Anne: When did you move from writing stories to writing poetry?

Duke: It was a transformation in middle school.
It was funny—it was me and Van and a guy named Jackie,
And we had drum practice.
After drum practice we just started makin' this little beat,

and then we just started rappin'.
It was funny—we was doin' it just for fun,
'cause he [the teacher] had us readin' different things,
and nobody liked to do it,
so then we got back—
it was a little music, and he say,
"Dot, dot, diggy, diggy, dot, diggy," explaining it out,
like how we should tap.
It was real borin',
and we were so tired of playin',
and then we made a little beat, like,
dot, dot, diggy, diggy, dot, diggy, dot (laughs).
Then we started (begins to sing)
"I was playin' my drums...."
Then we started rappin' just to—
That's how it started changin' into—
we started meetin' more often and doin' that.

That's when I learned to play the piano and drums,
and them things have my attention.
Those were more interesting,
So then I read less and less....
I loved rappin', and the first time I realized it's so fun,
I got a kick out of it, rappin'.

Discovery of a new interest means that earlier interests no longer get the time they once did. Music, especially rapping with his friends, began to occupy time that Duke might once have spent reading. But for Duke, reading less often came not only from discovering new ways to have fun; it also came from discovering that reading was becoming less and less rewarding. When I asked Duke about the shift in interest from reading to other things that had happened in middle school, he answered,

That's good, how you brought that to my head.
Yeah, that's—OK:
I started thinkin' that about that time was when
teachers really started makin' us do book reports.
And I remember Mr. Saunders'd have us do these little book reports
    that—
I'd never do 'em.
You know how you had to read 'em and then write what it was?

I made my thing up every time, every time.
I was readin' it at first, I was readin' the story.
And it's like, "Man, it would be better if I just wrote it down.
It's a lot better, and then I could express it the way I wanted it to
    be."
When I read books, I want things to go my way.

Either I didn't turn book reports in,
or I write 'em myself.
I honestly cannot say
a book ever that I've read all the way through
and wrote a book report on.
I do this sometimes: I just say to somebody that I've known read it,
"So what all happens in the book?"
Then I just write it out and throw some details in there.
Books started gettin' long and thick.
If I look at a book like this [holds up assigned paperback]
I don't want to read it.
I quit.
I just feel that there's gonna be som'n in there boring.

If the music and rapping with friends drew Duke's attention away from reading, the increasing academic demands for more and more reading (and writing about reading) made it easy for Duke to decide that reading took more time and effort than it was worth. In his account of middle school reading and writing book reports, several important developments become apparent. One is his dislike of long books, not because reading is difficult, but because the odds of the story boring him become too great. Another is his development of strategies to avoid reading—one of which is using a friend's knowledge of the book to get the assignment done. Most important is his discovery that he could invent a story to report on, so that he could make the story go the way he wanted even as he spared himself the labor of reading and the unpleasantness of being in the hands of an author who took the characters in unwelcome directions.

Reader, Writer, Text—Who's in Charge?

Duke is giving us important information about himself and a whole group of readers like him when he says, "When I read books, I want things to go my way." Readers who love to read *do* get to have things go their way because they find a match between what they are hoping for in a book and what an author provides. When things do not go their way, optimistic readers find other books. If those books are not satisfactory, a reader might eventually decide, as Duke had, that reading is not what it used to be, after all. Duke's observations elucidate an important reason that people who can read well may choose not to.

> I seem to lose interest,
> I mean, why didn't he [the writer] have it like...?
> Once I start readin' it,
> I feel like the author's movin' my attention to somewhere I just...
> [Duke's sentence fades away and he shakes his head.]

Duke was not impossible to please. He was enthusiastic about a writer who provides what he, as a reader, was looking for from an author.

> If I'm gonna read som'n, I like reading stuff like Edgar Allen Poe.
> I'll read his stuff, and it's just crazy (laughs).
> He just will sock you—
> I like his word play.
> He draws my attention.
> The play that we did was "The Fall of the House of Usher."
> I liked that one.
> But it left me in suspense at the end of the play.
> That's cool.
> I enjoyed that.
> I'm into Gothic stuff.

Duke is describing a basic relation of reader to text: When the story goes his way, his desires are satisfied by the author's work. During the reading, he feels that his attention is attracted, and after reading, he takes pleasure in looking back on the experience. When the story does not go his way, he feels that his attention is being moved to tedious ends and his interest fades. Naturally, he wants to take over the storytelling to make it go his way. He wants to see his stories (i.e., stories he finds rewarding) on the page. His purpose for reading is not to take on a completely different set of beliefs or someone else's vision of how the world works but to explore and reinforce his own. As Holland (1980) says, "all of us, as we read, use the literary work to symbolize and finally to replicate ourselves" (p. 124).

In *5 Readers Reading*, Holland (1975) presents in great depth the way in which the five college students he interviews respond to Faulkner's "A Rose for Emily" and two other short stories. He argues that all readers "re-create the original literary creation in terms of their own personalities" (xiii). This "re-creation" of the original literary work is also described as a transformation.

> In its most general terms, then, this model of literature as transformation suggests that the inanimate literary work is not that, not a work in itself, but the occasion for some person's work (in the sense we give the word when we speak of the "dream-work" or creative "work.") That is, a reader, as he synthesizes and re-creates a piece of literature, works; he transforms his own fantasies (of a kind that would ordinarily be unconscious) into the conscious social, moral, and intellectual meanings he finds by "interpreting" the work. (p. 17)

Holland's description of the reading process has been criticized for depending too heavily on the identification of a reader's identity theme—a basic way of relating to the world which is expressed in multiple variations throughout a person's life. Holland admits that although he speaks of his five readers' identity themes as if they are readily determined and verifiable, identifying a person's theme is itself an act of interpretation. Just as readers interpret literature through their identity themes, so Holland must "read" those readers through his own identity theme. This leads to an interpretation interpreting an interpretation, a situation of which Culler (1980b) and Bleich (1976) disapprove. However, for my purposes here, the identity theme question does not disqualify Holland's observations concerning the influence of a reader's psychological makeup on that reader's interpretation of and response to a text. I am not attempting to describe Duke's identity theme, assuming that he has one, as Holland says all readers do. I do find that Holland's psychological focus on why a reader engages with a text or not, and the form that engagement takes, illuminates Duke's reactions to his reading and writing. It is one way of understanding many of the differences between one reader's reading of a text and another's reading of the same text.

Duke had an extraordinarily active imagination, providing ample fantasy material to transform into meaning as he read. Furthermore, he was at a developmental stage of life in which he was focused on understanding himself and finding out how he fit or did not fit into the world in which he lived. He was engaged in the psychological, social, and developmental "work" of becoming a man in his particular culture, struggling with contradictions within himself and looking for ways to relate satisfactorily to others. At first glance, he seemed to be a person who had all the resources and motivations for being an enthusiastic adolescent reader, that is, being a person who can, in Holland's (1975) words, synthesize and re-create a piece of literature, thereby transforming his own fantasies into the "social, moral, and intellectual meanings" (p. 17) available in that work. In fact, however, Duke rarely found texts that allowed him to make such transformations.

Holland (1975) argues that "each of us approaches a new experience with a certain characteristic cluster of hopes, desires, fears, and needs" (p. 114). As readers approaching a new literary experience, we want to see these hopes, desires, fears, and needs presented or performed through character, plot, and language in a way that gratifies us because it matches or resonates with our own way of perceiving and managing internal and external reality. When this process goes particularly well, Holland says, "the reader merges with the book, and the events of the book become as real as anything in his [the reader's] mind" (p. 115). When a reader does not like a story, it is because he or she has not found the match.

When I asked Duke, as I asked all the students I interviewed, what popped into his mind when I said the word *reading*, his answer was immediate: "Boring." When I probed into his experience of *Go Ask Alice* (Anonymous, 1998), assigned in one of his English classes, he initially stayed with "boring" but then explained in more detail.

> For a while I was tryin' to read it,
> I was readin' it, actually,
> and then I got bored with it.
> It didn't relate to me.
> That's basically it.
> I mean, in a way it does kinda refer to me,
> There're a lot of times I have a struggle with my personality,
> and she had a struggle with her personality.

So in that way, I underst—I felt them—
it wasn't enlightening me any.

Anne: Watching her struggle did not help you understand more about
how to deal with your struggles?

Duke: Exactly!
Alice, I felt she's being pressured to lie,
and she was fallin' into it,
and once she got herself in,
it's hard to get out.
I feel she was havin' an internal struggle with herself,
and also with her friends after she was tryin' to get on the right
    track;
It's hard to ride back in.

After she had sex with that guy,
she was at her grandparents' house,
and her grandpa had a heart attack,
and readin' that...
I don't like readin' depressin' stuff.
Her life just started gettin' worse and worse.
I wasn't expectin' it.
I want som'n to get better....
It's bringin' me down.

If it had a different ending,
like if she hadda pulled through,
and turned around,
and she was helpin' everybody,
tellin' 'em how they could turn their life around,
then it coulda been an encouragement.

When you read som'n and it just goes to the peak,
then...like I did when once I choose—
it just went downhill.
When you read som'n like that,
unless you been through it like I—
I did in tryin' to have...
I went through som'n like that,
but then she just died
and everything was wrong,
It was kinda depressing.
I mean, I'm more of a hear person than to read,
that's basically it.

This lengthy quote is worth examining in some detail, for in it Duke revealed why and how he resisted this book. His first move was to use the word *boring* as a defense against the undesired experience of seeing Alice make mistakes like the ones he has made and spiraling deeper and deeper into self-destruction. As teachers, our response to a complaint that a book is boring should be to probe further rather than to take the complaint at face value or to assume that we know what the student means by the term. In this case, especially, trying to persuade Duke that the story is interesting would probably mean emphasizing exactly the trauma in the story that is threatening him. Many young readers do find Alice's descent into despair and death to be interesting. But rather than criticize Duke for being a judgmental or superficial reader, we can learn much about him and about readers in general by examining the ways in which his needs and expectations did not match the life-and-death drama presented in this book.

Duke held the story at a distance by attempting to say that it did not relate to him, but he immediately realized that it did relate, just not in a helpful way. He was clear about the way Alice's problems were "bringin' [him] down." He was clear about desiring a book that would inspire rather than threaten him. Alice's troubles reminded him painfully of his own, which he did not describe in detail, but said only, "I went through som'n like that." After a first attempt to push the story away by calling it "boring," he admitted that it did reflect his problems back to him. The story failed him, however, when it failed to provide defenses against suffering or defeat that Duke could identify and use. Reading the book, he felt defenseless against Alice's decline as long as he stayed in the world of the novel. The only way he could get out was to think of the book as boring and stop reading it. His use of the word *boring* served not only as an easy, familiar way to dismiss the experience but also helped to strip the story of its power to manipulate his emotions. If Duke admitted that he stopped reading because the story had too much emotional effect, he would not be able to shake himself free of it as effectively.

Striking, too, is Duke's final remark about being more of a hearing person than a reading person. He moved directly from stating that in *Go Ask Alice* "everything was wrong, it was kinda depressing," to rejecting reading altogether. If reading leaves him depressed and helpless, as it does in this case, such a move seems to be a necessary coping strategy.

Under the remembered influence of *Go Ask Alice*, Duke made a sweeping rejection of reading, but not all books leave him depressed and helpless. He had a happy story to tell about *Of Mice and Men* (Steinbeck, 1993).

I love that book.
Before I had ever read it or seen the movie,
my mom was tellin' me about it.
She made me feel it,
and then it was interestin' to see the movie.
I was sayin', "Oh, that's nice."
She had read the book version,
and she was sayin' how she had cried about it,
So now I'm, "Okay, I'm gonna have to see that,"
and she was lookin' to rent it,
but no place had the original.
She liked the original better,
so then it came on TV, and I saw it then.
I really liked it,
So when we started readin' it [in English class]
it was comin' back to me.
I could visualize the movie with the scenes,
so it was real good.

I saw somebody tryin' to help another.
George was tryin' to help Lennie a lot,
and that's cool.
He's bein' a good friend to Lennie.
He looked at his predicament,
he knew Lennie wasn't that smart,
but yet he was still there,
tryin' to support him.
Every once in a while,
he'd make little jokes about him,
but you could tell deep down inside he really loved him.
I liked that.
(Duke and I laugh together about George's telling Lennie again and again the story Lennie loved to hear. Then I ask about the ending of the story.)
That was kinda hard.
He felt he had to do it

'cause they were gonna torture him.
He felt it was the better way.
I don't know what I woulda did.
It woulda been hard to do,
I know it was hard for him to do,
but he thought it was the better way.

Duke's opposing reactions to *Go Ask Alice* and *Of Mice and Men* reveal more about Duke than they do about the novels. In other words, there is nothing absolute or universal about teenagers and Alice, or readers and Steinbeck. Duke felt threatened by the first story and reassured by the second. We cannot dismiss his depression while reading *Go Ask Alice* as a simple case of an immature person fearing conflict; as we will see in the next section, Duke was fascinated by conflict, and here he gave thoughtful consideration to the conflicts inherent in George's decision to kill Lennie. Nor can we say that the friendship between George and Lennie is universally appealing; every teacher who has assigned *Of Mice and Men* knows that it is not. Duke's reactions were personal, and the fact that other readers, even many other readers, agree or disagree with him should not obscure the authenticity and validity of those reactions.

As teachers, we can appreciate the affective and cognitive "set" that Duke's mother created for this book. It is interesting that the story Duke tells does not show her trying to persuade him to read the book; she first talked about it when she was looking for the video. But she "made [him] feel it," by telling him not only what the story involved but also how she cried over it. His own curiosity carried him forward so that when he actually read the book, he engaged with it; he understood it intellectually and emotionally. Seeing the movie before reading helped him visualize the story as he read it. And, having been helped to this point of understanding, he found in the novel a picture of a way to be a man relating to others that satisfied him.

Another rewarding experience came about the day one of his English classes read aloud a dramatic version of "The Fall of the House of Usher." Duke was thrilled. He wished the teacher had allowed him and the other readers to be on their feet, acting out the parts, but just having the opportunity to read in another voice in front of an audience was exciting and rewarding for him. He answered all the questions on the follow-up quiz correctly, too, providing further evidence that most of his academic problems were a result of his choosing to be engaged in life outside school rather than in it. He could do most schoolwork well when he was in class and awake.

However, Duke's reading prowess had its limits. One assignment that he tried to read but could not bring to life in his mind was Joseph Conrad's short story "The Lagoon" (1925). Students were expected to read independently, and Duke had a hard time understanding it.

> I try to get into it,
> but then they started gettin' into crazy talkin'.
>
> When I say "crazy" I mean
> they're flourishing together
> but they're not really making me visualize the scene.
> I had to look at the pictures,
> I was tryin' to think about it,
> but once they start usin'—
> I feel different authors try to be too descriptive,
> where they're using too-big words.
> I have a pretty wide vocabulary,
> but once they use a lot of words—
> big, intertwining together, then I can't really...
> (His sentence fades out here)

This story is generally considered one of Conrad's more accessible works, but Conrad always requires a great deal of skill, experience, imagination, and persistence from his readers. The vocabulary is somewhat difficult for adolescents (*somber, nipa palms, tendril, immobility, periodic, portals, enticed, astern,* and *discordant* are in the first few paragraphs). Other features that either challenge or intimidate readers are the long paragraphs and shifts in time.

I also had difficulty with the first few pages of this story. Duke identified the main problem right away: Conrad's description of the opening scene requires the reader to build a mental picture of a landscape—a Malayan river; the vegetation on its banks; and the position of the setting sun in relation to the sea, the river, and the boat—complete with emotional and symbolic layers. And then, of course, there are the characters of the white man and the Malayan oarsmen and the social relationships between them. None of this is familiar to me, so I had to read the exposition of the setting (eight paragraphs) carefully several times in order to form a picture of the scene. The difficulty was increased by my making several mistaken assumptions that I had to recognize and correct before I could go on, such as that the white man would face the steersman of his boat when he spoke to him (he did not, in fact, bother to turn around) and that the wake of the boat was behind it (the wake in question was the wake from the bow, however).

If I had trouble visualizing the scene from Conrad's words, I would expect that high school students would have even more trouble. This frustrating experience is characteristic of one of the ways that literature and Duke fail to connect with each other. Description is often a problem for him. He explained,

> Stories tend to get to a part where they're doin' too much describin'.
> It's too much of a break in the action
> and loses my interest and I never go back.

Duke did not have enough experience with or training in reading fiction to know that an author spends time painting a scene with words because he or she also is providing other kinds of information about states of mind, nature, and community. Duke did not have faith that such scenes are worth the time and effort they take to read, especially when the mental pictures do not form in response to the words. He felt that he was being asked to expend time and energy on useless description, and in this case, he never made it past the opening. He just gave up.

When Holland (1975) talks about readers finding or not finding a match for their hopes and fears in a piece of literature, he makes it clear that what he is describing is true of all experiences, not just reading (p. 113). We all go through life thinking, feeling, seeing, and hearing in ways particular to us—ways shaped by what postmodern theory describes as our decentered position in a network of possibilities (Eagleton, 1996). No such thing as an objective reading—or writing—of a text is possible.

The readings and writings that we do can reveal a great deal about us, especially when, like Duke, we resist practicing the school-taught literary conventions (see Purves, 1991, for discussion of this phenomenon). What can be learned about Duke is limited by the small number of literary texts he has read. However, there are stories that are extremely important to Duke. He does use the story form to accomplish much of the psychological work Holland observes in *5 Readers Reading*, with this difference: Duke's favorite texts are ones he writes, not ones he reads. The former are the stories that always go his way.

Duke's Stories

Many of the students in this study said that they would rather write than read. They enjoyed the chance to express themselves and to communicate with others. Whereas they often experienced reading as boring, pointless, and laborious, writing allowed them to tell their stories, in words of their choosing, so the labor it took may be forgiven. Duke was among those who would rather write than read. He negotiated a deal with his English teacher whereby he agreed to write a story using some of the themes in *Kindred* (Butler, 1979) in order to make up for missed work. He described his story, which, like *Kindred*, involves time travel.

> It wasn't my choice,
> I got transported without my consent.
>
> Somebody from the future has been watchin' me,
> and they said I had the qualities that they're looking for to send
>   me back.
> It starts out with a telephone conversation, where they call;
> the first time, I'm, like, 15.
> They call,
> and I can't hear—
> it's like a faint voice in the background
> and I can't really hear them,
> so then the phone line's cut
> and I hang up.
>
> Later they called me and then it was clear,
> but they didn't tell me anything—
> really, no instructions...
> they didn't even tell me my mission.
> I wrote it out like they was just telling me,
> "Don't let God see you in the Garden,
> and you gotta take a notebook, a Bible, a pencil,"
> all this different stuff I had listed, like a candle, or whatever,

and then it was, "You got two hours to get all this stuff together,
and then you gotta leave."
So I kept thinking it was a prank call,
they hanging up and stuff.
I watched my fish in my aquarium, and I got sleepy.
Then as I was asleep,
I woke up,
but then I'm outside.
During that time, I had got sent back to the past.

But I went back at the wrong time,
before God had created anything,
so it was just black, total darkness,
It was like, "In the beginning God created the Heavens,
and the earth was without form and void."

And I was wondering, Oh, where's everything at?
Then I woke up, I was back at home.
I was asking everybody where they was...
and they were like, "Oh, you were just here a second ago,"
so then I never fit in.
So that's where I'm kinda stuck.
I'm trying to see where I'm gonna take this.
I'm going back in time, to tell Adam "Don't eat the apple."
That would change the whole world.
I'm gonna try to do it in the way where you would decide your own
    ending.
Keep you in suspense.

This remarkable story speaks volumes about Duke. His desire for
the power to control momentous events, his fears of being controlled by unknown others (especially when he is unconscious), his
confidence that he would be chosen for a challenging task by the
powers that be, his concern with fitting in socially, and his awareness of how difficult communication can be are all here. Also present is the tension between the pencil-and-Bible world he inhabits
consciously and the dark, formless void to which his imagination
can send him when his guard is down.

But that darkness exerted a compelling attraction for Duke
even as (and perhaps because) it threatened him with confusion
and social isolation. He delighted in exploring it. He was constantly seeking to test his control over his own imagination by shaping

the darkness into a struggle between good and evil. He developed characters and plots in raps, songs, and poems (and occasionally stories, when school assignments required them) to dramatize this struggle. In this story, he went right to the top; God is the character he has to watch out for. God is not the enemy, but God is the author who has told a story with which Duke is not satisfied. Duke wants Genesis to go his way and he is unafraid of imagining himself interfering with God's plan. (See the section "Seeking Inspiration for Responsible Manhood" later in this chapter for further discussion of this story.)

Most of Duke's characters, he said, are vampires. He loved vampires and he identified with their power over others and over death itself. His interest in vampires was part of his love of competition and his admiration of a warrior's uncompromising standards.

> I love vampires,
> so that's my rap name,
> Prince Vladimir the Impaler.
> My image is a vampire—
> in rap, it's a challenge to who's the best,
> and I eat other MC's.
> I feed off 'em,
> they're nothing.
> I'm tryin' to belittle 'em in my rap name.
>
> I always liked Dracula,
> and I was watchin' the History Channel one day,
> and they was talkin' 'bout the first vampire—
> he didn't have fangs,
> but every Sunday it was a ritual that they wore the black with the
>   red.
>
> Just the whole concept of that, I just love this.
> It was sayin' how he was real mean, a cruel-hearted person.
> I wouldn't say I'm a cruel-hearted person,
> but he did what he felt was fair,
> and I liked that about him,
> even though it was kinda harsh,
> he did what he felt was fair.
>
> Like, this woman didn't have her husband's shirt the right size,
> he was wearin' a shirt that was too small for him,
> so he killed her.

Now that's not really how I feel,
you kill everybody,
but a lot of people think that about rap people,
they explain the story,
and just 'cause their story might have killin' in it,
they just tellin' what they feel
from day to day.

Anne: It sounds like a big part of what's appealing about vampires is they have the power to do honestly what they feel like doing, that the rest of us wouldn't do because we're too inhibited.

Duke: That's good, that's it right there.
Seems like I got this power trip.

I'm not afraid of blood.
I can work with it,
and that was a sense of how he succeeded.
He would kill people and then he'd actually drink their blood—
That was a form of takin' over 'em.

Competing, winning, belittling and consuming the enemy— these were warrior fantasies that drove one part of Duke's inner life. However, they were in conflict with his Christian family life and Duke worried about this. He used his writings to grapple with these conflicts and desires while he engaged in word play and creativity. Writing, not reading, gave him an arena in which to face his challenges and display his prowess.

The first piece of writing that Duke read to me came from his rap notebook, a standard school notebook with marbled cardboard covers and a taped spine. The tape was coming unglued, and the edges of the cardboard were a little worn because Duke had been carrying the book in his backpack for six months. I asked him if he could read me a rap from the notebook.

Okay, I'll find som'n, som'n kind of interesting.
I got some crazy ones in here,
just whatever's on my mind...
Okay, it's called "Why Must I Choose?"
This girl was tellin' me...
like, I was doin' a lot of things that was bad,
you know what I'm sayin',
I see, I know better a lot of times,

I know better than that,
I do, but I always wondered, why do I have a decision—
I'm glad that I do,
but I always choose the wrong, the bad things,
so I wonder why I got to choose.

When Duke read me this rap, he delivered some of the lines in a slow, half-sung measure and other lines in rapid-fire rhythmic speech. For the first eight lines he alternated between slow and fast and then he read the rest quickly.

(slow) I know that things aren't right,
(quick) sometimes they pressure me and I don't even know what to do—
(slow) When left, I told you right,
(quick) Lucifer is talkin' and my mind just got confused.
(slow) That pathway leads to doom,
(quick) I know a person fires 'cause I gotta let the gun go boom.
(slow) Turn right, or the end is soon.
(quick) I can see right now be another long day at the fork in the road,
so I got to jump, I got my ready to kill my foes,
should I kick in the doo' wavin' the forty-four?
I think about the penalty o' bein' on death row.
I don't know. Shall I put it to my head and pull the trigger,
let it blow? Hell no, when I'm thinkin' my mind's steadily twinkin',
I gotta stop drinkin'. Call my nigga The Max,
tell the man that I'm havin' second thoughts about the gig.
Shall I go ahead with the plan, blast him and his old man,
split the wig like I was Billy the Kid?
Man, I know I wanted to, but now I don't know what to do,
shall I go ahead and go through,
It's decision, decision to make and I don't even know.
That's why I'm sayin' that my mind's at a fork in the road.
[End of the rap]

Now this character came from my imagination.
I was thinking o' som'n real hard that people,
a lot of times they get pressured to do?
So I was thinkin',
my situation wasn't that deep,

but I was tryin' to make people feel that, you know,
how deep situations can get,
where you wonder,
you already set your mind to do it,
you're havin' second thoughts about it.

Anne: One of the things this character is thinking about is, "If I get caught, I could die," but I'm wondering if he's also thinking about whether he actually wants to be responsible for murdering somebody. Do you think that bothers this character?

Duke: Well, actually, in the end—
'cause I have more char—
more people in my head if I can—
I have Death featured in this,
And I have God featured in this.
Death is more like Satan.
And in this, Death is pressuring me to do it,
and God is tellin' me not to do it.
And at the end of the story I end up killin' him.

Well, it's not really me, it's just the rap—
God tells him,
"It's over, you're not my son, I don't know you."
It's kinda sad, to me.
I'm tryin' to make people aware of the bad things
that can happen from your decisions.

I really put myself in the character,
'cause I was feelin' it.
It was the same pressure
to choose between good and evil.

I asked Duke why he was depressed by reading about Alice's inability to make good decisions, but chose to create another character who also made fatal mistakes. He struggled with the question for a while, but finally realized,

When I write it myself, then it changes what I would do.
If I write it myself,
then I'm writin' it so I will make a different decision.
So when I write it,
I'm picturin' myself not makin' this mistake like he is.
I see what they're doin',

what's happenin' to them,
so I make sure I wouldn't do it.

But when I read it [Alice],
it's already over and done....
I guess that could be an inspiration too,
but I feel it more from my own writing,
to do the right thing.

This is an important insight into why, for Duke, writing was satisfying but reading was not. When he wrote, he engaged fully with characters and events that were important to him, and he resolved conflicts in ways that were most meaningful to him. He could imagine outcomes for characters who chose to be hired killers and, as a result of that imagining, resolved not to become one of them. Just as many readers love the alternate lives that their reading allows them to experience, so Duke loved the alternate lives that he created when he wrote. It is a testament to the authenticity of his psychological engagement with his characters that often, when he wrote, he did not feel in control of the process but rather as if he were a channel for ideas that must be expressed.

I kinda feel that [my characters] just do what they do.
It's funny,
I look at situations,
and then, it's like I go into another body.
And when I'm writin' it,
it just writes the way I...
would that be like a third person?
You can see a point of view,
I just look at it while my hand's writing.
It's like I'm readin' it.

His confusion over the meaning of the phrase "third person" suggests a way in which he has "read" a school lesson by transforming it into terms that make sense to him (or perhaps he missed the lesson on point of view altogether), but in any case he experienced writing as easy—"There's not really a time when I can't write," he said—and he enjoyed expressing himself, watching what his hand was writing, and engaging in creative word play. "I like to be entertained when I write," he said. But when he read, he felt constrained by the author's decisions.

When I write,
a lot of things come out.
I'm talking about what I wanna talk about.
[Reading] is adjusting to talkin' about what they wanna talk about.
To me, reading is like listening,
and you don't get to say nuttin'.
You just listen to the whole thing,
like somebody talkin' to you,
you want to input,
you want to say whatever...
"It should be this way,"
"No, you shouldn't do that!"
Just listenin' the whole time.
You can't argue with a book.

Limits of Reading

"Reading is like listening." No matter how much agency contemporary literary theorists take from authors and give to readers, Duke felt the constraints of the text. His frustration with being in the listener's position is understandable, considering how much he needed and wanted to find ways to deal with his internal conflicts. Reading or listening to a story someone else wants to tell but that does not help him with these conflicts made him feel that he was wasting time.

His problems arose, in large measure, from his being a highly social young man, as his algebra teacher observed, although being social involves more than hanging out with friends. The young men Duke liked to spend time with encouraged him to skip school and engage in exciting, risky, and sometimes illegal activities. Duke himself said that if he "didn't know anybody," he would "be doin' everything right," that is, spending time on academic work, attending school, and staying out of trouble. He referred to the exploits he enjoyed with his friends as "bad" behavior and as "sin or whatever," and his rap, "Why Must I Choose," was inspired by his feeling of being caught between his peers, who were pulling him into new and dangerous adventures, and his family and church members, who were pulling him back to culturally approved norms. "That's what I was goin' through," he said. He continued,

I know what's right,
I grew up normal, I had to do things, and everything,
and then with peers you're always gonna be introduced to som'n
     new.
They gonna try to get you to—
it might seem little, but it's wrong nevertheless,
and all these wrongs
will give you a want for wrong.
If you do one thing, then,
"Well, you did that, you can do this."
It's not that much worse.
It seems that way.
Then before you know it,
you'll be wrapped up.
You wanna experiment.
I mean, I know I'm not s'posed to do it,
but I want to do it
and I do do it.

Tasting adventure gave Duke "a want for wrong" and set him on
the slippery slope to trouble. Feeling caught, he looked up to men
who were no longer troubled by such temptations.

Then there's people that always do the right thing,
and I wonder how they got on that level.
I look at different preachers, and pastors,
they're always doin' som'n right,
you can never imagine them doin' som'n wrong.
They tell you, like they don't even want to do that,
but you think about it,
well, I'm young...I guess you think you grow out of it,
but most people don't.

And so I look up to them—
to be able to do that.
Losin' that attraction [to trouble],
I don't know how you do that.

Both groups—his peers and people associated with his family
and church—were important to Duke. He did not want either group
to be disappointed in him. But whatever he had do to gain admiration

in the eyes of one group was sure to garner disapproval in the eyes of the other. Under immediate pressures to graduate, earn money for life after school, and maintain peer friendships and family relationships, Duke was busy, psychologically speaking. The reading he was assigned did not help him with any of this. He explained,

> Thing is, you try to get into it [reading],
> but if you see somebody makin' the same mistakes,
> I look at my life,
> I do the same thing in life,
> but I don't want to read about it!

When reading goes well, it is not experienced as a passive experience by Duke or any other reader. Holland's (1975) theory of reading has an explanation for this: Engaged readers are busy using the story to transform unconscious fantasies into conscious meaning, which they find in the text. It is easy to see that Duke's pleasure in the bond between George and Lennie in *Of Mice and Men* reflects his interest in close social ties. (It probably also reflects deeper unconscious aspects of his psyche that this study does not probe.) When the reader cannot perform this psychological work with the text, he or she has the feeling that nothing is happening, that the book is boring, and that time is being wasted.

Of course, readers also can find reading unsatisfactory when it threatens their psychological well-being, as we saw when Duke talked about reading *Go Ask Alice*. Duke wanted to deal with these threats, but he had to work with them in ways that were useful to him, as in his own writing. He said, in fact, that he carried his rap notebook around partly because he liked to write in it, but also because

> It's som'n I care about.
> I put the ones I really feel,
> and sometimes if I want some comfort
> I come back to different ones I wrote down.

Stories can provide Duke with comfort and inspiration and with entertainment and lessons in the nature of good and evil— but they must be the right stories. When he was in school, talking to me about reading, Duke had a tendency to equate all reading with required school reading—not unreasonably because he did so little reading outside school (and lately, so little in school). He tended to dismiss reading in sweeping generalizations, saying that it is boring or slow. Looking at a paperback mystery story that had been assigned in his Recent American Novels class, he remarked,

> It hurts me to see it this long.
> But I heard people say once they read a book like this
> they feel like they accomplished som'n.
> Me? No.
> If I write som'n that much I feel like,
> "Oh, look at me!"

> They watched the movie in class.
> It sounds like som'n I woulda watched.
> But readin' it's a different story.
> I rather watch it than read it any day.
> Even if it is to a slow part in the movie,
> it still has my attention.
> But you gotta work to read.

Anne: If the movie is slow, I can just sit back and wait for the slow part to be over.

Duke: Yeah, if the movie gets slow, that's when you get the popcorn.

Anne: If a book gets slow, you still have to keep reading.

Duke: Exactly.
And that's what bores me.
Then I start losing interest.
And when I lose interest—
if I'm not interested, I'm not gonna understand it.
I'm gonna start just lookin' at it,
and it's just gonna look like words to me.
Like a whole bunch o' words,
and I'm like, "Okay, I'm puttin' this up."

Seeking Inspiration for Responsible Manhood

Duke was a young man who, like most adolescents, had formed strong opinions about what was important and what was not. He valued his peers: In addition to the obvious social acceptance they provided, they also took part in his rapping and provided ways for him to test certain aspects of manhood, sometimes in forbidden adventures and sometimes in fantasy worlds they shared, such as vampires or the cartoon *Dragon Ball Z*, which was Duke's favorite television show and yet another version of the battle between good and evil.

His large family (he has six siblings) and church also claimed his loyalty. His uncle was a preacher whom Duke admired, and through volunteering to play music at another church, he met a younger preacher to whom he loved to listen. His description of the two men's preaching styles revealed Duke's sensitivity to language and his emotional connection to religious inspiration.

> [My uncle] has everything he's gonna say wrote down,
> so he looks at it and he keeps talkin',
> like some type of oratorical speech.
> I have to say his vocabulary was bigger,
> he's older, he's been around, he's real smart.
>
> The pastor at this other church,
> he just comes from the top of his head,
> and he'll quote different things,
> or he'll look in the Bible
> and he just freestyles everything,
> I like the way he does that.
> I love his vocabulary,
> it's immense.
> 'Cause he says a lot of things
> and I remember 'em.
> When he's just sayin' it, seems like it's just coming directly from
>   God
> right then, at that time.
> I guess you could do that readin', but
> since I'm not really into reading...
> God's just talking to me right then.

No wonder reading ran a weak second to oral performance— this was a moment of heaven on earth. Duke sought the freestyling mode as well as the inspirational message repeatedly in various parts of his life. He loved the energy that seemed to be channeled from God through the preacher to him. He loved to perform and be entertained that way. He loved surprises, he loved stories that kept readers in suspense, and he loved watching and feeling creative energy flow. He felt that no human being really had control over improvised words or music; they came from mysterious and divine sources. They reminded Duke that the universe is full of treasures and pleasures and that the best way to find them is through spontaneous, inspired expression of feeling. The hand writes, the voice speaks, and Duke's responsive mind marvels.

But this view of life, this location of joy in the spirit of the moment, is hard to support in daily schoolwork. It is no wonder that Duke felt bored by school; in fact, school threatened to drain him of the wonderful energies that gave him his music and his stories. So he kept his energies alive outside school. In school, he kept his rap notebook in his backpack and his vampire lore in his imagination. He resisted reading that did not go his way and he kept his wits sharp (and his investment to a minimum) by guessing and improvising. For example, he received a point on an English quiz for an answer that had nothing to do with the book at all but which was creative enough to amuse his teacher (who wanted very much to pass him so that he could get his diploma). The teacher wrote in the margin of the quiz paper next to Duke's answer, "You win the creative wrong answer award." The question asked for a paragraph about the antagonist's scheme in Mary Higgins Clark's mystery *A Stranger Is Watching* and stated, "Be sure to include at least three specific details of his sinister plot." Duke wrote,

> The madman planned to kill off both the boy and his parents. He planned on brutally assassinating them both, impaling them from long, thick, solid oak poles, draining their blood into buckets and saving it to drink.

The vampires that populated Duke's imagination must have been active that day.

School seems made for a measured, sober, text-based approach to knowing and being. As an active, creative young man, Duke's response to the emptiness of school reading was to dream up some way out rather than just grit his teeth and endure. His mind was always busy, so he enjoyed the challenge of bringing his own ways into school through his stories, using them to dramatize and understand the consequences of the conflicts he struggled with. In his time-travel story, he brought his interest in power and control together with his religious life. His challenge in that story was to get into the Garden of Eden and change human history (and humanity's relationship with God) without getting caught—in other words, to make the story go his way. When I asked him how this could work because God is omniscient, he laughed and said, "God knows all, but don't let Him catch you at it. Don't be there when He come around."

In this fantasy, Duke does no less than confront original sin. If he can prevent Adam from eating the apple, humans will no longer feel the desire to go against God's wishes. The terrible "want for wrong" that plagued Duke and drew him into "sin or whatever" would never arise. If Duke could make Genesis into *his* story, then in the year 2000 Duke could be like those preachers he admired who had a manly gift for eloquence, the power to stir the community, and a connection with God, but who did not struggle with desire to engage in adventures that were ethically and legally forbidden. He would not be writing raps that asked why he must choose between what he wanted to do and what he should do. The radical nature of Duke's fantasy solution to this problem is a testament to both the depth of anguish it caused him and to his courage and creativity. It is also a testament to the psychological power of story.

Duke did not belittle reading in the abstract. He was clear about his personal taste being just that—his choice—and he knew that if he loved to read, he would be a much more successful student.

If I liked to read...
'cause I haven't really read any of these stories,
I'm just so happy to get good on the test,
I don't know how that come that way,
I do real good on tests regardless of whether I study,
but if I did read,
I could have a lot of my homework done,
I'd probably done more of my work.
I notice when people read,
they tend to do more,
they're more active and they do their work,
but I don't really do it unless I'm at school.

They always have their work and stuff,
in other classes they got their work,
they're the ones that have their work.
Not like me, I never read.
I try and listen in class,
that's the key.

What Has Duke Taught Us?

Duke's thoughts and energies were taken up by the problem of how to be a good man to others and still be true to himself. He desired self-expression with peers, adult guidance that he could respect, and freedom from dead ends and wasted time. These are valuable concerns—natural and healthy—that we should hope all young people think about. The sorrow is that the school institution is so poorly equipped to provide a framework in which Duke could explore these concerns in a way that was satisfying to him.

Thus, he presented particular challenges not only to his teachers and parents but also to the whole school institution. His rejection of reading was not a result of poor preparation; his family and early schooling provided a solid grounding in the affective, social, and cognitive aspects of literacy, and, in fact, Duke read well. When he read aloud the beginning of *A Stranger Is Watching* (Clark, 1977) to me, he read fluently and easily. He was able to describe the mental pictures he had formed as he read, all of which were consistent with the text.

But a good start does not guarantee continued involvement with reading. Duke's temperament and personal style led him toward performance, entertainment of others, music, and word play. Except for those times when reading became performance, reading did not provide for an expression of these talents. Of the Bible, which is one book Duke thought everyone should know, he said, "I'd rather quote it than read it." He used writing to express whatever was on his mind, usually in the form of stories in raps, but when he spoke of turning his Eden story into a novel, he said, "I could do it, but I wouldn't wanna read it when I was done."

I include Duke in these case studies because his use of texts (including those he writes) reveals a dense network of purpose, pleasure, and frustration—in other words, how he engages and why he resists. Duke's story shows how social and cultural forces collide with or reinforce personal needs and preferences. Each influences the other. In this way, Duke shows how the work of growing up that all young people must do and finding and making a place for themselves takes on the particular form that it does for him. Unless we keep both the large goal and Duke's individual path to that goal in our sights, his patterns of engagement and resistance will be either invisible or nonsensical and will likely generate frustration in those who try to guide him.

In fact, Duke's patterns of engagement and resistance had a deep internal consistency. School was not going to change these patterns, so teachers must learn to work with them. By this time in his school career, Duke was so practiced at avoiding reading, and so convinced that he could learn what he needed to know without doing any reading, that trying to force him to read when he did not want to was pointless. He might have been enticed into reading more if he could exert some control over the choice of texts. He might have been enticed into reading more if texts that connect with his interests were presented to him with those interests in mind. Conrad's story, "The Lagoon," for example, turns out to be filled with drama, danger, and romance, potentially very appealing to Duke. Duke might have persisted with this story, even reading alone (although he much preferred to have members of the class read aloud) if he had known that the rewards of adventure lay ahead. If his reading of the story had been set up so that he had been helped to visualize the opening scene—if, for example, the class had collaborated in drawing on the blackboard a map of the river, land, and sea, and then a picture of the boat and the men in it—Duke might have continued reading the story. It might have contributed to his understanding of what literature can do by contributing to his understanding of a way to be a man.

"Duke is learning to be a man, but not a *responsible* man," his algebra teacher said. She was frustrated by Duke's choosing to put his friends and his music—what he saw as preparation for his future—ahead of school, which to her was the more important preparation for his future. In fact, Duke agreed that getting a high school diploma was important, and he wanted to graduate. The difference between his viewpoint and his teachers' was that he believed he could get the diploma with minimal schoolwork, and all he cared about was passing. High grades did not matter to him. Required high school subjects did not seem important, either.

What did matter to him was moving into adulthood toward a career in music and becoming a man who expressed himself honestly and had good relationships with others. He sought experiences that gratified his desires, of course, but he also sought knowledge that helped him understand and manage those desires. He felt conflicted about his "want for wrong," the thrill he got from being part of a group of young men who challenged limits and created adventure, because he also admired his parents and the preachers who told him that wrong is wrong. He was aware of the serious consequences of getting caught, only one of which was disappointing his family.

He was at a stage of his life that was almost completely taken up with action. Reading was useful only when it helped him do other things such as find information about vampires. Adults who read know that reading could contribute much to Duke's desire for adventure and understanding. In fact, Duke knew it himself; when I asked him why a person should read fiction, he first said, "For entertainment," and then, "I guess it's always in the way of teaching a lesson." But he was not finding school reading a source of either entertainment or lessons. Part of this was due to the choice of texts, in which Duke had no way to participate (although the teachers did consider the students' interests when choosing from available texts) and part of it was a result of the presentation of the texts, which often was done without scaffolding (Applebee, 1991; Bruner, 1986; Wood, Bruner, & Ross, 1976), so that whatever Duke might need in order to enter into the fictional world he had to supply himself. He was not always up to the task.

If high school teachers, especially English teachers, were taught to teach their students how to read the texts they assign (see Schoenbach, Greenleaf, Cziko, & Hurwitz, 1999, for a successful schoolwide reading program), they could show their students that reading includes arguing with the book, something that Duke longed to do but believed was impossible (see Beach & Freedman, 1992; Corcoran, 1990; Kutz & Roskelly, 1991; Langer, 1990; Purves, Rogers, & Soter, 1995; Slatoff, 1970; and Smith, 1992, for discussion of how teachers might do this). Teachers' first and main concern usually is that the students understand what the author said, and curricula are set up on such a tight schedule that little time exists for students to talk about how they respond to the text.

For teaching purposes, it is important to distinguish between interpreting the text and responding to it, even though in theoretical terms, such a distinction is not possible. (For example, Gadamer [1975] identifies interpretation with remaking the content of the text into the interpreter's own meanings.) The difference I intend is this: Interpreting requires readers to stay within the circle of the text, generating ideas about why characters do what they do or why the author chose to emphasize a particular detail or moment. Readers' responses, on the other hand, come from stepping outside the circle of the text and examining the interactions between what readers bring to texts and what they find in them. Responses are reactions to texts, usually feelings and associations. Of course, both interpretations and responses will come from the readers' personal and cultural experiences, but Duke's feeling of being ambushed by the ending of *Go Ask Alice* is not an interpretation. It is a response. Teachers (including me) feel a responsibility to make sure that readers spend enough time and energy in the text to know (or create or recreate) what is there. But when readers have a strong response, it is important for them to express it and compare it with others' responses. Duke might have felt much better about the ending of *Go Ask Alice* if he had been able to discuss his dissatisfaction with other readers. In his earlier class, his appreciation of *Of Mice and Men* might have helped disaffected readers understand why the book is considered a valuable piece of literature, assuming, of course, that time had been spent arguing with the text and including it in a classroom conversation about people's responsibilities to one another.

Duke's problems with school would not all be solved by addressing his problems with reading. But clearly school reading was alienating him and contributing to his belief that school was not teaching him what he needed and wanted to know. If he were able to see (and feel) how the assigned stories spoke to him about his concerns, he might have turned to reading as a viable source of information, guidance, and comfort. If reading instruction and practice were aimed at helping him learn to argue with and debate about texts, he might have gained through reading with others some insight into serious questions that intrigued and troubled him.

Iser says that "literature gives presence to what otherwise would remain unavailable" (1993, p. xi). For Duke, trying to test his wits, develop his strengths, find his inspiration, and be a man among men, that which literature gives presence to might be exactly what he needed. The educator's task is to help him know it.

Chapter 5

Rosa: Fiction as Therapy

R osa loved to read. She carried thick paperback novels with her wherever she went, and all her teachers noticed her voluminous reading. When I asked what came to her mind when she heard the word *reading*, she answered,

> Relaxing, fun, quiet.
> I mean, I can read 7 books in one day
> if I'm not bothered.
> And that's on a school day,
> right after school.
> On Saturdays,
> I can read about 12.

These were big claims. But Rosa had staked out specific reading territory—romance, mystery, and fantasy—and because she had been reading in these genres for years, she had become an extremely fluent consumer of these texts. As Rosa's story will show, she read these texts for specific purposes, seeking a particular kind of satisfaction that she had become adept at finding quickly. She was especially expert in reading romance novels and proud of her expertise, even though her teachers routinely let her know that there was virtually no place for this reading in school.

Rosa, a senior in high school, was an adolescent mixture of child and adult whose pink cheeks and full figure brought to mind Victorian ideals of healthy young womanhood. Although lapses did occur, she usually was a conscientious student who worked to keep her grades in the C+ to B- range, and she had been accepted by a nearby state university for matriculation in the fall. She did not have any glaring academic problems, but she was not an outstanding academic success. Conventional wisdom would have it that a serious bibliophile should be an excellent student, but Rosa's story is a reminder that the equation is not so simple.

Rosa's chosen texts and her way of reading were not what most teachers mean by *reading*, and she implicitly challenged educators whose goal is to inspire students to love reading as they do. Are we, as educators, championing the development of a love of any kind of reading? Or do we really mean to teach students to value the same kinds of texts we value? Have we done our jobs as teachers if our students read only pulp fiction? What do readers need to know about reading (or about life) to appreciate different kinds of texts? As I dug deeper into Rosa's reasons for reading the novels she did, and deeper into institutional and academic positions about what and why educators want students to read, I found complexities and contradictions that are worth careful examination.

"Escape" Genres

The readers of romance novels that Radway (1991) studied said that they read them for escape—escape from the constant demands of their families and escape to a world in which a particular kind of romantic drama is played out. But the term *escape reading* implies an inferior kind of reading, a self-indulgent refusal to face one's responsibilities or at least a refusal to choose reading that will be useful or self-improving. I contend, however, that people use reading, including escape reading, for valid purposes that ultimately help them believe, learn, and be what is important to them. Reading helps people deal with emotions, including the most potent emotions—anger, fear, and desire (Coen, 1994; McNall, 1981). Reading popular fiction can, as Radway's readers insisted, give a reader renewed strength and inspiration for meeting responsibilities.

Rosa, too, read romances for escape from reality and to a world in which true love is possible. Because she did not have a husband and children demanding her care, the escape she was seeking was not from work but from blows of fate and fears of the future. In Rosa's life, the painful events and situations she could not control included numerous serious illnesses and deaths in her family and circle of friends, her parents' failed marriage, her tense relationship with her father, and what she saw as her own personal shortcomings. At one point she commented that she had never

been a sentimental person, and when I asked her if romance novels were sentimental, she grinned a little and said,

> Yes—
> To me, they represent
> what everybody wishes their lives could be.
> People that are shy wish they were outgoing like that, and—
> I mean, with other people that really don't know me,
> I am so shy....
>
> Once you get into real life, it's like,
> "Oh my god, can I go back, please...."
> It's like you finish this book, "Oh my gosh, it ended.
> Okay where's the next book,
> I need to get into it real quick."

When Rosa talked about escaping from reality, it is easy to assume that she was afraid to grow up and learn to live within actual
relationships instead of imagining living in idealized fictional ones.
In some respects, she was afraid to join the adult world. But fears do
not arise without reason, and the troubles Rosa witnessed are
enough to explain her seeking out a protected, predictable drama in
which everything turns out all right.

> I barely passed Honors English Ten.
> My parents got a divorce,
> a whole bunch of stuff happened.
>
> My dad had moved out of the house,
> but I was still close and I really didn't understand the concept of
>   divorce
> until it was final
> and I was doing mood swings and all that.
> Plus my aunt got real sick, almost died,
> my grandfather was in the hospital,
> he had a stroke,
> my other grandfather had three strokes at once,
> I mean, my whole high school so far,
> I mean, this year my uncle died,
> last year a real close grandmotherly friend,
> I always called her Granny,
> she got diagnosed with Alzheimer's,

so she barely remembers me now.
I'll go up to her and I'll go, "Granny, it's Rosie!"
She'll go, "You can't be Rosie, Rosie is only 4 years old!"
It's just really upsetting,
and in tenth grade with the divorce being final,
both my grandfathers having strokes,
and then my grandmother almost had a stroke
because her husband having the stroke,
and she also had blood clots
that if she would have waited two more days she would've—
they would've had to amputate her leg,
ninth grade, my aunt died,
they couldn't find out what was wrong until after she died,
they did an autopsy,
they found out it was her liver and her kidneys
instead of something else, 'cause she was diabetic
and she didn't take care of herself.
See, she kinda had Alzheimer's,
she kept on forgetting things,
and she would put her hairbrush in the 'frigerator,
all that kinds of stuff.
My brother was diagnosed with diabetes when he was 7,
so I'm 17 now,
I was 10 years old when he was diagnosed,
he had a relapse a couple years ago,
and he was in the hospital for two weeks,
I did not go to school for like, five days,
because I was so worried.

I include this speech in its entirety because it shows how many troubles Rosa carried and the way they poured out of her as soon as she was reminded of them suggests that she did not easily put them out of her mind. Although she returned more than once in our interviews to this unrelenting series of illnesses, she never spoke more specifically of her own "mood swings and all that." However, she made an interesting observation about Poe, one of several canonical writers whom she also admired,

> Eleventh grade, all I remember is the poems,
> like Edgar Allen Poe—
> I love him, he's been—

his poems describe my life in high school,
what it has been,
with the deaths and the strokes and all that.

When her uncle died earlier in her senior year, Rosa did not
let her teachers know that she was dealing with serious personal
problems. I learned, indirectly and after the fact, that something
was wrong when her social studies teacher mentioned that for a
few weeks earlier in the semester Rosa had stopped turning in assignments. The teacher, not knowing anything about a death in
the family, interpreted Rosa's slacking off as part of her ongoing
(but limited) rebellion against her mother's fundamentalist
Christian rules, but the teacher freely admitted that she was just
guessing because Rosa had not confided in her. I did not understand
how to interpret Rosa's failure to turn in work any more than her
teacher did. Knowing that Rosa cared about her grades, I was simply puzzled.

I was given a clue to her problem when I dropped by Rosa's
Computer Assisted Drafting (CAD) class later in the term to see
what she was working on. In our brief conversation, she mentioned
that for about two weeks earlier in the semester she had not done
any work in this class at all. This did not affect her grade because
the CAD class was set up so that students proceed through the list
of required assignments at whatever pace is comfortable for them,
and Rosa was far enough ahead to afford a slack period. She did
not tell me that she had been depressed because her uncle had
died; she said only, "I didn't have enough energy to do any work,
so I just came in here and read my books every day." She gave me
this explanation simply and naturally, with no indication that she
felt she was hiding anything. She may not have known herself just
what she was feeling; all her resources were channeled into avoiding the emotions the death aroused (hence her feeling that she had
no energy). I thought it was odd, at the time, but I could not guess
what was behind this period of withdrawal until she returned to the
subject of family deaths in a later interview.

I cannot deal with death in the family,
and this year my uncle died,
and two weeks later after that my aunt was put in the hospital
because she could not live without my uncle.
She's living now, she's doing a lot better,

> but she has blocked her husband dying.
> She doesn't even re—she remembers she has kids and everything,
> but she's at the point where she doesn't even remember being
>   married,
> 'cause that would bring back everything,
> and she would most likely die.

This account carries a belief that is consistent with the world-view promoted by romance novels, namely that two people who really love each other cannot or do not want to live without each other. Furthermore, it carries the sorrow of reality that Rosa sought to escape and the lesson she had learned about it: When loved ones leave (e.g., a husband dies, a father moves out), death threatens those left behind unless they can successfully block the pain. So when her uncle died, Rosa engaged in a romance reading binge that was, I believe, a two-week course of "medication" that allowed her to survive yet another loss. Months later, when I asked her why she had stopped working for those two weeks, she confirmed that it was because she was upset.

> Well, see, my uncle had passed away recently,
> and my aunt got sick right after him
> 'cause she was really upset about him.
> Instead, she kinda got kinda like an amnesia,
> she didn't even remember being married....
>
> And my dad really hadn't been coming to any of my concerts
> or anything, so I felt in a way
> that I wasn't as important in my dad's eyes as I should be....
> I would tell him as soon as we knew,
> and we don't usually know until, like, two days in advance,
> and he was all, "I'll see what I could do,"
> but instead of saying "I'll see what I can do,"
> he'll go, "I'll be there."
> And then I'll be there,
> and I'll save him a seat,
> and he won't show up,
> and when I call him and ask him what's going on,
> he'll say, "Oh, I had a meeting,
> I told you I had a meeting, that I would try."
> It's lack of communication.

Rosa's juxtaposition of her uncle's death, her aunt's illness, and her father's absence indicate that these were closely associated in her mind. In her experience, loss makes you sick. In her account of "losing" her father to his business meeting, I could hear Rosa's distress as her voice tightened, but I also could hear her calm down in her last statement. She was learning to come to terms with him.

It was during this same discussion about death that Rosa spoke about one of the most serious of the psychological traumas she had endured, the death of her best friend at the end of seventh grade. She had been talking about how much she loved babies and yet feared working as a caregiver or teacher because goodbyes were so hard for her.

> So, to me, that's the one bad thing about dealing with kids
> is to know you're gonna have to say goodbye,
> and I hate goodbyes.
> [pause]
> It's just a bad thing that I have....
>
> When my best friend Melissa died...
> when she died, I had totally—
> you know, I didn't wanna—
> actually, I didn't wanna live any more.
> 'Cause she was the one person,
> Melissa was the one person that, no matter what,
> she could get me to laugh...
> she could get me to admit things
> that I had never even admitted to my mom,
> and I tell my mom everything.
> She wouldn't even have to see me,
> she would kinda have this twin thing,
> and I would be, like—she would be on the other side of the state,
> or on the other side of the U.S.
> and she would know somethin' was wrong,
> and she would call me.
>
> **Anne:** Why did Melissa die?
>
> **Rosa:** Um...(pause) She was killed...
> she was killed in a drunk, with a drunk driver.
>
> She was killed instantly.
> She was about 14.

She was born two days after me.
It happened in seventh grade,
because it was, like, it was at the end of seventh grade,
and...[in eighth grade]
I was smiling on the outside, but I was like,
dead on the inside....

Rosa's references to mood swings, mental illness, and being "dead on the inside" suggest periods of depression with which her reading—of both Poe and the "escape" genres—helped her cope. In her fourth interview (at which her best friend Heather also was present), she was clear about this therapeutic function of reading.

Basically, ever since Melissa died,
my life has just been going zhoom, zhoom, zhoom
(making an up-and-down wave with her hand)
on a roller coaster, and it's just...how did we get on this subject?

Anne: Well, actually I was asking about what you were reading, and somehow we got onto these other things, I'm not sure. (Rosa laughs self-consciously)

Heather: Because you were—your childhood has a lot to do with what you were reading when you were a kid.

Anne: They're very closely related, I mean, I think that one of the things that people can use reading for is—

Rosa: Block everything out.

Heather: Get away...

Anne: To use it in whatever way they need to use it....

Rosa: Yeah, I didn't even tell her [Heather] about my uncle dying, I...
I had blocked that out, too,
until we started talking about death and all.

Anne: Oh, and writing, I was asking you about when you started writing.

Rosa: Writing...I write and I read mostly because I can, in a way, leave my body, and go into a happy place.

The theme of using reading and writing to go into a happy place shows up repeatedly in Rosa's reading story. She liked to talk dramatically about how preferable fantasy is to reality, but, in fact, when I examined the way she used fiction, I saw that she was constantly negotiating the gap—or abyss—between her fears for her future in the real world and the promises of happiness that her books offered. She was inching toward a reconciliation with reality, using escape reading as a buffer. Sometimes she found a writer who reflected the anguish of reality in a satisfying way, as Poe does, but more often she took satisfaction in dealing vicariously with the multiple problems besetting fictional characters. Although the genres she loved are infamous for predictable endings, it was exactly the safety of knowing that these endings were waiting that made it possible for her to dwell temporarily with the troubles of characters she cared about. In so doing, she was able to dwell on her own troubles, but at a distance made safe by the intervening presence of the story with the happy ending. While she was in the world of these stories, she was building up her supplies of hope and emotional strength before continuing on to her real-world destination.

Rosa's reading was remarkable in both the number of stories she consumed and the speed with which she consumes them. She said,

> I'll go in my room,
> close the door,
> turn on music full blast,
> and have a stack of books,
> and my clock's on the other side of the room so I can't see what
>   time it is,
> and I'll lay on my side and read the book,
> go like this (mimes tossing a book onto the floor)
> grab another book and read it.

Whatever Rosa was seeking in her reading of pulp fiction, she did not find enough of in a single story. Roberts (1990) notes this phenomenon in his argument that reading genre fiction is qualitatively different from reading "high-culture" fiction, in that literary texts are studied separately, each unique and valuable in itself, while each pulp novel should be understood as a "page" in the text of the whole genre. Rosa's reading of romances was a search for scenes that reassured her, but one book did not contain enough of them to sustain her. The writer's promise that life can be happy was at odds with what Rosa has observed, so, in order to be convinced, she needed a whole chorus of writers, characters, and plots telling her what she wanted to hear. One voice, one drama—no matter how pleasing—could not by itself counteract the weight of real anxiety that she carried.

Romance Reading: Seeking and Finding

When high school students recount their personal literacy narratives, they frequently tell a story of losing interest in reading in middle school. For Rosa, however, the middle school years were the time of discovering just how much reading could do for her. She was in seventh grade when she began reading romance novels, sneaking into her mother's room to read them while her mother was out. I asked her if her mother thought she was too young for them.

> She thought I was too young for a lot of things,
> but by that time my mom and dad were splitting up,
> and I wanted to have something that they kinda shared,
> or something, you know, close to that—
> 'cause me and my dad were never, ever close.

Rosa's words illuminate her reasons for choosing romance novels as her favorite means of escape. When Rosa's father moved out of the house, his departure left Rosa with a troubled daughter-father relationship and no model of a good marriage to use for her dreams of a happy future. When she looked ahead to her own adult life, she wondered what constituted love between a man and a woman. As she approached adulthood, her need to know about intimacy shifted its focus from her parents to the culture at large. Instead of her middle school question, What did my mother and father share when they were in love? Rosa wondered, What do men and women experience in the process of finding and marrying the right person?

It is easy to criticize romance novels as the poorest source of information about relationships between men and women—the plot lines are predictably unrealistic, the characters superficial, and authorial insight extremely limited. These novels do not demand the serious thought or reconsideration of unconscious prejudices and illusions that "real" literature does. But this is precisely their strength. Whereas classic literature includes, in its clear-eyed examination of human suffering, a critique of the human race (although it celebrates human wisdom and strength as well), romance novels offer a simpler, inspirational message about how good life can be. Clearly, Rosa needed—and searched for—information about how love works when it makes people happy. Radway's (1991) romance readers speak of reading as "a ritual of hope" (p. 207) that affirms their belief that true love can and does happen. Rosa, too, used romance novels to provide her the reassurance that her parents and the world she saw around her could not.

> Well, see, 'cause you know, in the romances,
> that by the end of the book, no matter how many times they fight
> or break up, or go through whatever they're going through,
> that by the end of the book they will be together,
> married, probably with a couple of kids.
> And you know that they'll live happily ever after.
> Well, in real life, you know that ain't worth it,
> 'cause it ain't gonna happen.
> There are certain types of people that,
> even if you go out with them you know it won't last two weeks,
> but you'll go out with them anyway.
> And it's really hard to get out of fantasy land
> and face reality sometimes.
> And I've faced reality one too many times,
> and I'd rather go back to fantasy.

This passage reveals the difficulty Rosa had in believing the worldview the novels offer and, simultaneously, the difficulty she had in facing reality. Loss had permeated her life; she was looking for a solid place to stand. Coming to terms with her parents' divorce had been especially difficult for her because it coincided with her friend Melissa's death.

> I needed my family with me,
> I didn't need them to separate,
> even though I didn't get along with my dad at all.
> I needed to have some comfort
> that if I needed to talk to him,
> all I would have to do is wake up at about 1:30 in the morning,
> and he would be in the kitchen.

During Rosa's senior year of high school, her relationship with her father was improving. But during those important years between the ages of 12 and 17, Rosa came to depend on romance novels to keep her hopeful. At one point, she stopped reading romance fiction for about six months and found that she did not like the person she became without a regular infusion of optimism.

> I quit reading the romance novels,
> and my personality totally changed when I did that.
> I was kinda—I felt that I was turning into a little skeptical—
> that's not the word I'm looking for—kinda, like, uh....
> I had turned—I didn't believe in romance any more,
> I didn't think anybody could fall in love any more,
> it was nothing but
> you get married,
> you have a couple kids,
> you get divorced,
> break each other's hearts,
> that kind of thing.

> And once I got back to reading romance novels,
> I was like, "I was actually like that? I can't imagine myself like that!"

Rosa also suggested that reading romance novels helped her develop a more mature response to the idea of emotional and sexual intimacy with a man.

> [Romance novels] helped me be kind of like a romantic at heart,
> because before, you know, (imitates her own reaction)
> "Oh my gosh, eeyew"—you know, that kinda thing,
> I find a little piece of the kind of guy I want
> through all romance things, you know.

> And no matter what, no matter how many fights we have,
> by the end of the day we have always made up.
> And not once did I ever see that with my parents.

In Rosa's talk about optimism and relationships, we also can see evidence of what McNall (1981) argues lies beneath the surface of romance novels.

> These stories, from early to late, are about the fear of doing with-out, of being without, one exclusive love, and about the anger that accompanies this fear. In these stories, possibility after possibility is sacrificed, to prevent the realization of that deep fear. (p. 120)

If we understand that Rosa turned to these books for help in managing her feelings of fear, anger, and longing, we can understand that what she got from them was far from "trash." Cohn makes a related point about the deeper reasons for reading romance novels that pertains to Rosa's enjoyment of them as well. In *Romance and the Erotics of Property: Mass-Market Fiction for Women* (1988), Cohn states,

> It is my thesis that power, not love, lies at the heart of the fictions of popular romance. In the fantasy gratification offered by contemporary popular romance are not only the secret sentimental and sensual delights of love but the forbidden pleasures of revenge and appropriation. In heavily coded structures these stories redistribute not only the power relations that exist within marriage, within the patriarchal family, but through and beyond that threaten existing gender relations in the broadest areas of power in patriarchal society itself. (p. 3)

I think that Rosa would be genuinely confused if I asked her whether she found romance novels disrupting existing power relations between males and females in our society because she wanted to take these novels at face value and usually did. Even when she thought one was silly, and so did not succumb to the enchantment of that text, she did not reflect on the culture that produced it. She did not want to analyze the social context of these novels; she wanted to use them to be happy in her social context. But she would understand and appreciate Cohn's (1998) observation of the power struggle embedded within the love story when the hero admits he loves the heroine:

> It is a confession, as something wrung from the hero.... The naming of love stands at the heart of the ritual that popular romance reenacts for its readers.... It is necessary as well that the hero's long struggle against love be made clear. He has loved long and in silence, a silence, moreover, that represents his allegiance to some other powerful force, a masculine principle of sexuality whose very potency depends on its freedom from commitment. The hero, then, like the heroine, has experienced conflict, has been caught in a struggle between two powerful forces until at last he surrenders to the stronger force, to the heroine and to love. (p. 33)

Rosa's favorite part of a romance was the capitulation scene, in which the man says he is sorry and sweeps the heroine into an embrace. She was sensitive to the way power works in relationships; at a number of points in my conversations with her, she mentioned how much she loved being right and hated being wrong. She remembered numerous instances in which she was able to say to her mother and her friends "I told you so," which she recounted with great pleasure (although she hated to hear "I told you so" directed to herself). I never heard Rosa talk about wealth and I do not think that property as such was a concern to her, but being able to participate vicariously in the psychological journey of a heroine who ultimately is recognized as being right in the most important kind of conflict—relationship conflict—so that she wins both love and the argument, must be sweet indeed.

The Critics Speak Out

Feminist critics such as Christian-Smith (1990) oppose romance reading because it may provide a kind of life script that induces young women to submit to the oppression of a patriarchal culture. Christian-Smith's (1993) investigation of teenagers' romance reading includes a review of the numerous individuals and groups who oppose romance novels for reasons that range from the narrowness of their worldview to their alleged promotion of promiscuity. Christian-Smith's most serious concern about the teenagers in her study is that they do not understand that the lessons these novels teach about gender, sexuality, power, and class not only are quite limited but also are controlled by large political and economic interests. By appealing to readers' desires and emotions, the multinational corporations that publish romance novels keep readers in the position of consumers of romantic fantasy. Christian-Smith surmises that one outcome may well be that heavy romance reading consumes attention that young women might otherwise invest in getting an education for an economically and socially successful future. As McNall (1981) writes, "In these stories, possibility after possibility is sacrificed, to prevent the realization of that deep fear [of being without love]" (p. 120).

It is too early to tell whether Rosa will pay such a price for her reading, but the following conversation revealed that she was more aware of her need to take charge of her own life than critics might give her credit for. Among those critics were Rosa's grandparents, who threatened to take romance novels away from her if

they caught her reading them again. Of course, this did not stop her
from reading them out of their sight, but when I asked her why
they disapproved, she said,

> They just think it's filth,
> that it rots your mind,
> that I need to read ed-u-caaa-tion-al things.
> Man, they read education, education, education.

> All their books are history, has to do with history.
> And it's all true.
> And it just bugs me,
> 'specially when they go,
> "Here, why don't you read this for a change?"
> It's like, No thank you.
> The books just sound so boring.
> They don't catch my attention,
> they use these big huge words that I don't understand,
> and then they go into detail over what the whole thing is,
> and it's like,
> why in the world would we want to study this anyway?
> It doesn't make sense.

When I asked Rosa how she interpreted her grandparents' des-
ignation of romance novels as filth that rots the mind, she first said
that "trash" is whatever you are not interested in, but then reflected
further.

> I think my grandparents are afraid that
> if I get more involved with the romance novels
> I won't pay much attention to my studies and college,
> and I might end up trying to base my life on one of the books.
> And they don't look at how old you are now and how you were
>   raised.
> They look at what, basically what you read.
> Who you are—
> what you read is who you are.
> I don't think that.
> I think who your parents have raised you—
> I mean, if you will stop,
> if you see a homeless person on the street that is hungry,
> actually hungry, and is asking for money to get food,

and you give them a couple of dollars,
that is a good person.
And if a person kinda like totally blows them over,
I think they need to work on their social skills.
But you know, you totally base the person on who their parents are,
who, um...not totally on who their parents are,
but how they were raised,
how they treat people,
not by what they read,
because I mean, you could be a terrible person,
a murderer, and you could read these (voice becomes light and high)
little fairy tales, you know, (resumes normal voice)
everything's perfect, and if you base it by that,
you think it's—the murderer's a good person,
when he really isn't.

Rosa honestly did not know the standards by which literature is judged, although she did imply that a reader should not base her life on romance novels, which is an indirect acknowledgement of those standards. Furthermore, in this conversation Rosa demonstrated her own agency as a reader. She did not see readers as passively constructed by the texts they read, and as much as she actively tried to use romances to help her "be" optimistic in some sort of essentialist, enduring way, she had learned that that could not happen. In fact, we can guess how tenuous her hold was on the novels' view of life when she said that "little fairy tales" in which everything is perfect might be a murderer's text of choice. She evaluated people by the way they treated others—a lesson, it could be argued, that her novels support. After all, the heroine marries a man who treats her well, a man who makes up after a fight, a man who sticks around.

Rosa was constantly reminded of how much real life is not like fiction. When she said that she did not believe that what you read is who you are, and that the measure of who you are is how you treat real people, she was clearly identifying the difference between the world of the novel and the world in which she lived. At another point she said, "I can read almost any kind of book as long as it's not true," indicating that for her, reading and fantasy were tightly woven, and she was fully aware of using her imagination.

Rosa's novels were not welcome in school any more than they were in her grandparents' home. She read in class whenever she thought she could afford to stop listening to the teacher, and although she was often told to put her book away, some teachers allowed her to read if no assignment was due because she usually was conscientious about getting her work turned in. When her English teacher told the class to choose a book to read and write about in a series of short writing assignments called levels, Rosa selected a romance. The teacher rejected it for reasons that Rosa did not understand.

> She said, "No book that you can buy at the drugstore."
> I was like, "I didn't buy this at the drugstore.
> They don't sell this series at the drugstore."
> She goes, "I don't care—they sell romance."
> I was like, "They sell a lotta other books at the drugstore."
> Me and her had a difference of opinion on that.

From this excerpt, Rosa's characteristically literal way of interpreting words and events is clear. She really did think that the teacher cared most about where the book was bought, and whatever else their conversation might have included, this was what she remembered. When I asked the teacher about the book Rosa had chosen, she said that Rosa was reading a fantasy after trying unsuccessfully to get three romances accepted. The teacher said, "I haven't read this one, but she showed it to me and at least it looked like a real book." It seemed obvious to the teacher that Rosa's romances were not worth school time (and this teacher herself occasionally enjoyed reading what she referred to as a "trash novel"), but when I asked Rosa why romances were not acceptable for this assignment, she paused, thought about it, and then said,

> You know, I honestly don't know.
> I just thought—I think it was because
> you had to tell the setting and the plot and all of that,
> and what parts you liked best,
> and with romance novels,
> you're gonna like the part where he finally says, "I'm sorry,"
> and totally wraps 'em up
> (mimes the hero embracing the heroine) you know, goes into that,
> and kinda goes into a little detail,
> and you don't wanna put that on a report.
>
> **Anne:** Okay, and so you as a student don't wanna get into that in school papers, is that what you're saying?

Rosa: Um...I'm saying that she probably wouldn't, that's why she didn't say it.

The teacher was both surprised and amused when I asked her if she had said anything like this to Rosa. "No, I was coming from a completely different place," she said.

I didn't want her to be reading a book that was entirely plot-driven. I wanted the kids to choose books that would allow them to write about theme and culture, and the book she finally chose did allow her to do that.

Rosa's explanation of her teacher's rejection of a romance novel for this assignment revealed that analytic or aesthetic approaches to romance novels did not interest her, and she assumed that her teacher would be embarrassed by talk about the emotionally gratifying scenes. Critical or ironic distance was outside her reading realm. Booth (1983) argues that "only immature readers ever really identify with any character, losing all sense of distance and hence all chance of an artistic experience" (p. 248), but Rosa, in her need for the protection that romances provide, did not see any virtue in giving up that protection or in attempting to adopt a less involved readerly stance.

Her gender also heavily influenced her way of reading. Bleich (1986a) concluded from the classroom study that he and his students conducted of their readings of a novel that "women enter the world of the novel, take it as something 'there' for that purpose; men see the novel as a result of someone's action and construe its meaning or logic in those terms" (p. 239). Rosa was expert at entering the worlds created by romance writers, assuming that the emotional and imaginative rewards she found were simply "there" rather than created by her interaction with the text and that to talk about the novel was to talk about the events that led to those rewards.

Rosa also encountered criticism for her reading choices from her best friend, Heather, who sat in on three of our interviews. Heather also loved to read, had divorced parents, and described her father as strict and demanding. Heather, however, chose to read psychology and Christian science fiction. Even though her mother read romances and offered the novels to her, Heather disliked them because they were "fake and mushy." Rosa was equally dismissive of Heather's interest in what she calls "the psychology crap" and told Heather that

> If you look at certain people's lives,
> it's fake to you, but it's not fake to them,
> and with all the books that I've read,
> the authors have put their lives basically in it.
>
> They might embellish it a little,
> but it always ends in the happy-ever-after things.
> Because they'll tell you from the beginning
> that the author will kind of like
> put a little bit of her and her husband and their kids
> into the characters.
> You don't know who's who,
> but you know that her life, or his—
> the author's life is in that book somewhere,
> so you know it's kinda reality a little bit.
> It might be embellished, but it's still reality.
> It's just put to the point where you can deal with it more.

In her last statement, Rosa was revealing not only why but also how she used this fiction. Rosa's life had been so traumatic that she was engaged in a constant struggle to control a flow of events that was completely beyond her control. She wanted to slow down the onslaught of sickness, death, and rejection to a manageable rate. She could not; all she could control was the degree of her own conscious immersion in this onslaught, a control she exercised largely by reading. Reading allowed her to regulate the amount of time she had to spend coping with reality and to create a more comfortable pace of coping with trouble, a pace better suited to her own pace of growing up. She used romance novels to protect her childhood and adolescence from too much, too soon.

Mysteries: Another Genre, Another Purpose

Rosa also loved mysteries. She did not read as many of these books as she did romances, but they are an important part of her reading story. She used mysteries for the intellectual pleasure of solving problems and—this is very important—the reassurance about her own intellectual capabilities that comes from finding the correct solution.

> **Rosa:** I read 'em
> because I wanna see if I can guess who did it with what,
> and see if I'm right (leaning forward to emphasize each word)
> I like to be proved that I'm right.
>
> **Anne:** Unhuh. So it's a kind of a puzzle to solve?
>
> **Rosa:** Yeah.
> One of my pet peeves is when people prove me wrong,
> I can't stand it.
>
> **Anne:** When people—? You mean just in life, or are you talking about mystery reading?
>
> **Rosa:** Uh...well, in mysteries, I have never guessed wrong,
> but with other things, like with in life,
> like with teachers proving me wrong,
> and—Heather's only proved me wrong once,
> and I don't think she really wants to prove me wrong ever again
> (half laughing), 'cause she—we call each other on it,
> and we both hate it when the other person does it.

Elsewhere, Rosa claimed a 90% accuracy in identifying the killer in a mystery and demonstrated a knowledge of the genre superior to her mother's.

> I love mysteries,
> I mean by the fourth chapter I could tell you
> exactly who did it,
> with what,
> and why.
> My mom will get halfway through a book,
> and she goes, "I don't understand this,"
> and I'll explain it,
> "Oh, it's this person, he did it like this,"
> and why he did it,
> and my mom goes, "Hold on."
> She'll go to the very last chapter,
> read the chapter, "Oh, my gosh, you're right."
> (Laughs) And I'll be right like 9 out of 10 times.

Sometimes it bothers me...
I want a book that will keep me on my toes,
and not let me know the ending,
'cause by the time I know the ending
I don't wanna read the rest of the book,
and I'll go straight to the last chapter to see if I'm right.

Rosa's command of mysteries came from reading the books and from participating in an online solve-the-mystery series that taught her the parameters of the genre. She also learned a real-life version from her brother: He set up pranks that made Rosa look guilty of some misdeed, so she learned to look for one of her belongings that he had left in an incriminating spot and replace it with one of his. She said, "Once you get used to doing that, you kind of really pay attention to who done it."

Rosa was not repelled by the fact that mystery stories are gruesomely concerned with people killing one another; the fact that murder happens in a story without deep emotional consequences for Rosa is further evidence of her feeling that the world of fiction is fundamentally and qualitatively different from the real world. If events that are only the building blocks of the plot-driven novel did not connect with her life experience or her desires, they did not arouse her emotions significantly. On one level, mysteries are designed to be enjoyed as a game, such as chess, in which known symbolic actors go through a repertoire of moves. On a deeper level, mysteries are satisfying because their characters play out a drama of the triumph of good over evil and the maintenance of social order as the detective uncovers the crime and brings the criminal to justice. Rosa never indicated that this was a source of her enjoyment of mysteries, but it is interesting to juxtapose her reasons for reading mysteries with her reasons for reading romances. Both genres offer reassurance. And I have to wonder, given the criticism of her romance novels that she faces almost every day, does being right about "whodunit" allow Rosa to feel that she also is right about romance reading? For her, both reading and writing are a way of going "into a happy place." The "happy place" of romances solves one kind of problem, while the "happy place" of mysteries solves another.

Writing: Another Pair of Wings

Mysteries and poems are the only kind of writing Rosa liked to do. I asked Rosa whether she had any interest in writing romances, and she said that she could not write a romance because she could not write the requisite sex scenes. Also, she said, romances have to follow a "concept" [formula], which she ticked off: meeting, pursuing, arguing, separating, reconciling. Mysteries, she said, can be written any way you want. For her class called Working as Writers, she produced most of a mystery story. Her teacher told me,

> The only due date in this class
> was the end of the semester
> when the portfolio was due.
> There were about eight different pieces that were required,
> but Rosa was fixated
> on the mystery story she was writing.
> Her story was getting to be thirty, forty pages—
> well on its way to being a novel—
> but she didn't want to work on anything else.
> She had to pull the other writings together at the last minute.

The stories Rosa wrote are about teenage girls who kill or are killed. Some of her stories involve cursed objects taken from ancient tombs; some of them involve people thought to be dead returning for revenge. Rosa learned these traditional turns of plot, of course, from her reading. Many of her ideas came from stories that the author brought to a close but that Rosa imagined further.

> I'll read a book,
> and I'll go, "You can't end it like this,
> you need to continue it!"
> And from that, I'll just start writing
> and what I picture happened after it,
> and then what I'll do is I'll put that into a whole 'nother story.

> I love fantasy.
> I'll read Piers Anthony, and once his books get done,
> I'll spend like an hour and a half
> adding to his books.
> What I'll do is, I'll copy his last chapter
> and then I'll add to it.

Through Rosa's writing, she shows her readers, as all writers do, something of what was in her mind: what she noticed and what she ignored, what she took time with and what she passed over, what she knew and what escaped her, and how she spoke of it all to her readers. Her mystery stories show a remarkable mastery of certain aspects of the genre, such as situating the story in ordinary life (i.e., a girl moves to a new high school; a girl is looking for a shirt that she thinks her sister has taken). Her chapters are only a page long, but they end with drama: "Now that got me thinking. Could it be true?" or "That reply hit me like a solid brick wall." She begins her stories quietly and quickly moves to the discovery of the death threat or the dead body. In presenting dialogue, she has characters "snap," "yell," and "cry," and if they only "say" something, they usually say it tiredly, or angrily, or while sticking their noses in the air.

Her stories also show a writer who is almost exclusively concerned with plot. A girl is murdered, another girl is trying to find out who did it, various characters appear and disappear, and yet another girl is discovered to have committed the crime. Finally, a confrontation between girl-villain and girl-detective occurs. However, great chunks of connecting logic between one event and another are omitted, suggesting that Rosa had more in her mind than she was putting down on paper. She generated many characters, all named, but having almost no observable characteristics. A few are described by others as being "nice," or "pretty," and the villain of one piece is "snobby." Otherwise, they are interchangeable, without distinct personalities. Description of the setting is nonexistent. Rosa did not see these features as deficiencies because she herself did not want to read descriptions of character or setting, and she herself did not notice characterization beyond who is good and who is bad. However, even though she was generally satisfied with her writing, she recognized that she had trouble with some aspects of storytelling.

> [Dialogue] is my problem.
> I'll get the whole thing written out,
> and I will have to put dialogue in
> and I can't—I hate writing the two little [pause] quotations—
> I think that's the right word—
> And then putting the words in between 'em
> and then putting comma
> and then "she said," or "he said," and—

with the action, I can't stand writing it.
I like reading it,
but I have a hard time putting into words
what I want them to say.
'Cause I'm not a very verbal person.

It is surprising that someone who loved to read and write described herself as "not a very verbal person," but Rosa recognized that she was "not very verbal" in terms of academic literacy. She did not seem to find it odd that she was not good with dialogue, but her recognition of the fact suggests that she may have been ready to learn how other writers use it.

Rosa said she loved to write, but what she loved was being in the "happy place," absorbed in the plot, thinking about the action when she was inspired by her reading. The actual writing was a labor that slowed her down, requiring an attention to detail that annoyed and confused her. She said she would like to use a computer to translate her spoken words into written ones so that she could keep track of her thoughts as she composed; as it was, she often forgot where she was going with an idea. School writing was often difficult for her, as is evidenced in her description of writing a murder mystery for English class, an assignment for which she received a failing grade.

It had to have a whole bunch of strict guidelines
which I'm not that good at following,
and then it had to have a certain amount of dialogue,
and then it had to end with the murderer getting caught.
Well I had to—I totally switched it around,
and made it look like somebody else was the murderer,
and then at the end,
without showing any proof,
it was his brother.
And I hardly did any dialogue,
she wanted about three pages long,
I didn't really do it three pages long,
'cause with the dialogue it would make it three pages long—
I'm just not good at dialogue
and that's one of the reasons why I got an E.
But I liked it! I thought it deserved about a C, not an E.

Rosa's writing is narrowly focused on the elements of a mystery story she valued—here, the surprise ending, with no time wasted on dialogue. Another point (discussed in detail later) is that Rosa needed inspiration from either her reading or her dreams in order to write. She did not come up with plots, much less characters or settings, unless she was in a fictional or dream world. This school assignment did not allow her to draw from what had come up for her in those worlds, but instead required her to invent, consciously, a story that met the teacher's requirements. Rosa had not learned to work through her plots methodically, but this, like dialogue, might be a writer's skill about which she is ready to learn.

Another one of Rosa's difficulties was that her vocabulary was limited. She often was left feeling that she did not understand the language of school.

> **Rosa:** With me, you need to explain it out in clear English
> and not use the big words that teachers use,
> 'cause my vocabulary is of a two-year-old.
>
> **Anne:** Yeah? Even though you read all the time?
>
> **Rosa:** Yeah, I don't use and I really don't understand big words
> and you could say a word that I would probably know
> but would have, like, two or three different meanings,
> and I wouldn't understand,
> I would need you to st—I have to do it step by step by step by step.
>
> [The teacher] will even write it in big words on your paper,
> and I know teachers are s'posed to kind of do that
> to broaden your horizons with bigger vocabulary and everything?
> But I mean, I've always been like this,
> and a lot of people, no matter how hard they try,
> they can't learn what those mean.
> [When I don't understand the words] I space out.

Some of the school standards of good writing were quite visible to Rosa, and she was frank about admitting that she had weaknesses as a writer. She talked about these when she described the question about writing on the state proficiency test that required students to list strengths and weaknesses of their own writing.

> I was, like, I can't spell to save my life,
> I can't and I don't understand big words,

so I don't use 'em in my writing, um...
another one of my weaknesses was I can't go on and on and on
to make one sentence into a paragraph.
I'm one of those people that will say
whatever I need to say about a person in one, maybe two sentences,
and when it's a paragraph you have to have like five to seven,
and that don't—that doesn't work with me.
It was—the writing portion was kinda hard.

It is interesting to note what Rosa did and did not see about her writing. She never talked about characterization, for example, nor did she talk about organization. She was clear about certain technical weaknesses of her writing, but the world of literary values, with its appreciation of technique, aesthetics, insight, courage, and imagination was only sporadically available to her.

Rosa's writing gives us important clues to the way she reads. The stories she wrote and her talk about reading show almost identical concerns. She wrote for action, just as she read for action. She was not interested in language, background, or characterization. She liked situations, feelings, and events. She read rapidly, skimming expertly over the scenes she did not like in search of scenes that satisfied her. Her writing, too, skimmed across the surface of plot. The following is all of chapter 4, "The Suspicion," of her book in progress, titled *Members of the Family*.

As the days went by, I got more and more clues of who the person was...[Rosa's ellipses] and more suspects. Now instead of six suspects, there were twelve. They were Ryan, his gang, Cynthia, her follower Jennifer, Mitchell, Rachel, Shelley, Robert, and Julie. I sat down with my list of clues and suspects. Andi was with me. "Okay," I said. "We know the suspect was a female. That leaves us five suspects. The person didn't have dark hair, so it wasn't Rachel. The person was big boned, so it wasn't Cynthia, or Jennifer." "So we have two suspects left. Who is the murderer?" Andi asked. "We need more clues." I said even more confused than earlier.

That night I thought about the clues. Suddenly I sat up. All the clues matched Chrissy's description too. "Oh, great! Now my own sisters [sic] a suspect. But Chrissy's not the type to go running around killing people especially her own sister, or is she?" I thought aloud. Little did I know that my answer was about to come forth soon, very soon...[Rosa's ellipses]

The next afternoon, I told Chrissy of my suspicion. Chrissy stared at me with wide, hurt eyes. "Why would I kill anyone especially my own sister?" "I know." I cried. "The clues match your description, but it's not like you to kill people." "So I'm not a suspect?" Chrissy asked hopefully. "I guess not." I agreed.

The more I got into the murder mystery, the more confused I got. Amidst all the confusion, I met a snobby girl named Tanya. Tanya said she knew who killed Angie. I've heard that line before, and all it was doing was getting me into a maze I could hardly get out of. But I followed along anyway.

Rosa's previous chapters did not lay the groundwork for the conclusions drawn here. We are not told how the detective knows that the murderer was big-boned and fair-haired. And we have not met most of the 12 suspects listed.

In both her reading and her writing, Rosa avoided dwelling on setting, characters' histories, and contextual information, wanting instead to get into an individual's situation.

> There are some books where it'll take place during the [U.S.] Civil War
> but it really doesn't go totally into the war,
> it goes right into their lives.
> And you don't really pay attention to the war and stuff,
> so that's when I'm still interested in it.
> But when it goes straight when you're on the battlefield,
> I'm not interested.

> It's just a different way of being boring,
> and I'll get to the first page,
> and sometimes if it doesn't catch me,
> I'll go (mimes tossing the book away)
> "My mom can read this, skip it."

She dismissed setting with "you don't really pay attention to the war and stuff," although she also knew that her mother and other readers have interests different from her own. The mystery stories she wrote show her "just getting on with the story," sometimes so quickly that essential information about what happened is omitted. Her rapid reading worked to the same end. I asked her whether there were parts of her reading for which she wanted to slow down.

Rosa: (smiles) Yeah. There's this one book I just finished,
the plot's basically this millionaire found twins on his doorstep,

baby twins, okay?
And he goes through the thing of trying to find the mother and all
    that,
and then—
he had just given the two a bath and forgot to put—
he put clothes on 'em and everything,
and the kids had just learned how to take their clothes off,
so they're going naked under the beds and everything?
They're slick with vaseline.
Somehow he got vaseline all through his hair trying to catch the
    kids,
and the woman was like,
"You coulda moved the bed,"
and he just gave her the dirtiest look—
I thought that was so hilarious.
And the guy's brother and his wife are just sittin' there laughing,
aren't even helping or anything,
then it was like, "Oh, step back,"
and starts playing peekaboo,
and then she stops and the kids will come out,
trying to get her to play peekaboo again,
and that's how they get 'em out,
but I thought that was so hilarious.
Vaseline in his hair, I was like, "Oh, my god,"
and they were at the back of that bed, and like,
three lines later, she goes,
"Well you're gonna kill yourself when you realize tomorrow
that you could've moved the bed."
I was like, "Oh boy."

Anne: So that is a scene that you would like to slow down and—

Rosa: Yeah, what I'll do is—
I'll kinda read, skim it,
and all of a sudden I'll burst out laughing,
and I'll have to go back up
and read what really happened, you know?

Rosa's account of this passage shows what she notices and remembers. The man's clumsy ignorance about how to handle children and the female character's triumph are particularly salient. Rosa delighted in dwelling on the woman's cool competence and enjoyed her belittling remarks to the man. The scene gave Rosa a chance to identify with a woman who can say "I told you so" to a man. The absence of character also is noticeable; only the question of who wins came into Rosa's account of interactions between these characters. She got a great deal of emotional gratification from this scene, laughing throughout her retelling.

Rosa also revealed her reading method here. She flies over the surface of the narrative, looking for rewarding scenes or events. She picks up enough information to recognize what kind of scene she is reading (her genre expertise in action) and then, when she finds herself pleased, chooses to "go back up and read what really happened." Her recounting of the plot of this novel was typical of her conversation about her reading. In our five interviews, she repeatedly volunteered plot summaries of stories she liked—nine in all, none of which I asked for. They just poured out of her when she talked about reading. But she never talked about character, description, or theme.

Rosa deliberately entered another world when she read. Her writing often came from this reading world (as in the Piers Anthony example), and sometimes it came from still another world which, like the fictional world, is psychologically but not literally true: the world of dreams. She kept a tape recorder in her bedroom so that she could save her inspirations when she awoke in the night.

If I have story ideas,
I push record and say what happens,
because if I write,
I'll get like to the third word and I'll forget it.
I just keep on playing it over and over again,
and then I'll kind of write a rough draft of what I have,
and then I'll show my mom,
and my mom usually gives some insights and changes some of my
    words,
and that's how I get my stories.

The fact that story ideas, as far as Rosa is concerned, do not come from ordinary reality, but from dreams or from other stories, is yet another indication of the separation between fiction and reality with which Rosa lives. However, she worked hard at using her writing to bring the imaginary world and the real world together. She repeatedly said that she preferred fantasy to reality, but in fact, her reading and writing are full of indications such as this that she was working to bring her interior life into the open.

Rosa appreciated dreams even when they were not happy, such as the dream that gave her the idea for a favorite poem.

> I write a lot of poetry.
> One of my poems was called "Will You Remember Me?"
> It was about this person who is dying
> and is just wondering if its spouse will remember
> when they first met,
> their first kiss,
> when they got married,
> their kids,
> and will you remind the kids about me,
> and how I—what I did with my life.
> And then it goes into,
> "As long as I am in your memory
> I will live on in their hearts."
> It goes on like that,
> it's really good.
> I had a dream that I was the person.
> And it was to where nobody visited me,
> I knew I was married
> 'cause I was wearing my wedding ring
> and there was a picture of my kids on the table beside me,
> but nobody visited me,
> and I wanted—
> I was always wondering,
> will I be remembered?
> And if I will be remembered, what will I be remembered about?
> When I woke up,
> I was, like, "Hoo boy! I need my recorder!"
> And I totally just said what was in my dream,
> and then after that,
> once I got home from school
> I played that like four or five times,
> and I just started it,
> "Will you remember me?"

This excerpt provides further evidence of Rosa's concern with death and loss. What particularly strikes me about this account is the deep loneliness and isolation of the character in spite of the fact that she has a husband and children. Rosa seemed to be unsurprised by this situation. It also is interesting that instead of being overwhelmed by the sadness of the dream, she turned it immediately into a poem. As she used reading to shut out her real-life losses, she used writing to transform reminders of losses into a poem, an artifact that held the emotion for her in a form that, like other reading and writing, provided some protection from raw feeling. She liked this poem a great deal and used it to fulfill a poetry-writing assignment in her Working as Writers class. Her teacher said that although he did not try to tell students how to make substantive changes in their poetry because they insist that the way they have written it is the way the poem "is," he did make a few suggestions about word choices. Rosa would not even consider such changes. Her peer-editing group was confused by some of the punctuation in her poem, but again, she refused adamantly to change anything. The poem, as she wrote it, served its purpose for her, which was to capture the story and emotion of her dream, and to change it further would be to take it further from its origins. Because Rosa did not feel a need to become a better poet or to accommodate her readers, and because the poem is already as close as it can be to the dream state, revision (literally, changing the dream vision) would be more destructive than improving. By refusing to consider alternate wording, she demonstrated that personal expression was more important to her than pleasing an external audience. She herself is the audience for which she writes.

A discussion of Rosa's writing is not complete without including the role that her mother played. Rosa depended on her mother for help and guidance with most things, including schoolwork. In describing in more detail what the state proficiency test required her to do, she revealed her mother's hand in her writing.

> **Rosa:** You had to...in essay form,
> explain your strengths and your weaknesses,
> and list your examples from your actual writing to prove it
> or somethin' like that,
> and I picked my two pieces of writing,
> and my mom had helped me with those two,
> and they had big words in 'em,
> and I really didn't understand what I wrote, either.

Anne: When your mom helps you, does she just suggest it orally and then you write it down, or does she actually—

Rosa: She types what she thinks
and then she'll put what I think within it.
One of my pieces of writing was—
it was called "A Mountain Stream,"
and I just totally talked about a mountain stream,
described it in real vivid detail,
how the water trickled, and was cl—
I used like four verbs before the actual thing, you know,
and that isn't me.
I can't think of four verbs to describe water in the same sentence.
That was one of my weaknesses.

Rosa's identity as the author of "A Mountain Stream" first included her mother. Saying "I really didn't understand what I wrote" implies that there is no distinction between herself and her mother; both are "I." This blurring of identity continues in "I just totally talked about a mountain stream," but separates into two people when she says, "that isn't me." This passage also emphasizes that she does not have powers of description in her writing repertoire. I think this is primarily because she does not read description, and one reason she does not read it is that her way of using reading and writing to escape reality is antithetical to description: To slow down in order to read and write descriptive details through imaginative observation means paying attention to what is going on in one's environment. At the very least, slowing down means postponing finding what she is seeking. Rosa is not looking for a place but for people. By focusing on human action, she has honed her reading and writing styles to suit her purposes.

Rosa also described an assigned essay about the people who had made her the person she is today. She wrote about her mother, her grandmother, her friend Heather, and a teacher-friend at the school, Mrs. Leyton. She said that it was relatively easy to write about Heather because Rosa "just said what she had done for me," but that it was difficult to say more than two sentences about her mother. She explained,

Rosa: But I couldn't branch off.
So my mom looked at it and she put all the things she did for me.

I would have like two or three sentences,
and she would stretch it out,
that's all she did.
More of a detail.
I would say, "My mother has done this, this, this, and this,"
and my mom would describe how she did that, that, that, and that.

Anne: So how does she do this? So she sits down at the computer, and...

Rosa: And adds to what I had on the computer.
We work on it a little bit together,
if it needs to be worked on,
and then I turn it in.

Anne: Do you sit down and read what she's written, and then you tinker with it some more?

Rosa: Not usually [laughs a little].
Well see, with my mom,
she uses the big words, like in every other sentence,
and I wouldn't understand anyway,
even if she tried to explain it to me,
'cause she would explain it in even more bigger words....
She'll use *ambivalence*, stuff like that,
and I'm like, "Huh?"

Anne: She uses these big words—does she use those words when she just talks to you every day? (Rosa nods affirmatively) But it hasn't rubbed off on you....

Rosa: [sounding amused at the preposterous idea]
Noohohoho...(laughs)
My mom will read my stuff,
and she'll just shake her head, and she goes,
"You cannot be my daughter."
(imitating her own incredulous voice) "Why not?"
(returning to her mother's voice,
somewhere between accusing and matter-of-fact)
"You can't spell, you can't e—" (breaks off, begins again)
She was, like, "You need to work on that."

When Rosa was recounting a conversation, her voice was full of drama. She imitated the tone and expression of the speakers, and in this example she sounded not only incredulous but also genuinely hurt when she remembered responding to her mother's saying "You cannot be my daughter." This moment revealed the fragility of her self-esteem and the paradox of her position as an adolescent daughter who desires to be strong and independent like her mother but who is still quite dependent on that very mother. Rosa did not tell her teachers that her mother helped her with her writing because she knew that if she did, she would not get credit for the work. But when I asked her how she felt about turning in papers that included her mother's contributions, her answer indicated that she valued her mother's help for more reasons than just getting a better grade.

> **Rosa:** I'm happy she does it,
> because it's another way for me and my mom to get together,
> have more in common,
> keep us from arguing.
> When somebody plays softball,
> or somethin' like that,
> their parents are teaching them how to play softball,
> there's automatically gonna be that person,
> a part of that person in you,
> it's just how much you use.
> And with me, I just use it more personally than when...
> more on the outside than on the inside,
> I guess is what I'm tryin' to say.
> Instead of...inheriting it,
> because if they did it,
> I can do it, you know,
> that my mom and me do it together.
> It's more of an "out" thing
> than an "in" kinda thing.
>
> **Anne:** Okay, so you're saying, if I've got this right here, that there's at least two different ways that you can get things from your parents, one is to be born with them—
>
> **Rosa:** Yeah, genetically,
> and the other is getting involved.

Rosa's understanding of this moral question of getting credit for writing her mother contributed to is interesting. She clearly put her relationship with her mother ahead of the school's rules about independent work, and she showed no sign of guilt or conflict about doing so. In this regard, she supports Gilligan's (1982) view that female moral standards are based in relationship rather than in rules of behavior imposed by outside authority. When I asked her if she felt that she was learning about writing when her mother put new words on her papers, she put the whole picture of learning, feeling, and relating into perspective.

> Yeah, I learn that a lot of my ideas are good,
> and I learn that I just need to branch out more,
> and talk about that stuff more,
> and if your parents aren't involved,
> or someone that is real close to you is not involved,
> then you're not gonna really learn anything,
> or as much as you would with your parents
> who are your best friend helping you with your life.

Rosa's Way of Learning

Rosa revealed that for her, emotional support is a necessary prerequisite to learning: "If...someone that is real close to you is not involved, then you're not gonna really learn anything." Just as her ethical sense is built on a foundation of relationship, so is her intellectual functioning. Her emotional connections to others are the paths to her understanding. Abstract concepts, in particular, do not make sense to her unless they are reached through an emotional connection or personal experience. This means that it is much harder for Rosa to learn when she and her teacher do not like each other.

> If you don't get along with somebody,
> you're less likely to pay attention,
> which means you're less likely to understand the part that you
>   missed.
> Even though I would pay attention,
> it really doesn't get into me.
> I'm like, with certain things, I can read and understand,
> with other things, I actually have to do with my hands,
> and with social studies, science,
> that kinda thing,
> I need to do it with my hands,
> and we didn't do anything with our hands,
> so it was really really hard.

Rosa moved seamlessly from the importance of liking her teacher to the importance of real-life, hands-on experience. In her mind, the routes to learning are emotion, relationship, and experience—preferably all three together. Crawford and Chaffin's (1986) study of gender and comprehension showed that a person's preexisting schemas determine whether new information will be understood and remembered and that "[g]ender and gender-typing are among the most powerful influences channeling the experiences of individuals" (p. 14). When we put this together with Gilligan's (1982) finding of the importance of relationship in females' lives, it is not surprising that Rosa's feelings about her teachers and her relationships with them determine how well she can learn from them. Unless a channel of personal connection is open between her and her teachers, the subject matter does not "get into" her. Learning depends on activation of a person's mental schemas, and activation of Rosa's schemas depends on emotion and relationship. She feels lost and confused when she is expected to learn abstract concepts through language alone, especially when those concepts appear to be free of affect and connection to others. She says that she learns through her hands, but hands-on experience is not always enough. She had great difficulty learning government and economics, even though both of those classes included simulations, one of elections and the other of running a small business. The simulations occurred at the end of the semester, and by that time Rosa already felt sure she did not understand what was going on. She did manage to pass both classes, but she felt shut out of the subject matter because she did not find a pathway she could use to enter into it.

School Reading

The only good texts, in Rosa's mind, are those that engage the reader's imagination. Textbooks do not qualify; they are "boring."

> With books that have history and all that,
> you can't really use your imagination,
> and what will happen is that I'll start reading it,
> and I'll soon fall asleep.
> So that's how I am in government and history and all that.

She emphasized that she had to work hard to get decent grades in most classes, and she knew that she learned best through stories. She asked her mother to make up stories about history assignments because she knew that she would not be able to understand or even read what she was not interested in. She had become expert in her own ways of reading, but she was still a beginner in virtually all other kinds. When I asked her if she could read any book as fast as she reads romance novels, she emphasized the importance of being interested in what she was reading.

> If it's a book that I'm not interested in,
> even if it was assigned,
> then I can't really read it.
> If it was a book that was assigned but I'm actually interested into
>   it,
> I can finish it real fast.
> But if it's like somethin' like a history book or somethin' like that,
> I don't get into it,
> and if I don't think it's interesting,
> I don't really read it.

Rosa knew that she did not really read a text she did not understand, but she phrased this in terms of interest—"I can't really read it," and "if I don't think it's interesting, I don't really read it" (note the conflation of "can't" with "don't"). Rosa did not distinguish between understanding and feeling interested. For her, these two qualities went together, as did their opposites—boredom and confusion. Rosa had her own analysis of what made a text difficult to comprehend.

> I never understand [my history textbook]
> and once I get done with it,
> I can't remember any of it.
> It uses big words so you basically have to have an understanding
> of what words mean what,
> what the spellings are,
> 'cause if you don't know—
> aren't a very good speller,
> you won't know what the word is.
> I'm not a very good speller,
> so I have a hard time...

it goes into detail, but it doesn't go into detail, you know what I
    mean?
To a certain person it's enough detail,
but for other people,
you need to explain it step by step,
and this will go step one,
and then step four,
and then step ten....
Also, it's basically true, all of it,
and I'm not really a realistic person.

Rosa's confusion comes from words she does not know, insufficient detail, incomplete explanations, and a focus on reality that inhibits her imagination. She described her difficulties with new vocabulary in terms of spelling, a concept that is familiar from grade school—if you can spell a word, you know it. Repeatedly in our conversations about school texts, Rosa complained that the explanations for concepts were inadequate. Speaking of her economics book, she said,

[It would help] if they would act like they're explaining it to third
    graders.
I'm totally confused.
They give you a whole bunch of graphs,
and it doesn't really explain the graphs.
They defined *demand*, but not *demand curve*.

Rosa was probably not the only student confused by the illustration of *demand curve* in the textbook. It is not a curve at all, but a straight line. The authors of the book never mention, much less explain, this apparently nonsensical technical language. They do provide examples for many of the terms students are expected to learn, and although Rosa understood the narrative examples, she still did not feel secure about the working definitions of the terms themselves.

What I hate is where they explain it,
they'll give—they'll go,
"In fact the effect prices have on our buying
is so common and important
that economists have a special name for it,

the price effect." (Junior Achievement, 1996, p. 21)
They don't say what it is.
They give you the example,
but they don't explain what it is.
It's confusing.
I don't understand it.

Rosa's reading style had been developed using texts that are the opposite of school textbooks in most important ways. Romance novels are written in a flowing narrative full of events, scenes, and people. Abstractions do not interfere with the reader's mental creation; everything in the novel has an obvious counterpart in the real world. Emotion is an essential part of the story, and the language is designed to be as transparent as possible.

In contrast, texts such as the economics book are dense statements of ideas that have only abstract counterparts in the real world. Events, scenes, and people are presented only as minor explanatory devices, not as the substance of the text. Emotion is nonexistent, and the language is solid, opaque, and heavy. Language becomes an object of learning in itself as new terms are presented for the student to memorize. In this particular case, the authors have buried the definition of *price effect* into a sentence that hides the fact that it is a definition. The sentence does not declare itself to be a definition because the focus seems to be on the economists' decision to give the phenomenon a name rather than on equating the phenomenon with the name as a good definition does.

Of course Rosa had trouble reading, understanding, and remembering such texts: They lack everything she liked about reading and imposed a burden she did not know how to carry. She recognized that some readers enjoy nonfiction, but she had only the most rudimentary idea of how to cope with it herself.

[Reading a novel] you understand what they're going through
'cause you put yourself in their shoes,
and history, you can't—
history, or science, or something like that,
you can't put yourself in their shoes.

Her first assumption about comprehending a text is identification with a character, a reading strategy that works beautifully with romance novels but fails utterly with nonfiction textbooks.

When Rosa read textbooks, she experienced confusion and boredom; when she was reading her genre fiction, she put herself not only into the characters' shoes but also in their minds and bodies. She had what amounts to a genius for exercising her imagination this way when she read a romance novel.

> When I'm reading it,
> I actually picture myself in the outfit.
> I'll put down my book,
> and for like two minutes while it's still fresh in my mind
> my whole room will turn into what the setting is.
> In my dreams I'll totally live through the whole thing,
> I get to the point where I can see it,
> I can smell it,
> and I...I mean, the part where she was getting raped,
> I could feel the little hairs in my neck stickin' straight out,
> and I could almost feel the brutal force of him
> pushing her against the wagon,
> and it said that there was a board that was sticking up
> that was jabbing in her back,
> and I could almost feel that,
> so I...I can...to all five senses when I read.

> But [history or econ textbooks] I can't get into at all.
> I feel like I'm out looking in, and since I can't—
> it's like you're outside,
> people are talking
> but you don't hear what they're talking about.
> All you see is that they're extremely happy or extremely angry,
> and that's all you understand,
> and that's how I am with history, econ, science...
> and sometimes math,
> and then the teachers get mad when you don't understand any of it.

Rosa was wonderfully articulate here about the difference between a text she could experience bodily and emotionally and one she could not. The fact that she could recall plot summary after plot summary of her novels indicates that she learned these stories, while her textbooks left her with only the most general impressions of their subjects. It is interesting to note that even when she was describing nonfiction textbook information that she did not understand, the analogy she used involves people, scenes, and emotions.

If nonfiction textbooks were almost impenetrable for Rosa, and her genre novels opened effortlessly to her, the fiction she was assigned in school fell somewhere in between. She remembered being confused by *Death of a Salesman* (Miller, 1998) because "it would fade in and out," and she remembered that *Of Mice and Men* (Steinbeck, 1993) was a mixed experience.

> Some of it was interesting,
> and some of it got so boring....
>
> I got real angry when they shot the big guy
> just because he did something that he didn't understand.
> It goes back to understanding certain things,
> you have to explain it to certain people, you know.
> I don't think it was right of the guy to kill the lady or the little
>   puppy,
> but I also didn't think it was right for them
> to shoot the guy just based on that
> 'cause he didn't understand it.
> And it was like a second grader
> in a 32-year-old's body.
> I feel like
> sometimes I'm basically a second grader
> in a 12th-grader's body.
> 'Cause there's a lot of stuff I don't understand,
> and people don't explain it.

Rosa identified with Lennie's difficulty in understanding, and, in fact, she was enacting that difficulty in understanding as she spoke here. The story Steinbeck presents, like all stories we recognize as "great literature," is far larger than Rosa's conception of it. She did not put herself in George's shoes but only in Lennie's, and she did not know how to read a story from any position other than in the emotional center with which she identifies. She did not know how to recognize that Steinbeck is, among other things, asking us to consider the paradoxes of the human race: The cruelty of men like the character Curley coexists with the benevolent (but troubled) humanity of a simple man like George, who saves Lennie from torture by taking responsibility for Lennie's death as he has earlier taken responsibility for his life. In Rosa's reading, one man unfairly kills another. She had no awareness of the possibility of moving outside that action and examining the larger contexts that bring about the killing. Nothing in her genre reading had prepared her for the moral complexity—or the characterization—of Steinbeck's novella.

In her 12th-grade Recent American Novels class, Rosa read *Go Ask Alice* (Anonymous, 1971), a simpler book than *Of Mice and Men*. After she had read the first few pages, she said,

> I'm curious if she kills herself.
> I'm kinda like wanting to read the last page.
> I don't like doin' that,
> 'cause then you get all the way through the book
> except for the last chapter,
> and then you're like, You know what?
> I already know what happens to it—skip it.

> I'm gonna read it because I have to,
> but I really don't mind that it's about somebody's life
> as long as you know it's interesting.
> I hate books that you know are so boring,
> they go, this happened this day and this happened that day,
> and it really bugs me.
> I had to read the biography of Martin Luther King,
> and it was all boring except for when he started getting into the
>   civil rights.
> And even that I kinda like skimmed
> 'cause I already knew the facts.

Rosa learned that unless she enjoyed being in the world of the book, she would need curiosity about the ending to sustain her interest in reading it. She was unsure whether she should apply her romance-novel reading style or her mystery-novel reading style to *Go Ask Alice*. She was somewhat fearful that the story would consist of the wrong kind of detail, the kind that bored her with the book about Martin Luther King, Jr. She had no reading method to cope with that situation. Ultimately, she was optimistic because it is about a protagonist she could imagine and is a book that gets into people's lives.

Later, after the class had finished with the book and moved on to the next one, I asked Rosa what she thought about it.

Go Ask Alice was a good book...
because it deals with teenagers' problems,
one problem that teenagers have always had and will always have,
no matter what.
That's dealing with drugs.
Not to take 'em, to take 'em, that kind of thing.
And it touched bases on popularity, too,
if you were not part of the "in group,"
if they were kinda like really going after you....

I didn't like it, how they killed her off?
I didn't like that at all.
We had to figure out why she was killed,
and I basically said, "No, she didn't do it on her own,
'cause she was clean for a long time.
I think it was Jan and Marcie,
since they tried to drug her before,
and this time it actually worked."

None of the students I spoke to about this book liked the ending. Duke said, "I wasn't prepared for it," but the others, such as Rosa, just said, "I didn't like it." In the novel, after continuous ups and downs with drug use, Alice's last diary entry shows her to be healthy and happy, reunited with her loving family. Everything seems to be going well for her. Only in an epilogue do we learn that she was found dead of a drug overdose a few weeks after she wrote this last, optimistic diary entry, but no explanation for her death is provided. This is too large an indeterminacy (Iser, 1978) in the text for these readers to fill in, so they felt let down by the story. The text did not uphold its part of the reading bargain. When the teacher asked Rosa's class to write about what they thought caused Alice's death, Rosa treated the story as if it were one of the mystery stories she writes, blaming the two young female characters who had been responsible for giving Alice drugs earlier in the book. Rosa usually disliked books that are this close to real life, but because she did not identify with Alice or her problems, she did not feel disturbed by it.

She did, however, feel disturbed by another book assigned in the Recent American Novels class, *Kindred* (Butler, 1979). Rosa's reading of this novel shed more light on the way she read fiction.

Rosa: I didn't like [*Kindred*].
I mean, it was a good book,
I think it was important to read,
but I particularly didn't like all the graphics
and how they were whipping the slaves and all that.

Anne: Yeah, so reading it was just painful, it sounds like. Is that true?

Rosa: Yeah, mmhm.

Later, I returned to the subject of *Kindred* to find out more about why Rosa did not like the book even though she thought it was important to read it.

Anne: Another thing that I was wondering about is when you were saying that you didn't like the real violence in *Kindred*, the real pain that those characters suffered. You've also told me about some books that you've read where it sounds like pretty awful things happen—people get raped, and people get kidnapped....

Rosa: But that's not as awful as...
I mean, it's wrong, you know, but then (pause)
with the slaves and everything, that was morally wrong,
it wasn't just wrong.
They had—it was a whole bunch of things wrong,
and I can't—to me, I couldn't imagine anything or anybody
being treated that way even if it was slaves,
no matter what, and that totally brought me to real life,
and I was like, "You know what? I don't like this book."

Anne: 'Cause it was too real?

Rosa: It was too real, 'cause it was...
it put too much history in books,
and even though I like the um...the Harlequin westerns,
where they go back to 1800s where it's Indian country,
and (voice becomes high and light)
the little white woman gets kidnapped by the Indian
and she hates him, she hates him, "Oh my gosh, I love him!"
(spoken with a mocking imitation of the silly tone and attitude
evinced in Harlequin westerns)
You know, and even though they'll mention a little bit of history,
the whole book is not based on history,
and with *Kindred*, it was based on history,
and that was why I didn't like it.

Rosa knew when a writer was serious and when a writer was merely entertaining. Although she loved feeling the emotions and bodily sensations of characters when she identified with them, she needed the security of a safe genre frame in order to throw off her fears and identify with a rape or kidnap victim. But it is not safe to identify with the protagonist of *Kindred* because she is not safe. The story connects in essential ways to the real lives of real people, and no happy endings are guaranteed. I think this is what Rosa meant when she said she did not like too much history; for her, history seemed to be synonymous with either painful or boring aspects of reality.

Rosa was teetering on the brink of a more mature acceptance of what the author of *Kindred* accomplishes in this novel. Rosa began by saying that it is a good book and important to read, and she seemed to be able to separate this evaluation from her own emotional response to the brutality in the story. Further, when Rosa contrasted the Harlequin westerns that she liked with *Kindred*, she clearly saw how absurd the former are. Yet she ultimately fell into her old pattern of concluding that because *Kindred* is based on history, she did not like it. She was not yet able to sustain a set of conflicting evaluations of the book; she was not able to say, "It was emotionally painful for me to read about the horrible treatment of the slaves, but it was also a gripping, well-written story." Again, nothing in her genre reading prepared her for an ambivalent reading or ambivalent response.

Rosa's favorite book of those assigned in Recent American Novels was the mystery, *A Stranger Is Watching* (Clark, 1977). Rosa was unequivocally enthusiastic because the story combined a mystery, which she said she solved by the fourth chapter, with a romance that kept her reading so she could enjoy the happy ending.

> Even though I know who did it
> and how he did and why he did it,
> I will want to read it even more to see if—
> because with Mary Higgins Clark,
> she'll put a little romance into it, so you want—
> not only do you want to find out who else gets killed,
> but you also want to find out if those two get together.

Part of Rosa's reason for finishing a mystery novel was to see "who else gets killed." This desire seems odd when juxtaposed with Rosa's intense discomfort with the suffering in *Kindred*, but she matter-of-factly accepted the mystery on its own terms, as a game in which reality is kept at a safe distance. This genre form allowed her to be coolly analytical, in contrast to the romances, which engage her emotions fully. Both genres are in contrast to *Kindred*, which engages Rosa ethically, an uncomfortable engagement because the suffering in *Kindred* can never be justified. Rosa does not know what to do with history's reminders of human cruelty and injustice.

Rosa's second reason for wanting to finish *A Stranger is Watching*, which was to "find out if those two get together," reveals the difference in practice between reading for emotional gratification and reading to solve a puzzle. Rosa knew perfectly well that the lovers would be united at the end of the story, but she wanted to experience the final union. Ultimately, this book provided Rosa with pleasures of the head and of the heart.

What Has Rosa Taught Us?

Recently, some scholars and educators have advocated including students' reading choices in the curriculum and making them the subject of classroom discussions. Lewis (1998) argues that students may be making surprising meanings of popular culture texts, so we should be listening to their explanations of how they make use of them. She also argues, as have others (e.g., Alvermann & Hagood, 2000a, 2000b; Bean & Moni, 2003; DeBlase, 2003; Finders, 1997), that teachers should help students examine the production and ideologies of these texts to see whose interests they serve and how they position readers. Otherwise, Lewis warns, students will continue to use the texts but without the benefit of adult insight into how they work in the larger culture.

A number of studies of the romance genre have investigated the psychology of their appeal: Modleski (1982) saw their purpose as "neutraliz[ing] women's anger and mak[ing] masculine hostility bearable" (p. 58). Juhasz (1994) argued that women are looking for the love and acceptance of the perfect mother; Moffitt (1987) and Christian-Smith (1993) found that teenage readers used romances for information about males and sex, to escape their lives, and to experience romance vicariously. Moffitt also saw teenagers' romance reading as a way for girls to begin to separate from their parents. Cohn (1988), as we have seen, focused on the power relations between men and women. Clearly, multiple readings of this genre exist. My argument is that Rosa, like other readers, has purposes for and ways of reading romances that cannot be known until she explains them. Students' chosen reading, perhaps especially when it is as extensive and determined as Rosa's, must not be dismissed on the basis of adult assumptions.

Some arguments in favor of including students' popular fiction in the classroom have gone beyond using those texts as a platform for teaching students how to think critically about the culture that produces those texts. Alvermann and Hagood (2000a, 2000b) take the position that students have the right to enjoy their chosen texts and that the study of any disempowerment these texts bring about should not be aimed at diminishing the pleasure the students take in them. I concur, but I believe this point should be taken further. "Pleasure" is often an inadequate description of the benefit students may be getting from their popular fiction texts. Rosa says that she loves romances, but when I listen to her talk about her reading, it becomes clear that the meaning she makes of it is deeper than pleasure. Chandler (2000) describes in detail the tension between a teacher and a student over the student's desire to read Stephen King novels for a reading workshop, but the only insight Chandler reports into the student's reasons for being so engaged in King's plots and characters is that, according to the student, King puts a reader's deepest fears into action. This student's remark needs to be pursued if we are to understand what meaning she makes of King's novels and how they are helping her make sense of her life. Only then might we be able to help her take the next step in her reading development.

Students generally experience only one way—their way—of reading a text, so they are unlikely to explain these deeper experiences unless they understand that the experiences are not obvious to everyone. If the adults who disapprove of romances, science fiction, horror, westerns, and other noncanonical texts could read through students' eyes and psyches, they might be able to see why these texts give pleasure—and see what deeper feelings and needs are addressed and satisfied by the texts. For this reason, I urge care in plunging into critical literacy readings. If a student depends on a genre or an author to provide essential support and information to cope with fear, rage, or other strong emotions, educators must not expect to wipe away the student's reliance on that genre or author without first making sure that the support and information are still available, either through the same texts even after they have been deconstructed or through another source. Critical literacy readings of these texts ask students to see how they operate in a cultural context, but such readings may be resented if they destroy the deeply personal and important benefits of the texts that students depend on.

Even if a student is not ready for critical literacy readings, educators can learn to use these texts as teaching tools. Rosa could learn a great deal about writing (and, therefore, about reading) from the romance novels. She could begin by examining carefully the scenes that she finds so entertaining and using them as models for developing a greater level of detail and description than she currently knows how to do. She also could keep a vocabulary journal, and, probably more interesting to her, she could examine the ways that romance writers create characters and differentiate between them. She also has a great deal to learn about setting and plot that she could get from these novels—in other words, all the basic elements of storytelling. She would need to learn to read, or reread, not for plot but in order to determine how the writer accomplished the storytelling. In other words, she would have to learn to keep some distance from the emotional influence of the story as she reads, concentrating instead on how that influence is achieved. Because Rosa would like to become a professional writer, she has a good reason to examine the difference between a reader's complete surrender to a story and the writer's conscious control over its creation. She can begin to know as a reader and as a writer what Iser (1978) means by determinate and indeterminate meanings of a text (the former are facts clearly stated; the latter are actions left open to interpretation or imagination) and use these concepts to expand her repertoire of both reading and writing.

Reading is a much larger enterprise than just what teachers and students are expected to do with texts in school. School reading, whether of textbooks or imaginative literature, is set up to prepare students to be productive members of society. It is designed to put certain information into people's minds, not to help them cope with loss or engage in fantasy. Some teachers do believe, of course, that reading the fiction they choose for their classes will help students learn about life (I tend to think this myself) and that reading can help us deal with a variety of big questions. But the baseline of literary instruction in English class as it stands today is learning who Iago is and what the scarlet letter means. The personal and more lasting benefits of reading, such as getting through a period of stress or learning what you are looking for in a spouse, are purely incidental and virtually never part of the curriculum.

When the reading an adolescent loves is outside the realm of respectable literature, teachers are taught that their job is to move students away from their chosen genres and into the fold of "something better" as quickly as possible (e.g., Christian-Smith, 1990). Teachers are given the responsibility for making the young person a more mature reader and thinker who can look upon popular fiction critically and understand why it is "inferior." Yet making a person grow up is outside a teacher's capabilities. Teachers can encourage, but not create, analytical thinking and tolerance for ambiguity; they can offer texts that are within a student's *zone of proximal development* (Vygotsky's, 1980, term for the growth a person can achieve with help from an expert) and provide the scaffolding (Wood, Bruner, & Ross, 1976) when a student is ready to respond to a story that is more complex and ambiguous than children's stories. Dialogues with students about what they independently choose to read (or view as in Duke's example) will help teachers understand what lines of experience are already open. They should begin teaching from there.

I recognize that I am calling for what amounts to individualized instruction and that teachers do not have the luxury of spending that much time on individual students. However, the current system is not working—Rosa is not learning to be a more sophisticated reader either of fiction or of textbooks. She is getting through her classes, and through high school, without absorbing much of what is offered. Individualized instruction does not have to be an all-or-nothing practice; almost all teachers make adjustments for individual students every day. If teachers understood more of Rosa's reading story from the inside, they would be better able to work with her strengths and interests to move her forward.

Rosa's reading story is a reminder that students experience a number of different kinds of reading demands and that not all students are prepared to meet them. If educators think of reading as a single, homogeneous practice, we do not see that a person like Rosa can read expertly in one narrow frame but be bewildered by texts outside that frame. As a result, we incline toward giving her too much credit for being a good reader and, therefore, too much responsibility for reading texts she cannot handle, or we give her too little credit for her effective use of romance fiction and dismiss her chosen reading material as "junk." Getting inside Rosa's reading circle lets us see how thoroughly she has personalized the complex and multipurpose practice of reading.

Chapter 6

Valisha: Finding a Reason to Read

I first noticed Valisha when I visited her Recent American Novels class because she kept her head down on her desk, roughly pillowed on her backpack, for the entire 50 minutes. It was the Tuesday reading period, the one time during the week when a class (a different one each week) was devoted to sustained silent reading. Valisha had opened a magazine when she first sat down, and for 10 minutes or so held it in front of her eyes, but then the inevitable happened. She let it go and her eyes fell shut. The teacher, charged with modeling good reading behavior for the students during this period, sat at the front of the class engrossed in her own book. Once, halfway through the period, she got up and circulated among the students, telling those with closed eyes that they were to wake up and read. Valisha dutifully opened her eyes for a few minutes, but that did not last. Only when the bell rang did she sit up, shake her head as if to clear it of sleep, and pick up her fallen magazine.

Valisha was one of the quieter students in the school, not shy so much as self-contained. She dressed modestly in casual pants and big, loose shirts, unlike some of her classmates who wore short skirts and tight, cropped tops. She never wore makeup to school and pulled her black hair into a simple, short ponytail. When I asked the teacher about her, I learned that Valisha had a son who was about 1 year old, and as a result of her responsibilities to him, which she took extremely seriously, she often was sleepy in school. She was frequently absent or tardy as well. All her teachers agreed that she struggled to keep up with schoolwork, but they also all said that they cut her some slack because they knew she was taking care of a baby and because she was a nice person who was determined to get her high school diploma and make a life for herself and her son. During the time of her interviews, Valisha was in her senior year and almost certain to graduate, although her grades would not be high—mostly Cs and Ds. But grades were much less important to Valisha than the fact of getting her diploma. Like all the seniors I spoke to, she was extremely eager to leave high school. But what reading experiences would she take with her? What had she learned about the value of reading? What did she believe about herself as a reader?

Reading—and Not Reading—Then and Now

Valisha was the only one of the five readers in this study who said she had never liked to read and who had no happy memories of childhood reading. When I asked her why she did not like to read, she paused to think about it, and finally said,

> I have no idea.
> I don't really like it.
> I do it—I just don't like it.

Only later, in another interview, did she offer an explanation, one that raised uncomfortable memories for her.

> **Valisha:** Prob'ly cause we did it all the time when we were little kids. In school.
> I don't like readin' out loud in front of a lot of people—
> I always get nervous and start messin' up,
> and feel like I can't read....
>
> **Anne:** Oh, OK. Do you think maybe if you'd been allowed to read just silently that you might feel differently about it?
>
> **Valisha:** I prob'ly would.

I asked about Valisha's memories of reading in elementary school, which she attended in rural Alabama. Again, she mentioned reading aloud.

> **Valisha:** I remember...
> how we used to all sit in a circle,
> and you know, like, one person would read one sentence,
> and the next person would read one sentence,
> and it would just go on like that.

Anne: Do you ever remember reading books that you liked?

Valisha: Um...uh....unh-unh [negative].
I probably liked 'em, but I just can't remember.
I remember a report, Dr. King books,
stuff like that.
I was never into reading.
I really don't like reading in front of a whole bunch of people—

Anne: Reading out loud, you mean?

Valisha: Yeah, listen to myself....

Valisha immediately connected reading with reading aloud "in front of a whole bunch of people," which she did not like to do. I persisted in trying to find out whether she remembered any particular books or stories because other students I spoke with remembered at least one favorite children's book with pleasure. But other than the embarrassment of listening to herself read aloud, Valisha remembered nothing of elementary school reading.

I never really read them, them books back then.
I just go to school (laughs a little).
I don't even remember readin' a book back then,
'less it was like little storybooks we would read,
that's about all I remember.

Valisha was clear and consistent about identifying herself as a person who does not like to read. Judging from her answers to my questions, this identity was not something she had wondered about or tried to change. She read when she had to in order to write reports (such as one on Martin Luther King, Jr., in middle school), but whereas other adolescents I interviewed carried with them favorite fixtures of memory and imagination that came from being read to or finding stories they loved, Valisha did not.

And yet I believe that Valisha was more of a reader than she realized. She was an interesting person for teachers to know because her interest in reading and the practice of it were coming slowly and much later in life than happened with most students. Indeed, her reading story is the inverse of the more common pattern of childhood reading interrupted by adolescence. It is more accurate to say that her childhood aversion to reading was interrupted by adolescence, and late adolescence at that, because not until her senior year did Valisha begin to read voluntarily. Furthermore, Valisha, like Rosa, found an entree into reading through emotion and identification with characters. And like all the students in this study, Valisha used reading for her own purposes and in her own ways, which were rarely in confluence with the school's purposes and ways.

At the age of 18, Valisha had, by her own account, read two books on her own. Both are by the popular African American writer Terry McMillan. Valisha's discovery of this author is an interesting story in itself. It begins with Valisha believing that she dislikes reading and includes well-meaning teachers who have done everything but stand on their heads to get students like her interested in reading. The irony in this story is that Valisha's introduction to personal reading had nothing to do with school.

> **Anne:** What pops into your mind when I say the word *reading*?
>
> **Valisha:** A book.
>
> **Anne:** OK. (Both laugh.) What kind of a book do you imagine?
>
> **Valisha:** Um...like just a book, I mean, just like books,
> I like, it's like, I read a lot of Terry McMillan books,
> I like her books.
> I don't really read a lot,
> I only read two,
> but I really liked her books.
> *Waiting to Exhale* [McMillan, 1992] and *Disappearing Acts* [McMillan, 1989].
> I liked those books.
>
> **Anne:** OK, so when you think of reading, do you think of yourself reading, or just a book on a shelf—
>
> **Valisha:** Myself, yeah.
> Terry McMillan books...friends just told me about the books.
> I just go to they house,
> and I just read like the back of the book,
> you know I already seen *Waiting to Exhale* [Whitaker, 1995].
> I already seen the movie,
> and I just want—you know, there's more in the book
> than the movie,
> so I wanted to read the book.

[The book has] More space.
And more time.
It was long.
It was good, though.

I was off and on with that book, probably a month or two?
I took a little time off tryin' to read the book.

When Valisha heard the word *reading*, her immediate response was to picture herself reading a Terry McMillan book. She did not respond with "boring," as do most people who do not like reading. Valisha tells us about the reader she is when she said that there was more in the book than in the movie, that the book fills more space and takes more time, both of which are reasons to read, rather than avoid, the book. The fact that she took a month or two to read *Waiting to Exhale* (strictly on her own time; she did not get any school credit for reading it) shows persistence in the face of inexperience with reading novels. She was getting something important from the book.

[I liked] how she just speak her mind,
say anything, and you know, tell how—
that's how I like it, just tell it
'stead of beatin' around the bush with it.
If you're gonna say it, say it. (Snaps fingers twice for emphasis.)
[I liked] the people—the charackership.

Valisha was searching for information about how people relate to one another, how they handle problems, and what they think about big issues such as abortion or teenage parents. She clearly wanted straight answers to the questions she cared about. Her school reading, especially the fiction assigned in English class, only rarely provided the kind of information she was seeking. Outside school, however, in addition to McMillan's novels, she sometimes looked for information in newspapers and magazines about other adolescents.

Valisha: I read magazines, newspapers...
Teen, and just like, stuff talkin' 'bout teenagers,
things that's goin' on in teenagers' lives,
I like stuff like that.

I just like to read—with people my age,
I like to read like some of the stuff they be goin' through,
like little love thingies they be goin' through,
stuff like that, you know,
tryin' to get ideas, and um...dating and stuff like that,
how they can do it and stuff.

Anne: Mmhm. But when you're reading the Terry McMillan novel, is she also talking about love and relationships and...?

Valisha: Yeah, she just put it more clearly, you know, like, how things should be with you and your man.

Valisha recognized the power of fiction. McMillan can and does speak the truth as she sees it through her characters more effectively than teen magazines do with what are presumably nonfiction articles and interviews. In spite of Valisha's lack of experience with fiction, she understood and appreciated what it could offer when its subject was close to her heart.

Reading With the Inner Eye

Because Valisha had so little experience with reading, she also was inexperienced with thinking and talking about what happened in her mind when she read. Yet every reader has a personal way of imagining a story as it unfolds. McMillan's stories encouraged Valisha to imagine the future courses of the characters' romantic relationships with each other.

Valisha: With those books, um...
people who been in relationships,
I always imagine them,
they either gonna be with other people
or they're gonna break up or get married,
or stuff like that.

Anne: Mmhm, so you're kind of predicting what the future might hold for them?

Valisha: Yeah.

Valisha had no practice in observing herself as a reader or in analyzing how the experience went for her. As a person who was, in a sense, a beginning reader, she assumed that what happened in her mind when she read was "just reading," without realizing that reading varies from text to text and reader to reader.

> **Anne:** And as you're reading, are you visualizing the characters, or do you imagine hearing their voices, or do you just—
>
> **Valisha:** I just read.
>
> **Anne:** You just read, OK. Does it feel like work to you, if you're enjoying the story?
>
> **Valisha:** No.
>
> **Anne:** When does reading feel like work to you?
>
> **Valisha:** Like when Ms. A give me a book and say,
> You have to read this by Wednesday. Or Thursday.

I came back to the question of what went on in Valisha's mind when she read in an effort to understand better what she noticed and (unconsciously) selected from the text to work with. I wondered what mental pictures she found herself creating.

> **Anne:** How about the McMillan character, do you get a mental picture of what she's like?
>
> **Valisha:** I—like, *Waiting to Exhale,*
> I seen the story, the movie.
> And *Disappearing Acts,* um...I got a picture of her.
> You know, she described herself, like, straight out,
> so I pictured a person like her, and her friends,
> and her boyfriend,
> and, like, the abortions and stuff she kept goin' through,
> the clinic, I imagined that.
>
> **Anne:** Is it like seeing a movie in your mind?
>
> **Valisha:** Not really...well, I—it probably is.
> Yeah—
> Seems like a movie.

Valisha had more experience with movies than with reading, and because she enjoyed most movies but not most reading, her first response was to say that the two are different. But thinking about it, perhaps for the first time, she realized that she was creating her own movie-like images of the story as she read the print on the page. Of course, she could have been responding to the suggestion that my question put in her mind, but she was so forthright about and comfortable with saying no to other questions I asked that I interpreted this exchange (noting her body language and tone of voice) as evidence of her making a connection between reading books and watching movies.

In addition to creating pictures of characters and events, readers also find themselves in a position relative to the action of the story—a position that seems to evolve naturally, without being consciously chosen. Some readers imagine themselves in the thick of important scenes (Wilhelm, 1996b), but Valisha was a more detached observer.

> **Anne:** And where are you in this? Are you standing on the sides, are you sort of in a theater looking at a screen—how do you—where are you? Some people put themselves right in there—"I'm the main character," and some people don't, some people say, "Oh no, I'm on the side, I'm..."
>
> **Valisha:** Probably on the side.
> Witnessing everything.
>
> **Anne:** Oh, OK. And did you ever find yourself getting sort of emotionally involved, like upset, or laughing, or depressed because of the things that were happening to the characters?
>
> **Valisha:** Um...prob'ly upset,
> how Mildred was carrying herself with men?
> I mean, she just didn't care,
> it just—be with a man for anything—I didn't like that.
> And Freda, Freda too.
> Freda was one of the daughters.
> Just back-to-back to men.
>
> **Anne:** Do you ever feel like you want to talk to the characters?
>
> **Valisha:** (half laughs) No. It's just like,
> "Will you please understand?" No.
>
> **Anne:** OK, you're just watching, and...
>
> **Valisha:** Seeing.
>
> **Anne:** Do you ever get frustrated when you know they're gonna get into trouble because of what they're doing, and you can't stop it?
>
> **Valisha:** No, 'cause sometimes it gets better
> to see what's gonna happen.

Valisha was interested in seeing. She wanted to know what was going to happen to the characters, and, in the case of McMillan's stories, she trusted the author to tell her something worthwhile. She was comfortable on the side, watching, absorbing, and making her own judgments, but interested in seeing what the characters were going to do next rather than itching to interfere.

Reading for School

Valisha was frank about not reading much that is assigned in school, but when she had a report to do, she would read about the subject if it interested her. In middle school, for example, she read about African American heroes.

> **Anne:** Do you remember reading any books before the McMillan books?
>
> **Valisha:** (pause) Um...I read a couple Martin Luther King books,
> I was interested in him
> and Frederick Douglass books.
> We had reports and stuff like that,
> and like I'd get like a book,
> we had reports and stuff like that.
> And I just read it.

In high school, shortly after the birth of her baby, the subject she chose for another research paper was abortion. She felt burdened by the amount of reading she had to do because the project went on for about two weeks (a long time in Valisha's reckoning), but at the same time, she was interested in what she was learning.

> And I read some books about abortion, stuff like that,
> I had reports on that,
> so I did it.
> Teen pregnancy books, like...
> The abortion book was really, really interesting.
> Like all this stuff that they got now for abortions,
> but that still don't inspire me to do nuthin' like that,
> 'cause I'm still against abortion,
> and the teen pregnancy, you know,
> I wanted to see how other people feel,

as tryin' to be a parent now,
and a teenager, you know,
and knowin' myself how I feel about bein' a mother,
and I want to see how other people feel about it....

Sometimes I read to see what other people think,
but then, like, sometimes I just ask some of my friends...
I ask my best friend, like
How you feel about this,
or, How you feel about that?
She'll tell me.

For some people (Rosa is an obvious example), the main reason to read is to get away from real life and into something different. For others, such as Valisha, reading is a way to get information about real life, and the more honest and direct that information is, the better. The way Valisha phrased her story shows that the impetus to choose this topic was an interest in other people's feelings. Once she began to read, she became interested in the medical facts of abortions. As is true of Rosa, the route to Valisha's intellect is by way of her emotional engagement with other people. Warburton (1987) sees this as true for all readers.

> Emotion colours all our cognitive life as a result of its involvement in selection of information, in the storage processes for information, and the associated affective tone of information. In this colouring, the emotional and cognitive systems act reciprocally, each essential for the functioning of the person. (p. 214)

Valisha's way of learning became clearer to me when I talked with her business education teacher about her work in that class. He had come to know Valisha well because she had a great deal of trouble understanding the concepts presented in the class, and he had spent considerable time explaining them to her. Even the most basic business concepts, such as the difference between accounts payable and accounts receivable, eluded her. When I asked him why she had so much difficulty with such a basic idea, he said, "I think it was because she was looking at it from way out here," and he gestured with outstretched arm, "instead of looking at it from within. She wasn't thinking of it from the point of view of the person who was running a business. She was looking at it from the outside." In other words, Valisha was not imagining the function of the terms *payable* and *receivable*. She was not envisioning people paying and receiving. Human feelings and actions breathe life into language, and when those are absent, Valisha sees the words only as terms that she is supposed to memorize. They have no life or purpose, and, therefore, no meaning, to her.

The same thing happened with many terms in Valisha's government and economics classes. Her government teacher said that she, too, had spent extra time with Valisha outside class, going over terms with her and explaining what they meant. The teacher said that Valisha could memorize a certain amount of material but that she did not really seem to grasp concepts without a great deal of effort, and sometimes not even then. Valisha herself said that concepts eluded her "all the time." "Like the *judicial branch*," she said. "I have to ask the teacher or a friend to break that down for me, to explain it in regular language so I know what it means." Valisha, like Rosa, experienced what Belenky, Clinchy, Goldberger, and Tarule (1986) call "connected knowing," which "builds on the subjectivists' conviction that the most trustworthy knowledge comes from personal experience rather than the pronouncements of authorities" (pp. 112–113). Many of the women Belenky et al. interviewed "remarked upon the discrepancy between the kind of thinking required in school and the kind required in dealing with people" (p. 201), and they resisted when they were expected to accept abstractions without experiences to support them. Valisha and Rosa both had trouble with concepts that were not obviously an outgrowth of specific, believable events that they had experienced.

Valisha's economics class was filled with such concepts. When I asked her about the class early in the semester, she said she was trying hard.

> **Valisha:** Econ's OK, just difficult to understand.
> It's a lot of stuff like, just a lot of stuff, you know,
> like supplies, demands, entrepreneur, stuff like that,
> marketing, all that stuff.
> It's kinda hard, it's confusing, a little,
> but I'm trying to get into it,
> and I did, like, this week I did all my chapters
> without help from my friends,
> and I'm getting into it—trying.

Anne: Yeah...is the textbook just difficult to read?

Valisha: A little bit.
It's just, like, I think if somebody just sat down,
like the teacher, you know,
if we just had a day when you just,
on a certain chapter
you just go over that chapter
and talk about it,
it'd be OK.

Anne: But does the teacher do that?

Valisha: Sometimes—not too often.

Valisha had some of the terminology on the tip of her tongue but did not feel that she understood what it all meant. She knew she would benefit from some personal interaction with the teacher, but the teacher of this class believed that high school seniors should be able to handle reading assignments. In fact, he saw part of his teaching job as giving students the responsibility for reading on their own. But Valisha did not know how to make sense of the material, which was completely new to her. She had no existing mental schema into which to fit it.

As the weeks went by, Valisha's difficulties with the economics text increased. Although she knew she was not understanding the book when she tried to read it, she had adopted the official view that she should read, even though she had no way of connecting intellectually or in any other way with it. Eventually, she gave up on the textbook.

Well, I'm passing.
I don't even read the book 'cause I don't understand it.
I try to read the summary,
thinkin' that'll help me,
the summary of each chapter,
but it doesn't.
I know I should read the whole chapter,
but I don't.

She said that she got by with a passing grade because she was able to absorb enough from listening in class, and, she said, "because

I turn in all my work." Even if that work included many wrong answers, turning in all assignments and listening in class seemed to ensure Valisha's survival. Valisha was in a bind here: She felt she should read but knew that it was a pointless, discouraging waste of time because she did not understand any of it. So she (wisely) adopted another strategy that worked better for her, but she knew that just turning in papers was not the real purpose of being in class. She knew she was not learning economics.

Textbooks very rarely accommodate readers like Valisha who need an affective component in order to absorb information so that they can imaginatively "see" it in action, remember it, and think with it. Some teachers recognize the needs of students like her and compensate for the dryness of text by involving students in simulations or talking about the concepts in ways that stimulate the students' emotions and imaginations. When this strategy works, the teacher is recognized as being a good motivator, and students like Valisha are grateful. They also learn the material. The problem is that if teachers themselves do not value the role of emotions in learning, students like Valisha will be regarded simply as slow or not trying. Instead of seeing emotions and social interests as routes into intellectual activity, people who do not personally use them that way often regard them as a distraction or a non sequitur, and, understandably, resent being asked to learn to include their students' emotional responses in their teaching. Yet without some emotional engagement, Valisha literally could not read her textbooks.

Other kinds of school reading include, of course, fiction assigned in English classes. Valisha found most fiction to be outside her realm of interest, although the particular reasons varied from book to book. When her Recent American Novels class read *Go Ask Alice* (Anonymous, 1971) in class, Valisha yawned.

> I don't [like long books].
> In Ms. A's class we read books,
> whole books,
> —maybe they get better, but I don't like Ms. A's books [laughs a little]. They're boring.
>
> *Alice?*
> I didn't like that book.
> It was weird, how that book ended.

Like many people, Valisha used the word *boring* to describe a quality that she believed to be in the book itself, rather than conceiving of it as a way to describe an absence of connection between herself and the text. Like many people, too, she felt that she had satisfactorily described the book when she said it is boring. The judgment is an endpoint. She does not automatically analyze what lies beneath her reaction. When I probed, however, she revealed something interesting about herself as a reader and as a person.

> **Anne:** OK, when you were reading *Alice*, what were you thinking, or how were you reacting to the character of Alice?
>
> **Valisha:** I was thinking,
> another young person tryin' to find herself in life.
> That's how she was doin' it, but...
> and she was goin' through a lot of changes with her parents....
>
> It was, it was an OK book,
> I just didn't like the ending,
> how she just died.
> I didn't get that.
>
> **Anne:** You didn't like the fact that she died, or you didn't like the way that the story told you about her dying...?
>
> **Valisha:** I didn't like how the fact that she just,
> she just—I don't see how people
> can let a drug run their life
> or make them do stuff,
> and how people let other people just run their lives
> and do stuff like that—I don't—
> I can't see how peoples can do that.
> She let drugs run her life,
> and she let sex run her life,
> and friends,
> and men.
> I don't think—
> you should be a bigger person,
> not to let stuff like that run your life,
> should have control over your own life.
>
> **Anne:** Right. So I guess part of the question, then, is that sometimes a novel like that will try to help you understand, Why does a girl

like Alice let all these other things run her life? Does the book help you understand anything about why she does it that way?

Valisha: It's probably how she—
I don't know, I can't really blame her parents,
then again, I don't know.
How they—I don't know,
I can't say how she was raised,
because you can be raised the best
and still turn out for the worst, and...
I really don't know.

I like the Terry McMillan book 'cause it's more adult—
it's like, with me?
I don't think
I'm on the level that most of these kids are, I think.
I'm more mature—
I'm not sayin' than everybody,
but I think I'm on that level,
from everybody else,
and I like adult books, stuff like that,
that tells the truth,
tells everything,
tells how life is really,
and they just—
how they put it in there,
and no secrets, and stuff like that, you know?

Anne: Let me just interrupt you for a second to ask how old, roughly, do you think the main character in the McMillan book that you liked was?

Valisha: Probably 'bout—probably in her 30s.

Anne: OK, and the character in *Go Ask Alice* is just 15 or something like that. She's much younger.

Valisha: Yeah. And I'm past that stage.

Several important things are evident from passage. Valisha began with "boring" but moved away from a sweeping dismissal of the whole book to focus on her discomfort with the sudden and unexplained death of Alice at the end, a discomfort many students shared. She also revealed two qualities of her own character that created a mismatch between herself and the book. The first is her perception of herself as a more mature person who does not need to learn about 15-year-olds coming to a bad end because they use drugs. The second is somewhat more subtle but very important: Valisha was seeking models of independence, characters who do not let other people or drugs or anything else take control of their lives. Although many students in this class enjoyed *Go Ask Alice* because it does speak a believable truth about a teenager's life, Valisha was looking to her future, not to her past as a 15-year-old. In preparation for that future, she wanted to read about people who succeed in their struggle with forces that threaten to overtake them. Alice appeared to be succeeding, but suddenly, with no explanation, she was dead. This disturbed Valisha. She was not inspired or even informed by the story of a teenager who died because she could not direct her own life.

Valisha also was disturbed by the other serious book read in that class—*Kindred* (Butler, 1979)—and for the same reason: The main character does not have control over what is happening to her, which left Valisha as the reader feeling out of control as well.

> I don't like the last book, *Kindred*?
> That book is really really boring,
> and I don't really like that book,
> and that's why I'm not that far on it.
>
> It's really boring.
> I don't, for some reason I don't like it.
>
> I don't enjoy reading som'n like what happened
> back in the day when slavery,
> how black people was treated.
> I don't like that.

When I asked Valisha whether the main problem with the story was the fact that she found it boring or the cruelty and suffering of the characters, she said,

> I think it's probably more of that than boring.
> 'Cause I mean, like, when I—
> in the beginning, I said,
> you know the book will probably be good,
> but then it's probably just more all this slavery stuff
> and goin' back in time and all that stuff.

Dana [the protagonist in *Kindred*]—she, like,
another person, somebody else is running her life,
and got control over her life right now,
and you know how she keep switching back in the times
and I don't like that.
'Cause a little boy is running her life again,
and it's just not possible to go back in time like that,
at least I hope it ain't,
and how they just keep—
you know, she has little dizzy things that she come back,
and like it is real when she come back all hurt and stuff...
I don't like that.
Like you in one place one minute
and then you in the next place one minute,
and you hurt,
and you're sleeping—I don't like that.

Valisha began her discussion of *Kindred* with the dismissive "really really boring," but when she began to think about her own feelings, she realized that one of the things she resisted in the book was being forced back in time to witness the brutality of slavery. Because she was emotionally and imaginatively engaged, the experience was extremely painful and she shut it out with the first weapon that came to mind: "boring." As we saw with Duke, "boring" serves two purposes simultaneously: It puts the story in a category of writing that is inferior and not worth reading at the same time that it protects the reader's feelings by allowing her to say, "I'm not scared or hurting, here; I'm just bored." Berlyne (1974) found that too much arousal diminishes motivation just as too little does. The optimal amount of arousal is between extremes. Valisha was accustomed to rejecting a book because it failed to stimulate her imagination. She did not realize, however, that a book may be at least as uncomfortable to read because it overstimulates or stimulates in an unwelcome way. This is an insight into reading that might have enriched her understanding of herself as well as her understanding of literature had it been available to her. As it was, she did not ever quite put all the pieces of her discomfort and frustration together into a coherent whole, so she never fully understood why she disliked a book so much admired by many other people.

In addition to the specifics of these scenes of brutality, Valisha disliked the sensation of identifying with a character who is unable to control what is happening to her. Dana has dizzy spells that send her back in time to the early 19th century and across the United States from California to the antebellum South. Just as Alice was unable to control her slide into drug abuse, so Dana is unable to control her location in time and place. She is transported whenever the 19th-century slave owner's son needs her help—he is able to call her to him in some mysterious way neither of them understands. The situation was too threatening for Valisha to enjoy as a story. Furthermore, because she was inexperienced in reading stories that are told in creative ways, such as using time-shifts, Valisha felt confused by some of the narrative.

> I don't know. *Kindred*—
> (short sigh of exasperation or frustration)
> I don't know what to say.
> I did not like that book.
> She—maybe 'cause it was—it kept flip-floppin' back and back,
> future, and time and...
> and it married people in the past—
> I didn't understand it.

It is important to note that the time-shifts in *Kindred* are responsible for putting the characters and the reader in the midst of slavery, so Valisha's sense that she did not understand what the author was doing may be another way to insulate her at least a little from the painful scenes. She may have been unconsciously using the sense of confusion in the same way she used the sense of boredom, focusing on sense making (or not sense making) instead of on sheer feeling. She was torn between wanting and not wanting to read the book, however, because when I asked her how the rest of the class was reacting to *Kindred*, she said they had come to appreciate it.

> **Valisha:** I don't think—well, no—
> well, at the beginning,
> I don't think people liked it,
> but at the end, people were sayin',
> "It was really good, it was really good," you know.
> "You should read it,"
> so they probably liked it at the end,

'cause, like, give it time.
I'm on page, like—I'm on—I'm not even—
I'm on page 60-somethin'.
I just won't read it.

Anne: Yeah, so you just somehow gotta make yourself get past the...

Valisha: I will.

Note that in the space of a couple of seconds, Valisha said, "I just won't read it," and "I will." School requirements and peers' opinions were pulling her in one direction; her own sense of self-protection was pulling her the opposite way. As it turned out, in spite of her good intentions, she never did finish reading the book. I asked her if she had made a conscious decision not to read it or if not finishing was just something that happened. She said,

I didn't finish it.
I know I was almost at the end,
but I know I didn't finish reading the whole book.
We got done with the book,
so it was somethin' that happened.

Anne: OK, OK...so the class got finished before you did, so then you just dropped it? Did your opinion of it change as you read more?

Valisha: (shakes head negatively)
I can't remember that book,
I think she got killed at the end?
I'm not sure about that.

Anne: I don't think she gets killed, but I do think that she gets injured in the past, and she brings that injury into the present—

Valisha: Oh, she got her arm cut off.

Anne: Right, right, so it's a pretty serious story. I know you said you didn't like the book, but I'm wondering if you think it was a good choice for that class? Is there any reason for people to read that book?

Valisha: (pause) Well...unless...
Was that February when we was readin' that book?
It was prob'ly like some'n 'bout Black History Month.
I think in the past our schools done taught us a lot
about black history.
We up-to-date on that, actually.

You can always accept more, you know,
but I think we OK with black history.

Anne: OK, so that would be the main reason to read that book, is to learn about black history in America?

Valisha: I think we read the book 'cause
Ms. A said it was a great book.
(the words *great book* delivered with imitative emphasis and clear enunciation)

Anne: And you don't agree?

Valisha: Well, no, I don't like it....
It probably was good to read it.
Probably in the middle it probably got better, for some people.
I don't think it got better for me.
I just didn't like that book.

Anne: Do you get a mental picture of the character in *Kindred*?

Valisha: Yeah, somewhat.
Like how she got beat up,
and the scars, and all of that.
How she seen the guy get whipped, and....

Valisha and other sensitive readers who feel with the characters sometimes get taken by their imaginations into terrifying places, leaving no escape except to put the book down and declare that it is confusing or boring. The paradox, of course, is that it is imagination that can make reading so interesting and so much fun and that allows them to be fully present in the work so that they can remember it, think about it, and learn from it. Another point to be taken from Valisha's speech is that she deserves credit for understanding the fact that although other people enjoyed the book, for her it did not get better. She did not expand on this point, but it indicates that she was already beyond the fallacy of thinking that good and bad are qualities inherent in a text. She knew enough about reading to see that readers and texts influence one another.

Valisha found the right balance between fear and pleasure when she had a chance to choose a book to read for the final project in her Recent American Novels class. She was fortunate that McMillan had written another book, *Mama* (1995), which she had not yet read.

Valisha: Remember when I was talkin'
'bout those Terry McMillan books?
Well, that was one that was called *Mama*?
And that's the one I read.
I enjoyed that.
'Cause it tells the truth in life,
and it's like an adult book,
and I like books like that.

Anne: OK, Mama's the main character, so did you like her? Did you identify with her?

Valisha: I liked her, but I didn't like her ways.
She was, um, what's the word, she was very...
(exhales in exasperation as she searches for the word)
she was a very outgoing woman to men (laughs a little).
[I liked] her five kids,
there's Freda, Money, Doll, Angel, and Boosty [sic].
I liked it—prob'ly all—I liked all the kids.
Money got on drugs, but I still liked 'em all.
And Crook [Mama's husband], I didn't like Crook.
He was abusive,
he tried to make her mind him,
like her was her daddy
and she had to play a role as a child with him
instead of a grownup.
And he beat her,
and he was very jealous.
But he cheated on her several times.
I didn't like that.
After a while, she just got fed up with it,
and plus she found out he was still cheating with this woman,
so she told him she wanted a divorce,
and he moved out
and they got a divorce.

With *Mama*—I don't know—
it's like telling me—it's telling me another person's life,
another person's perspective.
Like, since I'm growin' up, you know?
About to be in the real world, how things will prob'ly be,
but I know that I can never be like them,

like Mildred [Mama], or Freda,
or any other of the kids.
I think they was good people, actually,
but Mildred was stuck in her ways,
if she said she's gonna do somethin', she's gonna do it.
And that's not really me.
If I say I'm gonna do somethin' it'll take me a while to do it.
Eventually I'll prob'ly do it,
and like, with the men and stuff, I don't believe like that,
with all those men.
And they drunk a lot, too.

I think Mildred was a real—a really, really good mom.
She never let anything come between her and her kids,
and even though the men that she was with,
and maybe she moved a man in her house or some'n,
but she never let them just take control of her house,
she always had control of her house,
and what went on with her kids.

Valisha began with her own concerns: She was growing up and needed to be ready to live in the real world. *Mama* gave her some information, some perspective, on what that world might require of her. But if these concerns provided Valisha's motivation for reading *Mama*, they did not restrict her involvement once she was in the story's world. Here, we see that Valisha moved beyond plot into character analysis. She abstracted information about the character of Mama (Mildred) from the action of the story and was able to step back and talk about the whole picture of Mama's character. She was able to hold conflicting feelings toward the character: Mama drinks too much and is too concerned with having a man in her life, but she is a determined person who gets things done, and she is a responsible and loving parent. Valisha could say, "I liked her, but I didn't like her ways." She was able to read with judgment and a degree of critical distance, or if she did not exercise that judgment and distance while she was actually reading, she did so when she thought and talked about the book later. For Valisha, reading *Mama* was more than an immediate experience of adventure or pleasure; it was an experience of life that rewarded Valisha's reflection on it. When I asked her if the book ever confused her, she showed how much she was involved in the reading.

Valisha: No, I—in that book, (grins with pleasure)
it was like I was there with them,
actin' out everything,
like the children was doin',
I was goin' to college, everything (laughs a little).

Anne: Mmhm, so you really had a picture in your mind of what was happening. And how were your mental pictures when you were reading *Mama*?

Valisha: A big ol' house, in L.A.,
with family coming,
and pools and all that.
Everyone, children all around,
like I was one of her children (half laughs).

Like when Crook was beatin' her,
I felt like one of her kids, standing by the door,
puttin' my head through the door....

Anne: Oh, yeah...that must be scary.

Valisha: Yeah, how they was reactin' with it.

Anne: Unhuh, yeah...but that wasn't enough to make you say, "Oh, I don't wanna be here"?

Valisha: No.

Anne: And in *Kindred*, it did make you feel like, "I don't wanna be here," is that right?

Valisha: Yeah. 'Cause you keep readin' on,
she did get a divorce from him.
Kindred, they had to keep goin' back and back
and takin' the abuse.

Through Valisha's eyes, we see the satisfying way that Mildred takes control of her situation by divorcing the husband who beats and betrays her. Dana, the protagonist in *Kindred*, is engaged in an entirely different kind of mission, one that is completely unfamiliar to Valisha. Dana finds herself charged with making sure the past turns out in such a way as to guarantee her own existence in the 20th century. Her personal life story has become entangled with the history of her ancestors and of the United States, so the journey the story chronicles is larger than an individual's life. Dana is not in charge of her life in the same sense that Mildred is—Dana's challenges are of a different order entirely. As Valisha observes, Dana has to keep going back and taking the abuse. Unless Dana's story is understood to be part of a mythic tradition, one that Valisha does not know, it will not be as satisfying to her as the more realistic McMillan stories with their reassuring correspondences to ordinary life. Valisha knew where she was in McMillan's world.

In addition to her Recent American Novels class, Valisha took another English class, English Twelve. The combination gave her a heavy reading load; in addition, the English Twelve class began at 7:25 a.m. This teacher said that Valisha slept through many classes (due to her responsibilities as a new mother) and did not turn in many of the assignments, although she did always have passing grades on her report card. Valisha did not do any reading outside class, but sometimes the teacher used class time to have students read aloud stories. They did not read novels, only poems and short stories in the school's anthology. One story that they read aloud and that Valisha told me about was "No Witchcraft for Sale" (Lessing, 1965).

> **Valisha:** I can't remember the name of the stories...
> I only read like one of them.
> About a medicine man or som'n like that.
> It was about—
> they lived in a house with these rich white people,
> he was black, and he was the cook,
> and the rich white people,
> they had a son,
> and um...he took care of the son,
> he was a really good friend to the son,
> and the owners,
> they really enjoyed how he put in time with their son,
> helped him out when he needed it.
> But he had his own family, too, that—let me see—
> it was like in the same country,
> but they lived somewhere else,
> and the cook lived somewhere else,
> but he didn't want to go back there,
> and they wondered why he didn't want to go back there,
> but—and then, one day the son—
> the owner's son and the cook's son met up,
> and the owner's son had just gotten like a new scooter

or som'n like that and he was spinnin' around the cook's son
and scared him
and then he tried to apologize
'cause he didn't think the cook liked him no more,
that's when he got older,
so then one day, the owner's son,
somethin' happened and a snake spit in his eye,
this book—it is really weird, the story—
and the snake spit in his eye,
and without—and the cook saved his life
by gettin' a medicine from, like,
from trees or som'n like that,
and somethin', some kind of medicine from trees
and saved his eyes,
and the owners were very pleased and all that.
And everybody wanted to know his secret,
to know what he do,
but he wouldn't tell.
I guess that was a religion thing
or a tradition thing or som'n like that,
he just wouldn't tell.

Anne: Yeah...so did you enjoy that story at all?

Valisha: No.
It was weird.
You know, it was, like, one minute the owner's son was a child,
and then next minute he an adult,
scarin' people and all that.

What is remarkable about this account is that Valisha has retold the story with great accuracy, even though she had read it a month earlier and had not liked it. Neither did she feel that she understood it, which might reasonably be expected to interfere with her memory of it, but the fact that she did remember it so well suggests that she understood more than she realized. But in her mind, confusion about some elements of the story threw all of it into confusion; although she could recite the events, they did not form a coherent story for her. Her retelling is distorted by her emphasis on aspects of the story that the author presented only briefly and by her condensing of aspects that the author dwelt on. These selective emphases can help us understand something about how Valisha read.

She spent most of her account on family and social relationships, noting the cook's distance from his own family and his affection toward the white boy. She also showed particular awareness of the relationship between the two little boys, a key element in the drama of race relations, but one that Lessing describes in only two paragraphs of a seven-page story. The white child's careless cruelty to the black child stood out in Valisha's memory.

The entire second half of the story is devoted to white men's attempts to discover which plant the cook used to counteract the snake's poison. But Valisha summarized this power struggle very quickly, as if it were the falling action rather than (as I read it) the enlargement of the stage on which racial tensions and colonial powers are generated and enacted. When important people hear of the cook's cure, the action moves from the domestic homestead to the broader countryside; the cast of characters grows to include a white doctor and other important people from the town, and the significance of the medicinal plant shifts from saving one boy's sight to having potentially large economic and scientific consequences for white people all over Africa and possibly the world. Although Valisha understood the master–servant relationships between the characters on the homestead and was particularly sensitive to the way one boy bullies another, she had neither the background knowledge nor the political interest to absorb the shift from the immediate and personal drama of the injured child to the general and impersonal drama represented by the resource-hungry white doctor. Her interest in children and families controlled her reading of this story, giving her access to its domestic beginnings but not to its judgment on colonialism.

Valisha did not like the story because it was "weird" and "confusing." She was confused by a time shift that she misread or misremembered (e.g., the owner's son is only 6 years old when he scares the cook's son, not an adult, as Valisha reports). The snake that attacks by spitting is completely new to her, which makes it "weird." Also, she had not been taught what she needed to know about colonialism in Africa in order to appreciate the cook's polite but defiant refusal to tell white people the identity of the medicinal plant.

And this is where an opportunity has been missed. Valisha's comments about the other books she had read show that she was looking for models of strength and independence. The character of the cook in Lessing's story is certainly such a model, but Valisha did not recognize him as such. If Valisha's teachers had time and opportunity to get to know more about how their students read, what they are interested in, and what confuses them, this could be an opportunity to scaffold her reading of literature, capitalizing on her interest in the children and the relationships between rich whites and their black servants, encouraging her to see other ways in which people can successfully defeat attempts to dominate them. But because her teachers almost never had opportunities to get to know their students well enough to tailor their teaching in this way, Valisha came away from this story thinking it was odd and confusing, and she was unwilling to read any more stories in the same book.

One final reading experience should be included in Valisha's case history. Because so many students I interviewed mentioned that they liked mystery stories because they enjoyed trying to figure out the puzzle, I was curious to know how Valisha would respond to *A Stranger Is Watching* (Clark, 1977), her first experience reading a mystery. At first she had trouble remembering it, but then she talked about it with more animation than is usual for her.

Valisha: Um...I can't remember that book...
A Stranger Is Watching...
oh, yeah (smiles).
I liked that book.
I read it all.
(pause) I don't even remember the book.
I know I read it, though.

Anne: (laughs) OK. I haven't really read it myself, so I don't know if I can help you remember from just the little bit that I've heard about it.... I think it opens with a man who's in a motel, he's watching TV—

Valisha: (interrupting) OK, now I remember.
I think it was like a mystery.
It was the wife, Nina.
Nina got killed,
and the stranger, I forgot his name, he was the killer.
He did a kidnap and all that.
It was a mystery, when, like, every chapter,
it kept me wondering what's gonna happen next.
It was good.

It was when we were talking about this mystery story that Valisha said, "I'll read something I'm interested in, and once I get into it, it's no problem." This was the most positive and enthusiastic statement I ever heard her make about reading as a general practice, and when she talked about the pleasure she took in McMillan's books and in *A Stranger Is Watching*, it was clear that her pleasure was genuine. I asked her if her imagination was as caught up with *Stranger* as it had been with *Mama*. It was, although she admitted that she had a little trouble getting into the story at first.

> I enjoyed that book [*A Stranger Is Watching*].
> That book kept me wondering,
> and I kept readin' it and readin' it.
> It was like I was there when they caught him,
> like I seen the bomb blow up....
>
> [Class discussions] helped to—
> 'cause we was all into it,
> and if I...I prob'ly woulda read it on my own,
> if I woulda—
> but when I opened it up, though,
> and I read, like, the first chapter, I was like,
> "This book is nowhere. The book is boring."
> And then they told me just to keep readin', keep readin'—
> Just keep readin', it gets better.
> So I kept readin', and it did get better.
> I got into the book like everybody else.
> Everybody enjoyed that book.

Valisha reminds us of the power of peer opinion. It is not always successful (it did not overcome her resistance to *Kindred*), but it worked well here, with a story that was not threatening because it was safely ensconced in the entertainment category. We also can see, however, that a certain degree of reading skill is necessary to "keep readin', keep readin'" as are persistence and faith in one's friends, all of which Valisha possesses. Her pleasure in the story was enhanced by her sense of community enjoyment (see Cone, 1994, for discussion of the importance of talk about books). Her friends' recommendations provided some of the emotional warmth that she needs in order to read well, and the story itself, with its good guys, bad guys, and romantic subplot, provided the rest.

Writing: "It's Talkin' 'Bout Me"

A Stranger Is Watching gave Valisha the experience of sticking with a book until she got into the story and could enjoy it. Further, this book was the basis for writing a story that she felt proud of. The assignment was to write a three-page story using the Mary Higgins Clark formula, which the teacher elucidated: Include a background story from real life, write about nice people whose lives have been invaded, solve the mystery at the end, punish the villain, and so forth.

Valisha's writing, like her reading, shows her interest in the world around her. It shows her learning how to find what she needs and using it productively. The basis for her story was a movie she had seen about a woman who is murdered by a hit man hired by her husband, but Valisha changed it into the story she liked better. In her version, the husband is a good man who loves his wife instead of the bad guy who wants her dead. Valisha said she enjoyed writing this story.

Valisha: It was fun, 'cause I remember, uh...I forgot...
I think the movie was called *Indecent Proposal*?
I think that was it, I'm not sure.
But I wrote it like,
I wrote it in my words,
in my way at first,
and then at the end I started gettin' it like when she got attacked,
like how the movie was,
but I switched it around because the movie—
like her husband was like a part of the, um...(pause)

Anne: The plot [against her]?

Valisha: Yeah, but I switched it around
like her husband was there for her,
and she was pregnant, and...

Anne: OK, so why did you decide to try to make the husband be a good guy instead of a bad guy?

Valisha: 'Cause that's horrible
for your husband to turn back against—

When Valisha said this last statement, she looked at me as if I had come from another planet, so obvious was it that a murderous husband was too hideous an idea even to contemplate, much less write into a story. She exercised her artistic control in creating a story she would want to read, a story reflecting obstacles overcome through personal strength and the support of loved ones. Valisha explained that in her story,

> She [the wife] saw a suspicious dude at the gas station.
> She shoulda been more suspicious of him,
> but she wasn't.
> He followed her home,
> and when he tried to strangle her in the kitchen,
> she remembered that she had done the dishes that morning
> and that a butcher knife was in the rack,
> so she grabbed it and stabbed him in the neck,
> and he fell down dead.

I asked Valisha if she thought she could kill someone that way, and she said, "If he was tryin' to kill me, I hope I could."

Valisha said the hardest part of writing this story was getting started, so she asked her teacher how to do it. The teacher advised her to work from the required background story in the news. Valisha found a report of a serial killer, making him the villain in her story. She modeled her heroine after another teacher, who quit her teaching job when she became pregnant because she wanted to "raise her children herself," as Valisha put it, and who was Valisha's teacher for about three months when Valisha was pregnant and then at home with her new baby. Valisha never took a class from this teacher at school, but liked working with her at home. The fact that the teacher herself was pregnant during this time helped create a strong bond between them.

Valisha was able to look around at the world, choose models, take control of a plotline she did not like, and replace it with one that met her need to concentrate on good relationships and successful counterattacks in the face of danger. Valisha was uncomfortable in the world of dreams and fantasy, and preferred to be grounded in conscious reality. Both her reading and writing reflect this preference.

Valisha was fortunate to be in a writing class during her senior year with the same teacher who had taught her English class during her junior year. This teacher said that when Valisha had begun 11th grade, her writing was at an elementary school level. Her knowledge of grammar conventions and vocabulary were quite limited; she did not have a clear idea of how to organize ideas into paragraphs, and she did not know that introductions and conclusions were expected. If Valisha had read more, she might have absorbed some of these features of writing, but because Valisha had always kept her reading (as well as her writing) to a minimum, it is not surprising that so many of the conventions of written English were unfamiliar to her.

However, Valisha was willing to work, and when she wrote the research paper that is required of 11th graders at her school, she struggled through numerous drafts, correcting mistakes but making new ones in the process; redrafting; and learning, finally, how to create an essay. The teacher, impressed with Valisha's persistence, said that although Valisha's writing was still not at the 12th-grade level, it was much stronger than it had been 18 months ago.

It is significant that Valisha was allowed to find her own topic for this research paper. She chose to write about deadbeat dads, her own father having disappeared from her life before she was even born. I hate to think what this research paper writing might have been like for Valisha had she not been able to investigate a topic that she cared about. From the teacher's viewpoint, the experience of working with Valisha on that paper made it easier for the two of them to work together on her writing the following year. The teacher knew where to pick up instruction, and Valisha trusted her.

A major writing project for 12th grade was a memory book, a form of autobiography. Valisha ended up writing a memory book for both of her English classes, one in the fall semester and one in the spring. Although some students would be impatient about repeating an assignment, Valisha felt it was beneficial.

> **Valisha:** We're doin' a memory book right now.
> On my life.
>
> **Anne:** OK, so are you basically doing the same thing over again?
>
> **Valisha:** Not really, 'cause like, I just,
> I still have the stuff from last time,
> and it's like she reads 'em,
> and if there's som'n that she thinks that should be right,
> I do it over the way that she thinks it should be, you know.
> Just some ideas about it,
> just put it all together,
> and it's better,
> it comes out better.

Anne: Yeah, so basically you did one version of it for Ms. A's class, and now you're doing kind of a new version of it for Ms. B's. And you think it's better 'cause you're working on it more?

Valisha: Yeah, plus you got two opinions,
two people's opinions.

Anne: Are you enjoying writing that memory book?

Valisha: Yeah. It's a lot, but I like it.

Anne: It's a lot of—

Valisha: Writing, typing...

Anne: Yeah. What is it that you like about it?

Valisha: 'Cause it's talkin' 'bout me (laughs a little).
In some of the chapters I made up my own, I think I made up—
I know I made up one about my son, Andre,
and I really like that one.
I made up like when he was—
when I was pregnant with him,
when he was born,
I made up som'n like that.

Anne: Mmhm. Now when you say, "made up the story," you mean you're telling the story the way it actually happened, or—you're not creating a fictional thing—

Valisha: No. I'm tellin' it like it really happened.
I made up another one about "Who Am I."
And I put it—what I'm gonna be doin',
and myself, and I put 'bout his dad,
and how our relationship is,
all that stuff about me.

I looked at the second version of Valisha's memory book, and it was clear that she put a great deal of work into it. It consisted of 15 chapters, each about one and a quarter double-spaced, typed pages. Valisha included photographs to go with most of the chapters. She did not do the last assigned chapter on what the writer would do differently if she had her life to live over again. The teacher speculated that Valisha might feel some uncertainty about whether having her son at 17 was a good idea. In the chapter about her son, Valisha says that he is wonderful, and she would not do anything differently; so I suggest that another interpretation is that

Valisha may be avoiding fantasies of "what if," preferring to deal concretely and positively with her life as it is. Both reasons may be factors. The point is that Valisha has reasons for doing what she does and for not doing what she does not do.

Valisha's actual writing in the memory book included many errors, even after editing and proofing (such as *mined* for *mind*), but the flow was smooth and the voice was clear. Valisha's feelings about what was happening come through to the reader, although she never indulged in exclamation points or even in repetition. She is honest in this writing, facing up to the consequences of getting pregnant so young. She says simply, for example, that when she found out she was pregnant at 16, she was scared. She is aware that having a son has made her take responsibility, and she writes about how happy she is that her son's father also is growing in maturity and is a good father and partner.

It is impossible to separate the subject of a piece of writing from its style and technique. In Valisha's writing, we see her willing to work on the mechanics and style of pieces that had personal meaning for her, pieces that provided her with another way to work out her feelings and ideas about how she is to live her life. Reading and writing are both tools that she used for these purposes. When the reading and writing assignments of school did not serve her purposes, she did not engage in them.

Reading as a Mother

Valisha enjoyed talking about her son. She was proud of the skills and knowledge he was gaining and she took pleasure in the role she played in his development.

> My son is 1.
> He bring me his little books
> and we sit down and read his little Barney books.
> or he want a pen and paper so he can draw me a picture.
> He can talk, just not very clearly, but he can talk.
> I know what he's sayin'.
>
> He don't know none of it, we just sit down—
> we just point to little words,
> and Mommy reads 'em—(laughs) I read them to him,
> and stuff like that.

If he sees something that he knows,
like a dog, or somethin' like that, or a cat—
he don't say "cat," he say "meow," or "wo-wo"
or truck or ball or football, he know stuff like that.

Anne: I'm wondering how important you think it is for a child as young as he is to have some books or have somebody read with him. Do you think it's important at his age?

Valisha: Yeah, I think it's very important.
He um...you know, like kids learn a lot round now?
And my child is very smart (laughs a little),
and he knows what books he wants.
He got little Tarzan books that make music,
he knows which books he wants to read.

Anne: Would you want your son to be a person who reads? Would that be important to you?

Valisha: Yeah...I would want him to do that.
You get more outta reading, actually.
And I don't want him to do what I do,
just 'cause I don't like it [reading].
I will encourage him to read more,
learn more.

Having a son has affected Valisha's life in obvious and not-so-obvious ways. One of her teachers remarked that before Valisha had the child, she was better about attending school regularly and turning in assignments. "But since she had that baby..." the teacher trailed off, shaking her head. Her business education teacher made a similar observation. But having a baby has focused Valisha's attention. Her child has become her primary responsibility, putting school lower on her list of priorities but at the same time giving her a compelling reason to stay in high school and get her diploma. That responsibility has made her determined to learn how to take care of herself and her son, rather than depending on anyone else to provide for them. Her realization of her responsibility has given her reasons to read and to write. It is worth noting that her willingness to labor through repeated drafts of her research reports and her memory books came after her baby was born. Her discovery of McMillan's books came after the birth of her baby as well. I have said that Valisha is a person who needs personal and emotional connections with texts in order to enter them imaginatively, and no better example of that kind of real-life purpose exists than her desire to prepare for entry into the adult world as a good mother.

What Has Valisha Taught Us?

Valisha was a remarkably successful reader of the books that engaged her. Her talk about these books revealed how readily and completely she entered the author's imagined world.

> **Anne:** Let me ask you in general why you think a person should read fiction? Why should a person read a story that's invented?
>
> **Valisha:** (pause) Prob'y because reading,
> it tells you more about the situation and it helps,
> in some books you learn stuff,
> and if you watch a movie,
> you don't get as much as you get out of the book from a movie,
> so—'member the movie, *Waiting to Exhale*?
> I read that book and saw the movie.
> I saw the movie before I read the book,
> but I got a lot more out of the book
> than I got out of the movie.
> Like, um...when she first went to Jamaica,
> how things were.
> She didn't take a friend,
> like in the movie it says she took a friend,
> she didn't, she went down there by herself,
> and that's where she met the man, and like,
> how it had it, like she just—after a while of pushing him away,
> she just went to him.
> She pushed him away for a long time,
> and then she just couldn't push no more,
> and she started to like him.
> And the movie,
> it just had, she just started likin' him.
> I mean, I got a lot out of the book, than the movie.
> It was a lot of stuff.
> How she related to him.

Reading this book rewarded Valisha's search for information about lives that have something in common with her own. In particular, she noticed and cared that the protagonist travels alone and does not immediately like the man she met and first goes through a period of "pushing him away." Valisha admired independent women who deal with adversity, and the fact that she got more from the book than the movie tells us how important the subject matter was to her. She not only found the detailed information she sought but also discovered substantial improvements in the character. But she will not read unless she finds what she is seeking.

> I'm not really [into reading].
> I just—I read every now and then.
> It's like I read,
> but I'm not like I'm just gonna, you know,
> just go and just find a book and just read it.
> But a Terry McMillan book I will.
> Any book I won't.

McMillan's fiction gave Valisha a chance to observe, in action, people with whom she could identify. The characters' problems with love, family, neighbors, money, and jobs were like the problems she saw around her in everyday life, and the ways that the main characters solved or survived these problems were comforting and useful to her.

On the other hand, when Valisha tried to read a text that was not connected to her interests and concerns, she had a difficult time keeping her mind focused. Describing her attempts to read a novel she did not enjoy, she said,

> I always—I always get sleepy, and I get to readin' it,
> or somebody distract me,
> and I'll just close, and like, "I'll read it later."
> And I start back.
> Some of the stuff I forget,
> but I start back and read it again.
> If I keep readin' I remember it.
> Eventually.

But she often did not keep reading it. Of the five books assigned in her Recent American Novels class, she completed the first, *Go Ask Alice*, but found it unsatisfying. She also finished reading the two books that she did enjoy, *A Stranger Is Watching* and *Mama*. However, she could not bring herself to read all of *Kindred*. She did not even attempt to read the last assigned book, *Rats Saw God* (Thomas, 1996), about a boy who is finishing high school and looking ahead to college, because, Valisha said, his problems are just ordinary everyday problems and not ones from which she could learn anything useful. In addition, he talks about himself all the time in a smart-aleck way that she sometimes found incomprehensible. But the primary problem was that he seems to be just wandering around instead of finding answers to his questions. In Valisha's estimation, Mama's everyday problems are more interesting because she handles them: Mama decides what she wants and goes after it. Valisha is like Mama in her determination to make her own decisions and do what she believes she needs to do. These very qualities that Valisha admired in Mama (and presumably tries to emulate) were qualities that interfered with being an honors student in high school. She did not do assignments just because the teacher had issued them; she did not spend time writing about or reading what did not interest her. If her baby needed her, she showed up at school late or not at all.

Of course, Valisha's independence is not the whole explanation for her low grades and disinclination to read. Her early reading experiences humiliated her. Once she had fallen behind, she found it more and more difficult to read assigned texts. Not reading made writing difficult. In addition to a paucity of experiences with text, she was handicapped by a personal learning style not well suited to school: She could truly make sense of school subjects only when her imagination was engaged and she was able to live within the subject with emotional warmth as well as intellectual light.

In fact, however, Valisha's reading was astonishingly good for someone who had done so little of it. She had the ability to bring a text to life; she just did not have much experience practicing that ability. She could and did read beneath and beyond the surface of text when her imagination was at work. What she needed was more of what has worked for her: more text choices so that she would practice reading more, and more writing projects on subjects she cared about, with coaching from her patient, generous teachers. Textbooks presented a particular challenge because her vocabulary and background knowledge were not up to the grade level at which the textbooks are written. However, Valisha would improve in both if her teachers could or would take more time to "break it down" for her and scaffold her attempts to break down textbook language for herself.

I asked Valisha if she saw reading in her future, if, for example, Terry McMillan wrote another book. Would she make a point of reading it?

> **Valisha:** Yeah, I prob'ly would.
> I prob'ly read other authors' books too.
> I just gotta find the good ones.
>
> **Anne:** The ones that you like, yeah. If Terry McMillan came out with a new book, would you read it more for pleasure, or more for sort of information about life and people that the books contain? Or can you separate those?
>
> **Valisha:** I prob'ly read for both—well...
> I try to learn on my own 'bout life,
> but I prob'ly read it for pleasure.

Valisha was in the process of a big change in relation to literacy, whether she knew it or not. She still carried the belief that she was not interested in reading, and, if that meant reading for school, that was true. But for a person who had no childhood history of happy or easy reading; did not voluntarily read any books until the age of 17; and usually felt bored, sleepy, or confused when confronted with text, Valisha had made considerable progress with only three McMillan novels and one mystery story. She could read to learn and she could read for pleasure.

In the last chapter of her memory book, "Who I Am," Valisha begins by saying that she is a strong, beautiful, black woman with beautiful brown eyes. She talks about her son, her family, and her hopes for the future. She believes that she has choices in her life. Of course, she does not mention reading or writing; for Valisha, as for most people, reading and writing are functional tools used when the need arises, not (as is true for many English teachers) an essential part of identity. But we have seen how much Valisha has gained from the few books that she has actually read, in the full sense of the word, and how much she has benefited from the writing in which she fully engaged. As educators, it is our responsibility to learn the lessons Valisha teaches us. She, and others like her, will read in spite of their beliefs about themselves as nonreaders when rewards of reading are visible to them. Valisha's discovery of

McMillan's books was more or less accidental, but it might have happened sooner, and so given Valisha more reading experience, if a teacher had been able to pay close attention to her interest in realistic stories and then guide and support her reading development.

Valisha, like all the students in this study and like virtually all high school students, needs to be taught how to read. She needs guidance through a story such as Lessing's "No Witchcraft for Sale," with particular attention paid to the characters' motivations. These motivations escaped her on first reading but could help her make important connections with the story and its theme. She needs frank discussion of the brutality in *Kindred*, with particular attention paid to the distress that the brutality caused her and some of the other readers in the class. She needs to think and talk about why she feels bored and alienated from some stories and how she and her classmates can help one another when that happens. She needs to hear and discuss reasons for her teacher's judgment of *Kindred* as "a great book." She needs practice in noticing and talking about the successful reading that she does, as she did with *Mama*, applying these same techniques to other texts that do not open so easily to her. As she learns more about herself as a reader, she will learn more about herself as a person.

Joel: Trying to Focus

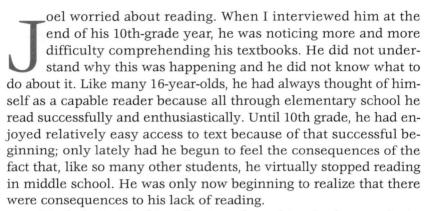

oel worried about reading. When I interviewed him at the end of his 10th-grade year, he was noticing more and more difficulty comprehending his textbooks. He did not understand why this was happening and he did not know what to do about it. Like many 16-year-olds, he had always thought of himself as a capable reader because all through elementary school he read successfully and enthusiastically. Until 10th grade, he had enjoyed relatively easy access to text because of that successful beginning; only lately had he begun to feel the consequences of the fact that, like so many other students, he virtually stopped reading in middle school. He was only now beginning to realize that there were consequences to his lack of reading.

I include Joel in this collection of case histories because he is, in important ways, *Everystudent*. The reading stories of the other four people presented in this study each tell us about a relationship to reading and purposes for it that are useful for teachers to know, but Joel's talk about his reading focused more on absence than presence and more on his confusion than on his purposes. He struggled with school reading but could not explain what the difficulty was. He talked less than any of the other case study students; he also was less articulate about his own thoughts and feelings than the others. Because he had so much difficulty explaining what the trouble was, I sometimes felt that the fog of confusion that enveloped him threatened me as well. I could not read the story he told me in the same way I felt I could read the others. In this way, he is characteristic of many students in U.S. high schools and middle schools—we who teach them never quite get to the core of their thinking and never quite figure out what they need from us, but even if we do, we never figure out how we can provide it in a form they can recognize and use.

Joel was somewhat diffident, although he was friendly and always courteous. Tall and lean, he wore the requisite baggy pants with shirts that, one way or another, indicated his love of sports. His straight brown hair was long in front, always falling in his eyes and partially hiding them, adding to the impression of shyness. I interviewed him three times at the end of his sophomore year and once again at the end of his junior year. In our conversations, he often did not say much beyond "yeah," although he had a wide repertoire of ways of saying that word. He could make it tentative, relieved, confident, or enthusiastic; he could convey "Sometimes," "Sure," and "You got it!" with "yeah." He did not smile often, and his face was sometimes a little stiff, as if he were reluctant to let it express whatever he was thinking. Yet he volunteered to be interviewed and he never forgot an appointment. He never seemed to be avoiding my questions; he just seemed unable to explain his answers, even to himself. Much of the time he said he did not know what he thought or felt, except that he was confused by one text or class or another. And he did not know why he was confused.

School Reading

A typical example of Joel's confusion came up early in the first interview when I asked him if he could remember learning to read.

> **Joel:** Not really.
> I mean, it just, just seems like I could always actually read.
> Like, 'cause I used to be able to comprehend words real good.
> And now it's like,
> if I read something I can't understand it sometimes.
> Like when we're reading our history books,
> I read something
> and for some reason sometimes I can't understand it.
> I have to read it over and over and I still don't understand it.
> I don't know why.

Note that he quickly jumped from the ease of early reading to his current difficulties with comprehension. At first, I asked the obvious follow-up questions.

> **Anne:** Do you think it's vocabulary? Or...

> **Joel:** I don't, I just—I don't know why.
> Just something,

I can't comprehend sometimes.

Anne: And do you ask for explanation from the teacher?

Joel: Not often, I mean,
I just try to understand it the best I can,
and write down from what I have, but...

I was reading something today,
and I couldn't understand it.
I mean, I read through the whole—
(pulls history book from his backpack and opens it)
I was reading this today, this section,
and I just read like over this whole—
where'd it go—
this whole page
and I couldn't hardly remember anything from it.
I don't know why.
I go back and I can't remember what I read.
I can't remember that much.

It's about the election in 1932,
that point in history,
just talking about all the stuff that happened after the [U.S.]
    Depression
and the crash...
(reads aloud) "Hoover tries to end the crisis." [Cayton, Perry, &
    Winkler, 1998, p. 629]

Anne: And do you know who Hoover is?

Joel: He was the president [of the U.S.],
he was the one blamed for it
'cause he was president at the time.

Anne: Right, OK, and do you know what crisis they're talking about?

Joel: The crash, stock market crash.

Anne: Stock market crash, OK. So it's not a question of background
knowledge, in other words you do—

Joel: I read over it, and I just can't like—(stops)

Anne: Make it stick in your brain?

Joel: Yeah.

Anne: Now, is that a question of not understanding, or is that a
question of just not being interested enough to really—

Joel: It might be that,
it might be not really interested in it,
'cause, I mean,
I used to be able to understand things real good, man,
I don't know why.

Anne: Sometimes I try to read something that I'm kinda bored with, and my mind keeps floating away.

Joel: Yeah, that's how it happens. Lots.
I'll sit down with something,
and just start thinking about something else,
and forget it's there.

In this case, Joel's problem was a combination of lack of interest in the subject and lack of sufficient background knowledge to comprehend the information as it was presented in the textbook. Or, framing the problem another way, politics of the past did not engage his imagination (at least in part because he did not know enough to make it come alive in his mind), and the textbook writers assumed more background knowledge than he had yet accumulated.

Background knowledge is like the receiving side of Velcro: When it is present, new information has a place to stick. When it is absent, new information slips away. Background knowledge is necessary for interest as well as comprehension. Wade (1992) notes that "Interest tends to be low with little or no relevant background knowledge, increases as more is known, and diminishes again as the reader reaches the point where nothing new can be learned from the passage" (p. 260). Of course, texts vary in the amount of background knowledge that they require, and this particular text assumed a great deal of prior understanding on the part of the reader. Here is the paragraph that Joel was trying to read:

> **Voluntary Action Fails** Hoover believed deeply that voluntary controls in the business world were the best way to end the economic crisis. He quickly organized a White House conference of business leaders and got their promise to maintain wage rates. At first, many firms kept wages up. By the end of 1931, however, many quietly cut workers' pay. (Cayton et al., 1998, p. 629)

Joel read this passage aloud easily and smoothly. When I asked him about the meaning of the term *voluntary action*, he did not know, although he did know the two individual words of the phrase. When we took the first sentence apart phrase by phrase, it turned out that, although he knew who Hoover was and he knew that the economic crisis in question was the stock market crash and the ensuing Depression, he could not find the story behind and around Hoover's action in this passage. What is missing from this abbreviated account is the alternative to voluntary action, namely governmental decree, which gives meaning to Hoover's choice. The term *voluntary action*, like any other term, does not mean much unless it is understood in context, a context that includes its opposite. When Joel read this paragraph, he did not see Hoover rejecting governmental intervention in favor of persuading business leaders to cooperate voluntarily, nor did he see the philosophical history of the debate about the proper power of government of which Hoover's rejection is part. Joel saw only a meaningless fraction of this picture. When I probed into his confusion over this passage, it became clear that although he understood generally that voluntary action is action a person chooses to take, he did not understand, because the text did not tell him, that the voluntary controls it mentions were part of a huge picture of human interactions and decisions. He did not understand how to apply his general understanding of voluntary action to the specific employment situation of 1931.

When I explained more of the story, describing Hoover's choices and decisions in the face of what was happening to bosses and workers, Joel understood the paragraph. He could see Hoover's position and he could see how bosses had reacted to Hoover's talks. Joel's conceptual understanding was fine when the information he needed was available to him. But when I asked him what went on in his mind after he read the paragraph for the first time, he said, "Nothing, really. It's just kinda blank." He was unable to make meaning from the words because too much was omitted, and he did not know how to identify what he did not know. Because he could read all the words, he could not understand why the meaning did not register in his brain. He could not ask questions to clear up his confusion because he could not identify what he did not understand.

The other school texts that Joel talked about were fictional works from his English classes. In the final weeks of his 10th-grade year, Joel's English teacher told the class to choose a book from the Accelerated Reader program in the library. Although in theory selecting his own book should have worked well for Joel because he needed to feel interested in a story in order to read it, it turned out to be too much for him.

> I picked *Cujo* [1994] by Stephen King
> 'cause I heard he's real good,
> so I picked something, not too long,
> because it's for the class,
> but something I can probably get done in plenty amount of time,
> get time to read it.
> I read a little bit more yesterday.
> I'm not understanding it still.
> Not at all....

> [Stephen King] makes it so confusing
> where he's gotta keep us reading,
> he makes it confusing
> so the reader will want to understand it more.
> I mean at first I wasn't understanding anything,
> and then it kind of got into something else,
> it kinda switched pace,
> and then I just keep reading,
> trying to figure out what's going on.

After Joel had read the first 20 pages, he and I spent most of one interview talking about the book, looking at passages, and trying to identify the sources of his confusion and disappointment with the book. One source of confusion was King's frequent shifting of the scene. King has a large cast of characters to introduce, and he does it by showing the reader these characters in small, introductory scenes. The reader learns some characters' names, locations, and a little about them and then shifts to a new scene and meets some new characters. Joel found this rapid series of changes to be disorienting.

> It's just he goes on from one thing,
> you start reading,
> and it's like switch to a different thing,
> and I just kinda got lost about what was going on.
> The problem is—I started to understand a little bit,
> I mean I knew what was going on,
> what, how it was starting,
> then it kinda like switched off into something else,

and then I got kinda lost.
It was kinda like on the one hand,
and then, I don't know if it was later or what,
he just kinda switched to a different thing.

Joel had done so little reading in recent years that he had not yet made the transition from middle school reading to more complicated stories that include multiple people, places, and events. He was accustomed to a story with a straightforward plot enacted by a few people whose relationships to one another are clear, an interesting series of actions, and a resolution. He knows that he does not know how to read fiction that asks more of its readers than this, but he does not know what to do about it.

Joel: I'm not used to reading big books like this—
I mean, I read books, but not like this.

Anne: "This" meaning that it's long?

Joel: Yeah, not like novels or anything like this.

Anne: If you were reading this as a class book, everybody in the whole class were reading it, what could the teacher do to try to—

Joel: Probably try to explain it.
Explain what's going on.
The only thing the teacher'd probably do best
is explain what's going on,
explain why or what's going on,
why he [the writer] is doing it.

Joel was uncomfortable accumulating characters and locations without getting on with the action. He could not see what they were doing in the story until they made something happen, and he was not experienced in suspending information that he did not fully understand until he (or the author) built enough of the story for it to rest on. His discomfort was aggravated by the fact that he was reading the book only at school and only when the teacher gave the class some reading time. I asked him if he ever read *Cujo* during the Tuesday sustained silent reading periods.

Joel: Mmm, actually, I never really thought about that.
That's a good idea.

Anne: So you have your Stephen King book compartmentalized into English class? I mean you said it didn't really occur to you to bring it for Tuesday, so I'm thinking, is that because in your mind it's just connected to English class?

Joel: Yeah, I forget about it until I get there.
The rest of the time I don't think about it.

Anne: Do you ever read it at home?

Joel: No. I never think about it—
it's like a school thing.

One of Joel's troubles with this book was simply remembering from one time to the next what was happening with the many characters in the story. A more important problem, however, was Joel's increasing impatience to get to something exciting, which would not only be more interesting but also easier to understand.

The book hasn't really got into—not that I know of,
and I'm supposed to understand it,
just from what I know,
it's like the dog, or Cujo, is like this—
might be a dream of the little boy or something,
not knowing that yet, but just guessing.

Joel admitted that the description of the dog in the boy's closet was neither scary nor interesting. I asked him what would be interesting.

Joel: If something happened,
like a climax of the story, anything, just—
anything exciting.

Anne: Anything except having characters be introduced?

Joel: Yeah (firmly).

Anne: And sit around talking about something that you don't understand....

Joel: Yeah (even more firmly).

Anne: OK. So it sounds to me as if—now, I don't want to put words in your mouth, so please, any time I say something that doesn't sound right to you, please correct me—but it sounds to me as if the problem you're having with this book is that it is taking a long time to set things up—

Joel: Yeah!

Anne: And you'd rather have something exciting happen a lot sooner.

Joel: Yeah (decisively).

Joel said he was "kind of" disappointed in the story because it was not as good as he thought it would be. Not only was the set-up going on too long, confusing him with multiple introductions and delaying the exciting parts, but he thought the vocabulary was too advanced as well.

It's such a big book
and it's one of the first books like that I read in a long time.
I don't read that much any more,
so it's just not registering.

Anne: Yeah, OK...what's the connection between it being a big book and it being confusing?

Joel: It's just—bigger words,
it's mixing words up,
using more of a thesaurus form,
using more words like that.

Anne: OK, lots of vocabulary—

Joel: Yeah.

Anne: That you're not used to, yeah.

Joel: Yeah. (sounds confident that he has been understood)

Anne: And when the characters are talking to each other? Are they also using big words that—different words?

Joel: Kinda. It's just termed in a different—
using different words to say stuff....

Anne: Mmhm. Right. Are the characters referring to things that you don't know about?

Joel: Yeah. Yeah.

Anne: So they're talking about things that you can't follow yet.

Joel: Yes.

The most recent scene Joel had read occurred between the father of the little boy and his business partner. They met in a restaurant to talk about their worries and plans for the future. I found their talk about the advertising business somewhat foreign, so I am not surprised that Joel had even more trouble understanding it. He could not see how this scene related to Cujo, and because he was far more interested in Cujo than in this young father, this scene looked like a pointless digression to him, just one more ball to keep in the air until the real story started.

The final outcome of this assignment was that Joel did not ever finish reading the book. He did take the 20-question test on the book (which is part of the Accelerated Reader Program) but did not pass. What remained with him was a sense of confusion, of not knowing what was going on, and frustration that the good parts that Stephen King fans rave about were so slow in coming. When he hypothesized that a teacher would tell the class what was going on if the class were reading the book together, I think he was speaking wishfully about somebody explaining sooner than King does what the plot entails and how each character contributes to it. In Joel's opinion, the sooner the threads of plot and character are woven together into a meaningful picture, the better.

A problem with a program such as Accelerated Reader is that many students do not read well independently. Of course the argument is that they will never learn to do so without practice, but if that practice is unsupported, as Joel's was, the student learns more about being frustrated and confused than he or she does about how to read. Joel needs help with scheduling his reading so that it gets done, and he needs someone with whom to confer when he gets confused or bored. (It is helpful to remember the way Valisha was supported by classmates who had read further than she had, and that their encouragement helped her stay with *A Stranger Is Watching*. Such specific support is not available in the Accelerated Reader program, in which each student is reading a different book, and the teacher has not read most of the collection him- or herself.)

Another problem with the program is that, because the books are all labeled according to grade level, teachers are sorely tempted to encourage or even require students to read at their grade level or above. This is likely to result in confusion and frustration because most readers read most comfortably and happily at a few levels below that which they can manage to achieve on a reading test. In fact, *Cujo* is rated as being at a grade level of 7.5, well within Joel's ability level. However, no system of identifying grade levels for reading materials can work without going beyond length of words and sentences to include the judgment of an experienced reader who can assess what else the text demands of a reader. Some works that have simple vocabularies, such as many by Ernest Hemingway and John Steinbeck, deal with adult themes that are inaccessible to young people who might be quite capable of reading the sentences. Joel's experience with the textbook passage about Hoover is an obvious example of word identification outstripping comprehension because of insufficient background knowledge.

Some degree of qualitative assessment of text difficulty is possible. Chall, Bissex, Conard, and Harris-Sharples (1996) have developed a set of difficulty scales for six kinds of text (literature, popular fiction, life sciences, physical sciences, narrative social studies, and expository social studies). Each scale consists of 7 to 10 samples of text in order of increasing difficulty. The user compares an ungraded text with the samples. Used correctly, this system requires the application of judgments about extra linguistic features of text that make it more or less difficult to read, such as necessary background knowledge and the ability to make inferences, understand symbols and extratextual references, and use imagination and intellect to fill in gaps (Iser's [1971] indeterminacies). Joel's difficulties with both his social studies text and *Cujo* illustrate the importance of these qualitative analyses.

In his junior year, Joel took two English classes—an English Eleven language arts class, the nonspecialized English class that most 11th-graders take, and an elective literature class called Prose and Poetry in the English Language. In English Eleven, he read some poetry and short stories, about which he did not say much. Prose and Poetry included two novels, one of which Joel enjoyed a great deal.

> **Joel:** (grinning a little) I liked that book,
> *One Flew Over the Cuckoo's Nest* [Kesey, 1989].
> That was pretty funny.
> It was funny, it was interesting.
> Ken Kesey who wrote the book just made it interesting,
> he like kinda would do different stuff in there,
> kinda based it on real life, in the asylum,
> but kinda just mixed it up,
> so it was pretty funny.

Like most people, Joel saw the quality of being interesting as something that resides in the story, as if it is intrinsically interesting to everyone (although some readers in this class, particularly the female readers, did not enjoy the book). He did not see that *interesting* or *boring* is a judgment about the interaction between reader and writer and, therefore, depends on a match between them of interests, desires, fears, and various other beliefs and feelings. But the match between what Joel was looking for and what *One Flew Over the Cuckoo's Nest* delivered became obvious when he contrasted the book with *Catcher in the Rye* (Salinger, 1991), the other novel assigned in that class.

> *Catcher in the Rye*, I didn't like that too much,
> it's just kinda boring.
> I don't know, it just kinda...
> 'cause the guy, he's like, I don't know,
> he kinda runs away from home for a few days,
> and it's just like he's criticizing everything, it's just...
> I wasn't interested in it.
> It was just—I mean, goin' through all this weird stuff....
>
> Holden was OK as a character,
> it's just I didn't like the way the story went.
>
> With *Catcher*, the problem was not really the character,
> just the way it turned out,
> the way he wrote the book,
> just kinda didn't make a lotta sense.
> I just didn't like the way he made Holden go through stuff,
> like how he went through—
> he got involved with those problems,
> and it just wasn't...
> I just didn't like the way the story turned out,
> or the way the story was goin'.

In this interview, I saw Joel's ongoing struggle to identify and articulate his problems with what he read. I had asked him if the trouble was that he did not really like the character of Holden, but he said it was not. He flirted with blaming the author, which was interesting because it showed that he absorbed a point his teacher emphasized: An author makes decisions about what happens next and how he or she is going to tell the reader about it. I kept probing into Joel's reaction to these authorial decisions.

> **Anne:** OK, where could the story have gone that you think might have been more satisfying or interesting?
>
> **Joel:** I don't know, 'cause it just started out—
> it started out bad, too.
> I mean, it's kinda like he got frustrated at school
> and then he just took off on his own, so....

I remarked that sometimes I got tired of watching a character mess up repeatedly, and Joel responded with one of his tentative "yeah"s, indicating that he did not disagree but was searching for something else, so I persisted in trying to clarify the important difference in Joel's mind between Holden in *Catcher and the Rye* and McMurphy—the protagonist in *One Flew Over the Cuckoo's Nest*.

> **Anne:** OK, and so how about *Cuckoo's Nest*? I mean, there's a bunch of crazy people—
>
> **Joel:** Yeah (agreeing).
>
> **Anne:**—they're doin' some really crazy things—
>
> **Joel:** Yeah (confirming).
>
> **Anne:**—but it didn't annoy you?
>
> **Joel:** No.
> It's kinda funny 'cause I mean, overall,
> everybody in the ward could actually leave if they wanted to,
> 'cause they weren't, they didn't have to stay there,
> it was their decision,
> and then McMurphy's thinkin',
> Why you stayin'?
> He was pretty cool.
> Just his attitude,
> the way he acted.
> I mean, he stood up for himself and everybody else.
>
> **Anne:** Unhuh, unhuh. (Holding up fists to indicate aggressive stance) Like he took on authority, you mean?
>
> **Joel:** Yeah! (with enthusiasm)
>
> **Anne:** Right. Does Holden take on authority, too?
>
> **Joel:** No.

Anne: OK, so you liked watching McMurphy—

Joel: Yeah (confidently).

Anne: —kinda engage in that.

Joel: Yeah (happily).

Joel is showing a satisfying connection between the writer's vision of the world and his characters in it, and the reader's vision of the world and the kinds of people he likes to get to know. Joel thoroughly enjoyed McMurphy's courage in engaging in combat with authority, and he also appreciated the character's concern for the other patients' welfare. Holden, however beloved of other readers, did not provide Joel with the model of courage and agency that he was seeking. On the contrary, Holden seems to complain, wander, go through a series of problems he cannot solve, seek what he cannot find, and apparently spend the whole novel running away from authority rather than taking it on. This was deeply unsatisfying to Joel.

The actual reading of these two novels was a problem Joel never did resolve. The teacher expected the students (11th and 12th graders) to read a certain number of pages for homework each night. Joel did not keep up.

I always forgot to read.
I just read it when I remembered.
I'd read it in class, or wherever else....

I can't really say I read 'em, but I—
I read 'em, but I actually didn't read it all.
I read selections.

Depending on where I was,
where the class was,
I'd read a little bit from there,
and then skip.
I just try to stay caught up with the class.
The quizzes were easy.
I understood the quiz, 'cause I mean,
it's kinda like—some of it was common knowledge
to what the story was,
and we watched the movie of *Cuckoo's Nest*, too, so...
[that helped] a little bit.

In spite of Joel's memory of success on quizzes, his teacher knew that he was not doing the reading; Joel would turn in blank sheets of paper in response to the brief questions given at the beginning of class to check on the previous night's reading. Speaking of Joel and his classmates, the teacher said,

> He may have out-of-school factors
> that I don't know about
> in terms of just doesn't know how to budget his time, won't sit
>   down for an hour
> and read 20 pages a night.
> They've got the paper, here's your reading assignment,
> it's got the date on it....
> And when you're doing a novel,
> every day there's reading involved.

But Joel had compartmentalized reading into something done almost exclusively for school. He almost never thought of it when he was outside the school building. He did, however, show up for class every day—unlike many students at this school, Joel had perfect attendance—so he read and heard enough about both *One Flew Over the Cuckoo's Nest* and *Catcher in the Rye* to respond to them and form strong opinions about them. These responses tell us something about what he looks for in his reading: He prefers a strong protagonist who dies in the course of fighting the good fight to a more ambivalent protagonist who does not seem to know how to fight but who survives.

Joel's interest in combatively engaging authority is evident in his response to the other major work, *Othello* (Shakespeare, 1993), read in Prose and Poetry. Joel liked this play, largely because of the villain's cleverness.

> **Joel:** It was, that was pretty interesting, too.
> 'Cause he—Shakespeare wrote it?
>
> **Anne:** Yeah.
>
> **Joel:** The way he—
> like Iago, the way he made Iago plan everything,
> how nothing messed up,
> everything went perfect,
> the way he had it planned...
> and the way he characterized everybody was interesting.

Another reason Joel liked *Othello* was that he could listen to professional actors read it instead of listening to himself and his classmates or the teacher read it.

Joel: We read it—
he had one of those tapes that read the book.

Anne: Unhuh, so you basically listened to actors—

Joel: And followed along.
That worked really good.
I didn't have to worry about depending on myself to read it,
or having to remember...(sentence trails off)
I always do better when I'm listening to someone read it.
All they have to do is read it and I get it,
it comes to me better.

Anne: Were you tracking along as you were listening?

Joel: Yeah. Most of the time.

Anne: Is that your choice, or would you like to just stare off into the distance and...

Joel: It's my choice.

Educators could debate whether following along while listening to another reader constitutes reading, but Joel certainly looked at most of the printed words and made meaning from them, albeit with the help of the actors' voices. When he said, "I didn't have to worry about depending on myself to read it," he was admitting that he worried about depending on himself to do assigned reading, although the worrying did not seem to produce useful results. He implied that he was in conflict about this lack of dependability. Part of the conflict came from being concerned about his grades (which were low in this class because so much of the work depended on careful and thorough reading), and some of it probably came from his affection for this teacher. Prose and Poetry was Joel's first class of the day, and he always showed up before class began at 7:25 to talk with the teacher about sports, especially hockey, which Joel loved, and basketball, which the teacher coached. The teacher said that they had an ongoing cheerful rivalry about the two sports. Their friendly feelings for each other were not enough to make Joel remember or do his reading, however. From the teacher's point of view, the students' responsibility is clear, although he knows that sometimes other things get in the way. The teacher's decision to use the tape recording of *Othello* was based on his experience with teaching *Julius Caesar* (Shakespeare, 1992) to 10th graders. He explained,

> The kids that had had Shakespeare two or three times,
> I think you could allow 'em to read themselves
> and then talk about it,
> but a lot of those kids, they hadn't had—
> you know, *Romeo and Juliet* [Shakespeare, 1992] real quick
> at the end of their freshman year,
> and it went right over their heads.
> *Julius Caesar* at the end of their sophomore year,
> and then here we go again,
> so there's not a lot of experience there.
>
> And I didn't do that [use the audiotapes]
> the first time, three years ago.
> I handled that play like I did the novels,
> where you read Act Two tonight,
> and it's due, or whatever.
> And they come in, "Huh?"
> and it's like we'd never even get half through it,
> so we'd end up reading it in class ourselves anyway,
> so that...we'd hear it and then we'd go back—
> it's kind of tedious for some,
> but for most kids,
> like Joel,
> it probably works.

When Joel spoke of *Othello*, he turned immediately and exclusively to Iago's near perfect plan. It was the only content matter that he discussed. It had been discussed in class, and Joel used it as the basis for the paper he wrote about the play. The teacher described the way he presented Iago to the students.

> Evil for the sake of being evil.
> They instantly want to know what's his motivation.
> The fact that he thinks Othello says...
> maybe Othello slept with his wife, that's not enough;
> he didn't get the promotion, that's no—
> no way a guy can be motivated to be this evil,
> to explain that,

> but he wrote about that in his paper,
> Joel—although he doesn't approve of Iago
> he liked the plan
> and the fact that it almost worked to perfection.

Joel did not use the word *evil*, as the teacher did in talking about Iago, but focused instead on Iago's plan and how well it worked until the very end. It is interesting to consider what McMurphy and Iago have in common because they commanded Joel's admiring attention. Both are active rebels, undermining authority. Both declare war on the authorities immediately over them. Both make daring, high-stakes plans that they carry out in spite of the risks. Both make their plans work long enough to inflict damage on their enemies. And in the end, both die, although McMurphy dies as a hero who has sacrificed himself for the inmates in the asylum, while Iago dies after "cunning cruelty/That can torment him much and hold him long" (5.2.333–334). In contrast, the battles that Holden fights are against an amorphous enemy (the phoniness of society and the inevitability of loss of innocence), and perhaps most important, Holden fights in a confused, adolescent way rather than developing strategic battle plans as do McMurphy and Iago. Joel appreciated the direct, military approach. His teacher commented,

> Joel actually, for the first time all year—
> a couple times during poetry, 'cause I would call on him, and he
>   would respond,
> 'cause they had talked about it in their groups,
> but during *Othello* he—
> the hand went up a couple times
> (imitates a tentative hand raised as far as his own head)
> so I think it's in his capability.

I think that Joel was able to raise his hand to talk about *Othello* because he had read it and felt engaged with it. Both elements were necessary. He felt engaged with *One Flew Over the Cuckoo's Nest*, but he had not really read it. And he missed *Catcher in the Rye* in both respects.

Personal Reading

Joel's story of personal reading choices falls squarely in the middle of all the other stories I heard from adolescents about when and what they enjoy reading. He read about subjects he was interested in, and he had the impression that he read "a lot" about these interests even when the number of books read was small. When I asked him the question about his associations with the word *reading*, he spoke of the voluntary reading he was doing.

> Books and magazines.
> Mainly it's about sports,
> I like sports, so I read a lot of sports books....

> **Anne:** On a scale of 1 to 10, where 10 is "I love to read," and 1 is "I loathe it," where would you put yourself in terms of reading?

> **Joel:** Um...I'd say about a 7.
> I used to really like to read,
> but then I just got into a lot of sports and stuff
> so then I just don't read as much as I used to,
> but I still like to read once in a while.

Early reading success had a long reach. Joel's description of himself as a 7 on the reading-pleasure scale surely did not come from high school reading because he thought of it so rarely, actually engaged in it even more rarely, and was frustrated and confused by much of what he did engage in. I asked him to tell me more about when he really liked to read.

> Mainly I feel it was when I was in elementary,
> 'cause I was—then I used to really like to read,
> and I was a real good reader,
> according to a lot of my teachers,
> 'cause in first grade, um...
> I remember we had to get into groups to read,
> and the teacher put me and this other girl in our own group,
> she wanted us to read at a second-grade level.
> She made us do that—I don't think we did it that long,
> she put us back in our other group, but we used to read a lot,
> and I just liked reading...
> [I liked] anything I could actually read,
> a lot of things used to interest me.

I read a whole bunch of different stuff,
trying to read, like, harder stuff.

Anne: Yeah, so you would read in your spare time—

Joel: Yes.

Anne: —just because you liked to read?

Joel: I used to do that a lot.

Anne: And so when did that start to change?

Joel: I would say somewhere in middle school,
Seventh grade.
Sixth grade I still read a little bit.
Seventh grade is the one where you're able to start sports
in middle school,
so that's when I started.
In middle school I was in wrestling
and then here I'm in tennis and wrestling.

Anne: And so why does getting involved in sports affect your reading?

Joel: I think it's 'cause I'm like more focused on it,
plus I have whatever schoolwork to do,
so I just really don't think about it any more.

Anne: Yeah. So your schoolwork kind of takes up time?

Joel: Yeah, sometimes...
or when I have it.
And just 'cause I haven't read in a while,
I really don't think about that much any more.
I mean, I still read every once in a while,
sit down and read something, but....

The habit of reading falls away when a person's time and attention are taken up with other things. When it falls away as early as the age of 12, it may be difficult to reinstitute as a habitual way of spending free time. Joel and many other teenagers I spoke to had lost the habit of turning to reading for entertainment, relaxation, or the exercise of their imaginations. They have many other ways of achieving these ends, ways that are more socially and physically active than reading and hence more appealing to them. For Joel, sports and the Internet are the big attractions.

> Well, a lot of times in my free time
> I'll either go rollerblade downtown,
> or I'll play video games, or online....

Joel had Internet access at home and said that he spent a lot of his free time using it: "I always find som'n to do." In fact, when Joel was in 10th grade, before he had Internet access at home, he and two friends would show up at the school library every morning as soon as the doors opened (at 7 a.m.) to use the computers there. They would listen to CDs, investigate sports sites, and Joel, especially, would read and write e-mail. He had three or four accounts, all free, which he used "for different things." I asked him if one account would do the job, but he seemed to like using different accounts for different subjects. He said he corresponds with people he met online.

Joel's personal reading, at 17 and a junior in high school, consisted of online reading where necessary, occasional magazine reading ("If *Sports Illustrated* is there, I'll look at it,"), and even more occasional book reading—about sports. Although his main sports interest was hockey, he still liked professional wrestling, an interest that was much stronger when he was younger ("I watched it all my life; I used to watch it all the time, but I ain't actually into it the way I used to be"). For Christmas of his junior year, he asked his parents for a copy of wrestler Mick Foley's (1999) autobiography, which he told me he was still reading even though he had started it six months before.

> **Joel:** Right now I'm reading an autobiography.
> Mick Foley—it's a wrestler.
> I haven't read it in a while, but I started readin' it....
> When I first got it I started to read it,
> and I read it one time in here for silent reading
> but I don't think I've read it since then.
>
> **Anne:** OK. Do you think you will?
>
> **Joel:** Yeah, I will.
> I keep meaning to, I just keep...
> I forget it.

In his ninth-grade year, Joel had read another autobiography to fulfill a class assignment, which turned out to be a successful reading experience for him.

Joel: It was a hockey player from a long time ago, Rod Gilbert, he's a former hockey player.

[I got it from the] school library.
We had to pick a book, then we had to...
she'd pick a day out of the week to make us read,
and then we'd have to write about it....

Anne: Was that OK with you?

Joel: Yeah.

Anne: And you didn't feel like, Oh no, I've gotta read a book—

Joel: No, it was a real good book, too.

Anne: Good. Did it make you feel like, Gee, I could do this more often, or...?

Joel: Yeah, kind of.
It'd be nicer if it woulda told a little more, though.
They just kind of stop it after a while.
[I wanted to] See what else was gonna happen with him,
the rest of his career.

When a student finishes a book wishing it would go on longer, teachers have cause for rejoicing. In this case, Joel's wishing did not result in his reestablishing his reading habit, but it may have influenced his request for the Mick Foley autobiography from his parents. And it must have supported Joel's sense of himself as a reader.

I read...I still read what I want sometimes,
like the magazines, or books.
I'll read anything.
Whatever I think might be interesting,
I'll start it.

Joel did not say "If it's interesting, I'll read it." He said, "I'll start it." A minority of readers will determinedly finish anything they begin, but most, by far, are like Joel in that they try out the first few paragraphs or pages if the text looks promising, but put it down when they lose interest in it. Joel still saw himself as a reader, but after he began high school, he became much more discriminating in his reading than when he was as a young child. And although he still saw himself as a reader, he forgot about reading far more often than he remembered it.

Writing: A Fading Pleasure

Like Sting, Duke, and Rosa, Joel enjoyed writing outside of school. I include a discussion of his writing here because, like the other students, his writing provides important information about how he thought and what he was interested in. Although he did not enjoy or seem to benefit from much of the reading assigned to him (even when he remembered to do it), some writing experiences in school have made a lasting positive impression on him.

> In eighth-grade reading,
> we were required to write a book.
> Just any kind of book we wanted to pick.
> And I lost that book,
> but I did write another one.
> It was on a disk the teacher had, and see,
> I had it in my folder,
> and my mom went in to clean my room one day,
> and I guess she threw the folder away with it,
> and the disk I had got messed up, so....
>
> The book was about hockey.
> And I made almost a double to it,
> like a run-on from it, sequel—
> I mean, that wasn't like right after,
> it was a couple years later,
> and I just kind of went on with that.
>
> It's a fiction. It's fiction.
> The first book I wrote in eighth grade,
> and the second book I just wrote I think last year,
> during the school year [ninth grade], and stuff.
> [Not a school assignment] just on my own.

What stood out in Joel's memory was that the students were free to write "any kind of book we wanted to pick" and that he cared enough about it to write another one the following year on his own initiative and on his own time. Of course, I asked him what he had done with it, hoping to be able to see it, but he just laughed a little, said he had not thought about it in a while, and that "it's put up somewhere. I don't know where, but it's put up somewhere." He did, however, tell me a little about his creative writing, including the plot of this story.

> **Joel:** Some [things I write are] based on real life.
> With the first book, the wife—
> It was about hockey,
> and this was some of the things that happened
> kind of away from the story.
> Like the guy, he plays hockey,
> but then at home—
> I had his wife kill their little baby son,
> and then she died of cancer.
>
> That was later on in the book, near the end.
> That's just something to throw in there.
> I mean, I don't know why I did it,
> it was just som'n to throw in there.
>
> **Anne:** Wow. Is that a real-life news event that you read about?
>
> **Joel:** It could be, yeah, a while back, when that lady drowned her
>   kids in the car.
> That happened.
> It builds suspense.

When Joel was telling me this scenario, he was perfectly calm and matter of fact, as if a mother killing her baby boy were an ordinary event. His talk about the fiction he has read, including his aborted attempts to read *Cujo*, shows a pattern of interest in highly dramatic and brutal events. He was dissatisfied with the indecisiveness of *Catcher in the Rye* and frustrated with *Cujo* because, as I facetiously suggested to him one day, the story was not fulfilling the promise made by the cover picture of a huge drooling dog, looking insane and ready to attack. (Joel interrupted this remark four times with appreciative "yeah"s.) Although Joel's demeanor suggested constraint, his interest in hockey and admiration of McMurphy and Iago suggest, as does his fiction writing, that beneath his reserved and generally cooperative surface beat the heart of a fighter.

Joel mentioned his interest in creative writing every time the subject of writing came up, but although he repeatedly said, "I like to do creative writing," he said it in a tone that indicated that he did not really want anybody to take that too seriously, or that he did not want to commit himself to being a person who did creative writing in any sort of regular way. He said that he had not done any writing on his own time since the hockey book. His recent schoolwork had not included much creative writing either.

Anne: Have you had a chance to do much creative writing this year?

Joel: Not really. Not this year. I did a few things.
We had to do a story.
We had—we had spelling,
we did spelling for a couple times,
we had a book that we had for spelling,
and we had to use the words from that in a story.
It was OK.
We didn't read 'em out loud.
Just for the teacher to read.

Anne: OK, and when you write your stories using your spelling words and stuff, do you also go for the really big drama?

Joel: Not really. It's a smaller assignment,
and I always just write som'n real quick.
Just throw somethin' out.

Interestingly enough, Joel considered English to be his favorite school subject even though Computer Assisted Drafting (CAD) was his favorite class. And writing, or the thought or memory of writing, seemed to be the reason that he favored English.

CAD's my favorite class, but...
subject-wise, that's probably English.
I like writing sometimes,
I mean we do writing things, and I just like—
I like writing things once in a while,
creative writing.

I could do creative writing.
If I was going into writing, yeah,
I'd do creative writing,
write just a couple books, whatever.

Like so many of his classmates, Joel preferred writing texts to reading them. And although he never said it directly, I think he was quite proud of his story about the hockey player and the murderous wife. He had considered writing as a career, although as he got older and closer to graduation and further from actually doing any creative writing, that plan was losing its force. In 10th grade, he said his future plans were "going into computer drafting and then probably writing a little along the way." A year later, in answer to the same question, he said, "Go to college and major in CAD." I asked if he were still considering writing.

Joel: I think about it once in a while,
if I should or not....

Anne: What kinds of things would you like to write?

Joel: Um...anything.
Ms. B told me last year to go into sports writing,
like for newspaper.

Anne: Unhuh. Does that sound appealing?

Joel: A little bit. I mean,
it's fun to think about,
what other people think.

Joel was getting some encouragement from one of his English teachers to continue with his writing, but he had a difficult time in his other English class in which all the writing was in response to the reading.

Joel: [In Prose and Poetry in the English Language]
We do these lit-er-a-ry a-nal-y-sis
(speaks these last two words carefully and slowly,
taking time with each syllable to get it right)
things.
I don't always get it,
I always somehow mess it up.

Anne: Do you know what he's lookin' for?

Joel: Not really.
He knows I don't really get it that much,
but I try.
There's a certain way we gotta write it,
and I always write it
but I end up always somehow summarizing the story.

Joel's teacher shared Joel's frustration over this problem. The teacher said that Joel must have asked 10 times, "How do you do a literary analysis?"

> I kept tryin' to give him a different way.
> I said, "Theme is not the only way to do it,
> but I think it's the easiest way to do it,
> so just focus on a theme.
> You have to tie in the author,
> the author created every character
> and every word in this book,
> so what was the author trying to say?"
> He would talk to me;
> it appeared like he understood,
> and then I'd get another paper
> and he'd have another plot summary.
>
> I mean, he's got to have an original thought.
> He had a hard time with that.
> He would say, "*Catcher in the Rye* is about Holden..."
> and some of the things that we talked about,
> maybe a major theme,
> loss of innocence,
> he would cover that,
> and he'd give the real obvious examples
> of the things that we'd covered,
> but we wanted him to go a little further,
> come up with some angle of his own,
> but he just....

Joel, like many students, put a great deal of faith in class discussions as a way to learn about a book, not realizing that most of the book remains invisible if it is not read. He never mentioned his lack of reading as part of the problem of writing a literary analysis, but of course his teacher made the connection right away.

> Joel was not in a position to respond to the literature,
> so the best he could do
> was summarize what we were talking about in class,
> based on his memory.
> I didn't see him take any notes.
> I'd say his comprehension is probably,

based on some of the things I've read, his final exam,
it's probably somewhere middle to maybe even a little below, for
    whatever reason.
Maybe he doesn't read a lot.
His writing is typical of an average student [at this school],
some things are there,
he'll run six or seven nice sentences in a row,
and then all of a sudden, "What was that?"

This teacher saw the comprehension difficulties that Joel him-self mentioned at the beginning of our first interview. The teacher at-tributed it to Joel's lack of reading practice, which is a fair attribution, but I think Joel needs more reading instruction as well as supervised practice. It is interesting to examine in detail the ways in which Joel's reading has suffered from lack of practice and ways that it has not. His oral reading, which is very good, was the basis for his English Eleven teacher characterizing him as one of the best readers in his class. Because she gave grade credit to those students who volunteered to read aloud, Joel often volunteered, and she was happy to call on him. As he demonstrated when he read his history textbook aloud, how-ever, he did not always understand what he read. By his own admis-sion, his vocabulary fell short of high school expectations, contributing to poor comprehension. More damaging to his comprehension, how-ever, are two other large gaps in the fabric of his reading: (1) his inex-perience with different genres or storytelling techniques (exemplified by *Cujo*), and (2) the fact that he has not been accumulating general background knowledge that would enable him to understand new ideas and into which he could integrate those new ideas.

Joel did not see that writing well about literature is complete-ly dependent on reading literature. Like many adolescents, he be-lieved that he was learning what he needed to know about a novel from listening to others talk about it in class. He got the plot and characters down, as well as one or two of the major themes (be-cause the teacher emphasized themes), but he never saw what he was missing in these texts, just as he did not see what he was miss-ing in his history textbook. (In English class, the text was complete but Joel did not read it; in history class, Joel read it repeatedly, but the text was, in a sense, incomplete. So he missed important ideas in both cases but for different reasons.) The fact that the English teacher expected the students to come up with some original ideas about the books, some interpretation or "reading" that had not been discussed in class, made thoughtful and careful reading in this class imperative. Without experience in reading novels (Joel said *Cujo* was the first long novel he had tried to read), Joel could not understand the writer's moves, such as shifts in time and place that do not immediately result in action but instead require the reader to remember details that do not become important until much later. Joel did not have the knowledge of storytelling that a reader needs in order to follow the writer's design. His teacher remarked that he had made some good points in his writing once in a while, but other things he had taken very literally. Getting beyond the literal meaning of the words—understanding how to read figurative language and symbolic characters and events—takes practice, coaching, and a good imagination. Joel lacked practice, received coaching only in whole-class discussions, and could not engage his imagination unless he was interested in the story and remembered to read it.

Joel's English Eleven class did not require writing about novels but focused on short stories and poetry instead. He was asked to keep a journal, writing in response to the teacher's prompts. She said that he did what he was asked to do but that he always kept his writing to a minimum. As might be expected from someone who is impatient with set-up and wants action, Joel wrote succinctly for these assignments.

> The 4th is cool. We always eat good food and spend time with family. Then we got to watch some kick back fireworks.
>
> I can't wait till our on ice practice for hockey next Thurs. It's gonna be fun to get out there and work on ice YEA BABY!
>
> My weekend was ok. Thurs I ate. Fri I played my game all day. Sat. Played my game all day. Sun went out for breakfast.

His teacher was satisfied with these three journal entries because they fulfilled the assignment. She noted that Joel wanted to write about hockey all the time, which she agreed to for some assignments but not all. When I asked her about his comprehension of literature, she said that she thought he was doing fine, especially in contrast to the large number of other students in his class who hate reading and are not comprehending the stories. This assessment is a reminder that a student's performance is often perceived in the context of those other students who happen to be enrolled in the same class.

Generating Mental Events

Successful readers make meaning from texts by responding to print imaginatively and creating ideas, scenes, emotions, people, or events in their minds. Some readers, like Rosa, imagine vividly and physically; others, such as Iser (1978), imagine more conceptually: The character is "illuminate[d]...not as an object but as a bearer of meaning" (p. 138). As readers, according to Iser, we do not necessarily need to literally "see" characters and events so much as experience them mentally and emotionally, imaginatively knowing their presence through their effect on other characters and on us. This is a more conceptual than literal "seeing." But however it happens, reading generates mental events. Learning the nature of those events for different readers furthers understanding of what reading is or does for different people reading different texts. For example, when Joel said that his mind felt blank after reading the paragraph about Hoover, he was describing an absence of mental events that led me to surmise that he did not have enough information to generate the story that the textbook writers intended to tell. His persistent sense of not knowing what was going on when he read the first part of *Cujo* led me to infer that he wanted and needed to know how all these different characters fit together, or what they contributed to the story, before he moved on to meet new characters. He wanted resolution of one scene before taking in another.

This may be a characteristic of an immature reader, or it may be a sign of inexperience with longer novels. Whatever we call it, it is a stumbling block for many readers that generates their resistance to reading long books. It is important for Joel's teachers to know this about him and so many other students who share his inexperience.

It also is important to know what mental events Joel enjoyed when he read successfully. When he was reading something he was interested in, he visualized it.

> I'm just like, trying to picture it,
> seeing what's going on at the time,
> what's happening.

He spoke of his picture in active terms: He was seeing "what's going on," "what's happening." Because Joel's reading practice consisted of looking for and creating mental images of activity in a story, it is not surprising that he was frustrated by the long expository phase of *Cujo*. He was not finding anything to work with mentally or imaginatively in this part of the novel.

I asked him about listening to someone read aloud compared to reading for himself.

> **Joel:** Usually when I'm reading,
> I try to picture it,
> but when I'm listening, it's not as much.
> I just listen, and try to...
> if it's interesting, I'll try to think about it.
>
> I probably picture it more when I'm reading it,
> 'cause that way I can stay focused on it
> and see what happened;
> aside from when I listen to other people read
> I try to listen to them
> and not lose focus.
>
> I mean I try to follow along as best I can,
> but sometimes if somebody else is saying something,
> sometimes my mind just kinda floats off.

Joel is a reader who "sees" in his mind's eye what he is reading about, and he knows that he needs to envision the subject in order to stay focused and stay focused in order to envision it. But it was often difficult for him to corral his mind and keep it on the subject. Everyone loses focus at times, but Joel seemed to have greater-than-average difficulty in maintaining control over his wandering attention. When it came to his own reading aloud, his mood and energy level determined whether he was better off reading for others or just to himself.

> **Anne:** Sometimes Ms. R and lots of other teachers, too, will tell the class to "just sit quietly and everybody read this passage, you've got 10 minutes" or whatever, and other times they'll have students take turns reading out loud...what's your preference?
>
> **Joel:** Um...I don't know, it's dependent on how I'm feeling.
> If I'm feeling like kinda tired,
> I read better alone and silent,
> aside from when I'm awake and kind of hyperactive at the time,
> I like to read out loud better.

Sometimes I—yeah, I like to be called on sometimes to read out
    loud.
Well, sometimes I don't like doing it,
it depends on what it is, but...
sometimes I don't feel like expressing myself, or...
I don't feel like wasting a lot of energy, what I have left of it.

Sometimes, just 'cause you're not as focused,
and you just can't understand what you're reading,
and you have trouble trying to read it out loud.

Joel had learned to talk about "being focused" in connection
with reading and learning, which is certainly a useful concept for a
student to have. I do not agree, however, that lack of focus is always
the cause of poor reading comprehension. As with the history textbook, no amount of focus can overcome inadequate background
knowledge, and as with *Cujo*, no amount of focus can substitute
for knowledge of how to negotiate a writer's use of literary techniques. And in all cases, it takes self-discipline and commitment to
override lack of interest with an act of will. Joel tried to do so, reading his textbook over and over, but he only repeated the same trip
through an empty landscape.

What Has Joel Taught Us?

Joel's attempts to focus his attention on texts were repeatedly frustrated by his lack of interest in much of what he was required to
read. When I asked him about the kinds of reading he found distasteful, he did not mention conceptual difficulty or any other features of writing. Instead, he talked about how he experienced the
content of these texts.

> **Anne:** What is the worst kind of reading for you, I mean in terms of
> something you feel like you have to read but you really—it's the
> hardest or least appealing.
>
> **Joel:** It's...I'm not sure, it's just like things I don't—
> things that aren't interesting,
> like things that start off, like something that—
> they don't interest me.
> Things that I don't like, so....

Anne: Are you thinking of fiction? Or are you thinking of textbooks? Or, what are you thinking of?

Joel: Just...anything that really don't interest me,
that I really don't like to hear
or talk about
or anything.

This question of interest came up with every student to whom I spoke. All said that they would read something if they were interested in it, and all spoke of the misery of being required to read something that they were not interested in. And, of course, students are not the only ones. Everyone who reads knows what happens when the text is "not interesting"—how our minds disconnect from our eyes, how we realize suddenly that the last three paragraphs (or pages) of print have not penetrated the thicket of our unrelated thoughts. At least two of the teachers I spoke with at this school admitted that they do not read any more than they have to because their minds wander so quickly and far away whenever they try it. They are part of a very large group of people who share that problem. But they have never been taught to try to deal with it, so they just stop reading.

It seems like common sense to say that readers' minds wander when they do not understand the text or are not interested in it. Joel frequently mentioned the problem of his mind wandering when he tried to read. His only recourse was to try reading the same words over again, a tactic that usually failed. But he was inexperienced enough with texts, and obedient enough as a student, to assume that the problem was with his focus. He did not know that the problem might be with the text, the interaction between himself and the text, or some other quality of his own mind or personality instead of poor focus. And wherever the problem lay, he did not know how to begin to deal with it.

Because learning to control and direct one's attention is such an important part of reading, teachers would do well to teach their students some techniques for dealing with the problem of the wandering mind. Levine (1990) suggests using a television channel metaphor: Students learn to check to see whether they are on a school channel when they are reading. Levine also describes a concentration cockpit that encourages students to think of themselves as pilots in control of a plane, tracking their own moods, motivation, memories, and more (as cited in Schoenbach, Greenleaf, Cziko, & Hurwitz, 1999). Readers can learn to notice their loss of attention in its early stages and can practice focusing their minds on text features that are giving them problems. Instead of trying to read in the usual sense, they can use a form of metacognition to conduct a meta-reading, or analysis of their own reading process, with particular attention to the question of why they are not successfully reading this text. Does it not make sense? Where exactly does it stop making sense? Is a contradiction unexplained? Is a piece of information missing? Is some specialized knowledge of terminology required? Is prior knowledge of any kind assumed? Is the writer speaking from a set of assumptions that are too foreign for the reader to recognize, much less adopt? Can the reader visualize the subject? If not, why not? Often, the inability to visualize means either that the text does not provide concrete examples of abstract concepts or that the reader does not have the necessary background knowledge to picture the content. One of the most important insights to teach students about reading comprehension and attention to text is that if they experience a blank after reading a passage, that means that they have not connected what they read to previously existing knowledge structures (schema) in their minds, either because they do not yet have the relevant knowledge structures or because they have not activated them.

Joel's Prose and Poetry teacher mentioned several times that the subject of reading instruction comes up often in staff meetings, but the staff have not been taught how to teach students to be better readers. One characteristic of reading that makes it different from most other school subjects is that a noticeable percentage of the student population will pick up the nuances of skillful reading (which Joel has missed by not reading) on their own, seemingly without any teaching at all. English teachers, usually in possession of strong linguistic interests and experiences, are particularly adept at navigating a wide range of texts without consciously realizing how many skills and techniques they are using. When they were high school students, they were likely to be among those who did not need to be taught how to interact with texts. They discovered, through their extensive reading, writing, and talking about texts, many things that a student like Joel needs to be taught explicitly.

Joel's talk about his experiences with various readings provides information about how and why he does and does not connect with them. Joel's expectations and desires were not met by most of the books he tried to read. If a writer's beliefs do not mesh well with the reader's, a reader may feel alienated or simply puzzled. For example, Kesey's depiction of women in *One Flew Over the Cuckoo's Nest* as either controlling destroyers of men or submissive prostitutes does not leave room for many female readers to find a point of identification in the story, or a way to enter into Kesey's world, unless they learn to "read like a man" (Fetterley, 1979; Schweickart, 1986). Feminist critics such as Fetterley and Schweichart have pointed out that women reading the Western canon (written largely by men) must learn to adopt a masculine point of view in order to read with the text, that is, read it the way the author intended. Joel, trying to read *Catcher in the Rye*, was not able to read with the text because he did not recognize Holden's angst as a legitimate motivation, nor Holden's running away as a legitimate response to conflict. A similar mismatch between a reader's expectations of the text and what it actually provides also can result in a failed reading: Joel expected *Cujo* to be thrilling, full of mad dog attacks and deadly battles. When *Cujo* turned out to have a novel's cast of characters and structure, with lengthy exposition and traditional expectations of the reader, he was bored and confused.

Joel might have been able to understand what the writers did accomplish, even if he himself did not find it personally relevant, if he had had more preparation and guidance of a particular kind. Experienced readers are able to categorize texts quickly, predict what the texts will offer and expect of readers, and either adjust accordingly or stop reading. Inexperienced readers need guidance from experts—just enough prereading information to help them understand what the writer intends to accomplish, and enough insight into their own preferences and needs to avoid disappointment when those preferences and needs are not addressed by a writer in a particular text. Teachers can set the new text within the students' frame of reference if they know something of their students' interests. Richardson (1996) describes successful prereading activities with her secondary students, as do Rothenberg and Watts (2000), Robb (2000), Beers (2002), and numerous other authors of helpful books for teachers. I am recommending that teachers add to these activities a discussion with students of what kinds of information, plots, or characters they personally find compelling, and situating the new text in relation to those interests. In other words, Joel's teacher might say,

> I know that some of you love a story in which a strong hero takes on a powerful enemy, the way McMurphy did in *One Flew Over the Cuckoo's Nest*. *Catcher in the Rye* is a different kind of story, although the protagonist does have certain battles to fight. Let's see who or what he thinks his enemies are and how he deals with them. You will see that he is going through a kind of personal crisis in this story, and he is searching for something he doesn't quite understand.

In the process of reading the book, teachers can help readers see Holden's conflicts and realizations in a way that makes sense to them, even if they are accustomed to admiring a more obviously heroic protagonist. Seeing the ways in which the new text fits familiar paradigms and yet differs from them, students can learn that texts are not inherently boring or interesting. They expand their reading horizons by learning to do what Gregory (1997) calls assentive readings, even of texts that they think they will not like, if their guide helps them see that the text does accomplish something of value. Readers learn a great deal about the world from texts that are not perfectly matched to their personal desires. But this mismatch should be brought out into the open so that it becomes a point of conscious learning rather than another irritating but unexamined feature of required school reading.

Joel needs to be taught to analyze his interaction with a text that is giving him difficulty and to understand that the problem may be in the way the text is written, it may be in his hopes or expectations of the text, a psychological resistance to the subject of the text, or in that he is missing some vocabulary or other necessary background knowledge. There are many ways that readers can connect with a particular text, but there are just as many ways that readers and texts can miss each other. When we take the time to teach secondary students more about texts and about themselves, showing them how to take active control when things go wrong in their attempts to connect with text, they will be in a much better position to understand and direct their reading successfully.

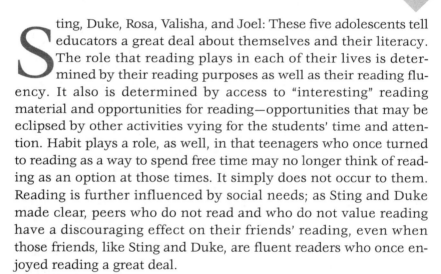

Chapter 8

Investigating Resistance and Engagement

Sting, Duke, Rosa, Valisha, and Joel: These five adolescents tell educators a great deal about themselves and their literacy. The role that reading plays in each of their lives is determined by their reading purposes as well as their reading fluency. It also is determined by access to "interesting" reading material and opportunities for reading—opportunities that may be eclipsed by other activities vying for the students' time and attention. Habit plays a role, as well, in that teenagers who once turned to reading as a way to spend free time may no longer think of reading as an option at those times. It simply does not occur to them. Reading is further influenced by social needs; as Sting and Duke made clear, peers who do not read and who do not value reading have a discouraging effect on their friends' reading, even when those friends, like Sting and Duke, are fluent readers who once enjoyed reading a great deal.

The role of reading in Sting's life became much more constrained than it was when he was in elementary school. As a child, Sting read widely for the pleasure of the imaginative journey to a new place. As an adolescent, he used reading for limited and specific purposes: learning about sports, especially professional wrestling; learning about other interests, such as science fiction; reading rap lyrics (some of which he writes); reading the professional wrestling stories that he writes; and reading the Bible. Reading helped Sting learn what he wanted to know, connect socially with peers and maintain a certain standing with them, enjoy the expression of his creative ideas and feelings, and participate in church life with his family. These are purposes that he chose. None of them are the school's purposes. It is true that the expression of creative ideas and feelings is part of the English curriculum, but because Sting's expression takes the form of raps, wrestling scripts, and journals about his extracurricular interests, he did not get much school credit for it. Sting did not see the need for more school, much less more school reading. Occasionally, he still engaged fully with an assigned story in spite of himself, but that was a relatively rare event.

For Duke, reading had become even more peripheral than it had for Sting. Duke found other ways to satisfy his curiosity about the world, although he would read if he were interested enough—about vampires, for example. But instead of reading, Duke would rather talk, watch movies or television, and participate directly in life. Duke and Sting both believed that they already knew enough about reading and had read enough school texts to obviate the need for more. The only reason they saw for cooperating with school reading was to earn a diploma and the social currency that it carries.

Rosa used reading for therapeutic purposes as well as instructional ones. But the instruction she was seeking in her chosen reading was not about the subjects school promotes; it was about relationships and, in a larger sense, taking a place in the adult world. She understood intellectually and felt emotionally that that place involved being in a happy relationship with a man without being too dependent on him. She turned to reading to see how others did this and to convince herself that it really could happen for her. Rosa's reading had everything to do with her family and her future and almost nothing to do with school. When she did read for school, she did not enjoy or understand her reading unless she could find in it some of the information and reassurance she was seeking about herself and her future.

Valisha, the one person of the five who described herself as a nonreader, was in the process of discovering what reading could do for her. Like all the others, Valisha used reading for specific purposes. Reading helped her find out what she wanted to know about the world and reassured her through literary role models that the kind of life she wanted was possible. And like the others in this study, Valisha found most school reading unrewarding and difficult to understand. She found meaning in school reading only when she could connect it with her particular interests and needs.

Reading was fading from Joel's life, just as it was from Sting's and Duke's. Whereas Joel once was able to rely on his reading ability to get through school assignments easily, as an adolescent he struggled to keep his mind focused on the text and to understand what he read. He was finding that he was not the excellent reader that he used to be—not so much because his reading ability had weakened but because it had not developed beyond a middle school level at which he, like Sting and Duke, more or less stopped learning to read. For Joel, high school reading was more confusing than helpful, more alienating than enlightening. And yet we see with Joel, as with all the others, that when a text provided what he was looking for in a form he could understand, he enjoyed it and benefited from it. He did not, however, read independently either of the two works he liked best, *Othello* (Shakespeare, 1993) and *One Flew Over the Cuckoo's Nest* (Kesey, 1989). He depended on a recorded reading in one case and on class discussion in the other. Joel was able to understand and enjoy these stories because his teacher spoke of Iago and McMurphy in ways that satisfied Joel's search for strong men who challenge authority.

The common theme in these case studies is the purposeful way in which all five readers used reading to accomplish their goals. All these students were concerned with their futures, and all of them were concerned about how to be a successful man or woman in their culture. Sting, Duke, and Joel all expressed their interests in strength and power as well as in how to be a good man among men. Sting and Duke clearly showed their desire to be admired for their strength: Sting was fascinated with the good-guy wrestlers who can defeat the bad guys, and Duke loved the lore of the vampire and the fearlessness of the rappers who metaphorically consume their competitors. But both Sting and Duke also showed their concern with the welfare of others—Sting in his concern for homeless people and his care for his family and Duke in his admiration of the relationship between George and Lennie in *Of Mice and Men* (Steinbeck, 1993) and in his responsiveness to Christian teachings. Joel's interests were somewhat more veiled, but even a brief analysis of his interest in hockey and the characters Iago and McMurphy is enough to show that his attention was drawn to strong men who test their courage and win. Joel's protective side did not show up as unequivocally in this study as Sting's or Duke's, but Joel did not express himself as readily as Sting and Duke, and

I was not looking specifically for evidence of this kind in the interviews. From my conversations with Joel and my observations of him interacting with other students, I have no doubt that he is fundamentally as kind-hearted as Sting and Duke.

Rosa and Valisha, too, were seeking understanding of how to be a strong adult who also is a good and loving person. Both Rosa and Valisha wanted to be capable and independent women who had happy family relationships, and the fiction they read well (or read at all) is fiction that provided them with models of this story. It is worth noting that neither character nor plot alone was enough to be satisfying for them; a good character must be living through a good plot with a convincing outcome for the whole story to be fully satisfying. Rosa might have liked Dana's character in *Kindred* (Butler, 1979) if the plot had not disturbed her so much; Valisha might have liked the character of the cook in "No Witchcraft for Sale" (Lessing, 1965) if the plot had not confused her with its foreign elements. And we have seen that Valisha did not like either the character or the plot of *Kindred* because neither gave her the satisfaction of seeing a strong woman make independent and productive decisions about her life. She was so frustrated by seeing a boy take charge of Dana's life that she did not finish reading the book, even though her friends encouraged her to do so.

These five students vary in their definitions of what constitutes a good character and a good plot, but each is consistent at the bedrock level of desires and needs. These students help us look beneath the convention of adolescent interests in fast action and teenage characters and show us something important about generating a connection between text and reader. The challenge ahead is what we do with this information.

In this final chapter, I address this challenge on two levels: (1) what teachers can do in their classrooms today and tomorrow, working within the confines of existing school structures, and then, (2) on a larger scale, what changes in that school structure we can envision and begin to work toward and in what ways we can apply a broader understanding of the cultural work we do in the classroom, especially, but not by any means exclusively, in the English classroom. These two categories are not at all separate; both rest on a foundation of information about readers and nonreaders to which all 25 of the students I interviewed contribute. Therefore, I begin with an overview of the study's findings. This is followed by some advice students have for teachers, which I expand on, offering some suggestions for classroom practice. The final section of this chapter deals with broader and more conceptual ways of thinking about reading and teaching.

Why People Read

When I brought up the question of why a person should read, most students mentioned learning new things. Some of them also made a distinction between learning something that they have to learn, such as for school, and learning about something they are interested in, such as sports or other teenagers. These are students who use reading as a tool to accomplish a desired end. They did not say, "I love to read." They said, instead, "I love sports, so I read about sports. And I watch sports on TV, and I talk about it with my friends." Reading is just one way to fill their minds with sports. It may not be the most effective or the most pleasing way.

The devoted fiction readers, such as Sting when he was younger and Rosa when she was reading romances, are different. They love being transported to a new world, swept away by the words that stimulate imaginative places, people, and plots. These readers talked about their sense that these events are really happening in another realm and how they can get so caught up in the character's emotions that they feel their own hearts pounding and their fists clenching. These are the readers who declare their love of reading because, for them, the experience of reading cannot be duplicated, much less bested, by other media.

Nonfiction readers also may enjoy reading immensely and spend a good deal of time doing it (see Alexander, 1997, for discussion of the motivation and rewards of reading expository text). However, the nonfiction readers I spoke to do not see why anyone would waste his or her time reading something that is not true. Facts and information are what they seek. Fiction-only readers such as Rosa, on the contrary, cannot understand why anyone would waste their time reading something that is true. The real world is all around us, pressing in on all sides, and these readers look for a chance to stretch the wings of imagination. Because so many English teachers love fiction, it is important for them to realize that fiction is regarded with suspicion, as something fake, by readers like Sting, and as a forced march through boring alien territory by readers like Duke. Although serious fiction readers trust authors to say something about the human experience that is worth knowing, not everyone shares that trust, even when the authors are famous. In fact, the opposite is true—according to many students I interviewed, famous authors assigned in school are likely to be the most boring.

Ways of Reading

The preceding assertions are rough generalizations about groups of readers; of course many people read both fiction and nonfiction, myself included. But there are major differences in both the purposes and the experiences of reading different kinds of texts, differences that Rosenblatt (1934/1978) characterizes as efferent (we carry information away from our reading) and aesthetic (we experience something that is beautiful because it is a true insight into the human condition). Although we usually think of imaginative literature as being read aesthetically and informational texts being read efferently, nonfiction reading may be aesthetic just as fiction reading may be efferent. A text that is primarily nonfiction may be written to give aesthetic and emotional pleasure, just as a piece of fiction may include much factual information about the real world. This softening of genre boundaries can be confusing to inexperienced readers, who may assume that if a story is set in a real time and place alongside historical events they recognize, it must be nonfiction. Sumara (1996) describes this confusion in students responding to historical fiction about the Beijing student revolution in Tiananmen Square. In this fictional text, the characters' journal entries were dated as if they were historical artifacts, persuading these readers that they were dealing with something "real." As teachers, we need to try to read through our students' eyes as well as analyze our own styles and tastes and recognize what it is that we expect of our students' reading. We need to recognize that many of our students will be quite different in their reading styles and tastes (see Cone's, 1994, account of her somewhat reluctant attempt to read science fiction and Sumara's, 1996, account of his reading group). We need to talk about these differences with our students. It is an essential part of learning how to read.

Reasons for Losing the Reading Habit

The students in this study showed wide variability in their relationships to reading, but certain stories were told again and again. One of these is the all-too-familiar story of having been a good and enthusiastic reader in elementary school and then when early adolescence hit at age 12 or 13, the reading more or less stopped.

When I probed into the causes for this, students answered in several ways. One common theme is that the family was going through some changes at the time, requiring, for example, transfer to a new school because the family moved. Or, the parents divorced and the child spent so much time and energy thinking about the breakup and going back and forth between parents' homes that reading fell by the wayside. One of the points to remember about this scenario is that moving may well mean a physical separation from books—the family no longer lives near a public library; the child's books get packed away; or the family no longer has as much discretionary income, so books are not bought as frequently—and these seemingly small changes can tip the balance from a child reading to a child not reading.

Teenagers in this study also told me that when they got into eighth grade, books got boring. When I probed into this answer, I often found that the students still read but chose to read magazines or books of a particular genre. This shift in attention away from the worlds of children's books to the more specialized interests of adolescents frequently coincided with a strong interest in peers. Reading about other teenagers, whether in magazines or books, was usually interesting to them. A teenage protagonist is not enough, however, to guarantee that high school students will like a story. Valisha did not like watching Alice in *Go Ask Alice* (Anonymous, 1971) let other people take over her life. Joel did not like watching Holden Caulfield in *Catcher in the Rye* (Salinger, 1991) running away and searching for something he could not find. Both students preferred books that happened to have adult protagonists when those books provided the kinds of characters, experiences, and information they were seeking.

Students also said that their reading diminished due to peer influence and lack of time; for example, one student stated, "I just started spending more time hanging out with my friends, and none of 'em read, so I just stopped reading, too." Time that once was spent reading, at home alone, is now spent out with friends playing video games or looking for other friends at the mall. Attractive alternatives to reading draw young people away from books, and at the same time, these teenagers may feel pushed away from reading by the escalating demands of reading in middle school. Duke pointed out that middle school was the time when teachers started requiring book reports on long books that he did not want to take the time to read, both because the books did not go the way he wanted them to, and because he wanted to spend time doing other things. For Duke, and for many students, this is a critical point of departure from the reading habit. It is a point at which learning how to get by without reading can take precedence over learning to be a better reader. As teachers, we need to find ways to stay involved in students' reading and to keep them involved in one another's reading through in-class book groups and other ways of talking and writing honestly about reading.

Three of the teachers to whom I spoke seemed surprised that I would bother to be researching the question of why so many high school students do not like reading. The answer was obvious to them: television. They all told me that their own children read because they had been brought up in a family that read instead of watching television all the time. However, in the interviews I conducted with all 25 students, I found that the widely held belief that growing up in a reading household makes children into readers is not founded on cause-and-effect evidence. It is correlational. In my particular case, and in millions of other cases, the correlation holds. But as a researcher and as a teacher, I have seen many students whose relationship to reading was significantly different from that of other members of their families. As a teacher, I have spoken to many parents who wonder why their adolescent son or daughter does not enjoy reading even though the adolescent's childhood was filled with intense parental reading guidance. This is not an occasion for parents or teachers to feel guilty; it is an opportunity to find out what reading means to the young person and to explore new reading experiences they can take part in.

What Makes Reading Interesting?

Another theme that emerges from these interviews is that virtually all students (except the severely dyslexic ones) insisted that they can and do read. They said that they even like to read, under the right circumstances. What they require, however, is something that is interesting. When I probed into this question of what makes reading interesting, most students could not explain. "Interestingness" is not an objectively identifiable quality, and certainly not a universally agreed-upon one, although Shank (1979) says that certain topics such as sex, death, and money (to name a few) are of universal interest. I agree that some version of these subjects is interesting to virtually everyone at some time in their lives, but not all forms are automatically interesting to all adolescents. Students may grow weary of extended study of one or another of these topics, or, like Valisha reading "No Witchcraft for Sale," they may not recognize that a story is based on a theme they are interested in.

When stating what they like, students mentioned stories about people like themselves or about characters with whom they can identify—and they were quick to say that they can identify with a character of a different gender or race as long as they can identify with what the character is experiencing. When the story catches the imagination, the student enjoys being in that world, working on the challenges the character is tackling. But inexperienced readers need a guide to help them see that the character's challenges are related to their own. They usually see a work as existing as a single object of study, complete in itself and isolated. They have a hard time seeing that a story is located in a network of human interests and endeavors, so, like Joel, they do not connect McMurphy's battle against authority with the rebelliousness of characters in professional wrestling; they do not easily see that Holden Caulfield, too, is fighting the authority of his culture.

When students talked about interest, they clearly located it as being "out there." Books are interesting or they are not; they either grab the student's attention or they do not. These students showed little sign of seeing that what they think is interesting, funny, or boring is as much a reflection of who they are as it is a reflection of the story. Another aspect of the question of interest is that most students mentioned that they need to be interested right away; they have little patience with stories that require a long introductory process. When teachers hear this about a particular story, they can devise ways to help students get into the text (see Allen, 1995; Beers, 2002; and Richardson, 1996, for books with discussions on prereading exercises). Teachers also can address the problem directly by discussing it as a challenge for readers, helping students understand that more advanced reading includes knowing how to work up slowly to the dramatic action they are hoping to find. Knowing that some readers (e.g., Duke) do not trust the author to provide an interesting story can help teachers understand that their students' impatience with slow beginnings may well be a fear of feeling imprisoned in future boredom. Thus, modeling one's own responses to introductory material can help students see that it does serve a purpose and can even be interesting.

It is notable that many students, both boys and girls, mentioned how much they like mystery stories. When I asked why, they said they like having a puzzle to figure out. Essentially, the story gives them something engaging to do; it is interactive. In contrast, boring stories are those that involve lengthy, seemingly irrelevant descriptions instead of characters doing something dramatic—or "interesting." Clearly, these students have not learned to read descriptions as more information from the author about character, community, and conflict as well as about what the person or place looks like. They have not learned to read interpretively and symbolically, although they know that teachers like symbols in literature.

Intrinsic Interests

These student interviews support the idea that by the time people are in high school, they have developed a number of interests and dismissed some things they have tried but not liked. These high school students may enjoy playing a musical instrument, or basketball, or reading romance novels and know that they do not enjoy golf, westerns, or science fiction. In other words, they have a more developed sense of their own tastes, based on their experience of the world. The omnivorous curiosity of childhood has been distilled into a more mature concentration of attention into fewer areas. These teenagers have begun to specialize, as all people do with age. Their interests are likely to be the basis of what they like to read, of course, as is true of everyone.

This is extremely inconvenient for teachers, whose job is to teach a curriculum that includes much that students have eliminated from their lists of interesting things. Tension arises when teachers, wishing to broaden students' horizons, require them to read or study something the students have already decided is boring.

And when the student wants to read about one of his or her interests, the teachers sometimes resist, feeling (as do some librarians, see Walker, 1981) that the student can do that on personal time, that school time should be spent on "better" or more literary readings. This tension is built into the very bones of an institution that attempts to direct the lives and thoughts of people who are actively moving from childhood to adulthood, from dependence to autonomy. Younger people and older people get to choose what to read; only in middle and high school are people's reading choices so controlled. There is no one right answer as to how to deal with this tension, but it is good to be aware of how pervasive it is and how deeply adolescents feel it (Allen, 1995; Bintz, 1993; Bomer, 1995; Christian-Smith, 1990; Evans, 1993; Mahiri, 1994). Repeatedly, teenagers say, "I'll read it if it's interesting. If it's boring, I'll skim or just skip it altogether."

Avoiding Reading

Students were frank about their decision not to read what they did not want to read. They skimmed and depended on class discussions for information about text content. In social studies or science, they used the textbook questions and section headings as a way of deciding what they needed to know about, and they read very selectively for those things (see Hidi, 1995, for discussion of readers' goals and systems of attending to text). In English class, they used the teacher's study guides to direct them to the points about a story the teacher considered important. A few used Cliff's Notes or other commercial study guides, but most did not bother. If they were going to take the trouble to find an outside source of information, they would rent the movie or ask a friend who reads well to just tell them what happens in the book. And they saw these strategies as successful; most could pass tests on a reading without having read the book themselves. I asked one 12th grader what the difference was between reading a book himself and listening to someone else who had read the book tell him about it, and he said, "There's no difference. Either way, I find out what happens." He has no way of comparing the knowledge of "what happens" that he gets from a friend with the much fuller knowledge he could get from reading, thinking, and talking about a text. If educators knew more about how to teach high school students to be aware of what they do when they read and how to get more from reading than just "what happens," students might understand that there is a big difference between reading and not reading.

Students' Advice to Teachers

Teachers are in a real bind when it comes to requiring students to read. In social studies and science, it is possible to learn a great deal about the subject without reading (e.g., through videos, oral explanations, and hands-on discovery), although reading has at least two advantages: (1) It is a highly efficient way to learn material, assuming that a learner is a good reader, and (2) knowing how to read a textbook is an important advantage for success in high school and college. Nevertheless, not all the teachers at Oak Creek High School expect their students to read textbooks on a regular basis, either because the teachers themselves personally prefer media other than textbooks or because they have found that a significant number of students do not read well.

English teachers, however, are mandated to teach literature and language use. They must require that their students read. Teachers in other disciplines, too, may decide that it is important to use textbooks regularly. When I asked students what advice about reading they had for teachers, the most common response was, "Choose interesting stuff. Don't try to make us read boring stuff." This advice reveals students' belief that interest is a commodity teachers can choose to include or ignore (and for some reason, they persist in ignoring it, according to many students). Furthermore, most students do not understand that teachers do not always have a great deal of choice about the texts they teach. English teachers may be able to choose among novels or short stories, but they still are required to teach literature, and literature is exactly what many of the teenagers I interviewed regard as boring. Knowing that this concern with interest is primary, teachers can choose texts that are more likely to appeal to more young readers, especially if they get to know their students' interests (see Allen, 1995; Barbieri, 1995; Bomer, 1995; Hosking & Teberg, 1998; Ivey, 1999; Smith & Wilhelm, 2002; Worthy, 1998, for teachers' discussions of the role of interest in reading success). Just as important, teachers can try to help students see why they should bother to read a particular text and help them see that certain themes that operate in their own lives, such as how people care for one another or how they negotiate with authority, are the concern of famous authors, too. Not infrequently, students reveal a belief that people of earlier eras did not think or feel the way we do now, a belief that leads them to reject texts that were written before they were born. If reading William Shakespeare or Robert Frost does nothing else for them, it can at least begin to disabuse them of this notion.

These case studies reveal that students' interests can be understood on more than one level. The three boys, for example, are all interested in sports; the two girls are interested in romance. These are the interests that students are likely to mention if asked. On another level, however, we can see that they are all interested in what it means to be an adult. The boys are overtly concerned with masculinity, power, and authority; the girls are overtly concerned with children as well as relationships of love and power between men and women. Joel's admiration for Iago and McMurphy and his discomfort with Holden are similar to Sting's fascination with professional wrestlers and Duke's interest in vampires. In other words, desire to understand how people experience and use power is an enduring theme in these three readers' stories (although if you asked them if they are interested in power, they might not answer affirmatively). Trites's (2000) study of young adult (YA) fiction concludes not only that adolescent literature is about power, but that it

> problematizes the relationship of the individual to the institutions that construct her or his subjectivity.... YA novels tend to interrogate social constructions, foregrounding the relationship between the society and the individual rather than focusing on Self and self-discovery as children's literature does. (p. 20)

Knowing this, teachers can choose texts that explore the question of how people experience power (either for whole-class readings or for individual recommendations) and situate the texts they choose in relation to that same question.

Talking with students about a book in terms of a character's conflict with institutions (e.g., Iago, McMurphy, Holden, Doris Lessing's cook, and millions of other characters who test their mettle through conflict with powerful institutions) can help young people see how literature can prepare them for life beyond school.

I urge readers and their teachers to recognize that surface interests are only that: on the surface. Beneath them is the real motivation for doing and learning what a person wants to do and learn.

For example, other students interested in vampires might ignore the power that Duke finds so attractive and be drawn to the alternate reality in which vampires live or to blood-drinking as a compelling symbol of intimacy. Both Valisha and Rosa are interested in relationships between people, especially intimate relationships. Although I have emphasized that Valisha seeks knowledge of reality and Rosa seeks escape from reality, both are seeking ways to be intimate with others while maintaining independence. Valisha confronts this more directly than Rosa, wanting to read about women who take charge of their own lives and successfully meet challenges to their independence; Rosa, too, seeks models of independent women who know how to love and be loved. Her interest in the capitulation scene in which the hero admits his love for the heroine is evidence of her desire to learn how love and power coexist. These deeper reasons for attraction can themselves be probed for information as to how the reader understands and uses them. Ultimately, what a reader learns about him- or herself does not have to be made public or even shared with the teacher. The teacher's role is to make students aware that their responses to text are based on personal emotions and experiences, and are therefore a rich source of self-knowledge.

Some fundamental questions are common to all these readers: How do I become the adult I want to be, living the life I want to live, in the face of the obstacles I see? How do I relate to others to get what I want? Do I dominate, submit, or negotiate? How do I deal with the fact that I feel in some ways as if I do not fit into my culture? How do I meet the demands of my culture so I can fit in but also be true to myself? If we teachers could keep these questions in mind as we present literary works (or history or science lessons), we could help students see that virtually all the human endeavors we require for study in school are aimed at understanding ourselves and our environments, both social and natural (see Wiggins and McTighe's, 1998, discussion of "the big picture" and "enduring ideas" for more information about connecting schoolwork to real life).

Teachers should choose texts that appeal to different kinds of readers in the class so that fiction and nonfiction are represented, as are stories with which different genders, races, and temperaments can identify. Teachers can help readers who resist a particular story by being frank about what the text focuses on and what it accomplishes as well as what it does not. This is most effective when it is done in the context of students' own experiences with various kinds of stories, and because students have different experiences, a teacher needs to situate a text in several ways for a class of 25 or more readers. If a teacher situates *Catcher in the Rye* in relation to *One Flew Over the Cuckoo's Nest* for students like Joel, he or she also will need to situate it for students like Rosa who are looking for successful relationships, and students like Duke who are looking either for examples of characters making good decisions in the face of serious temptation or characters who take care of each other, as George and Lennie do in *Of Mice and Men*. Another student, one who is starved for connection with others, may be profoundly uncomfortable with a text that celebrates a character's search for independence. Secondary students need practice in a supportive environment to get beyond "That book is really, really boring." Once reading has begun, open lines of communication allow readers to let the teacher know how they are doing with a particular text, talking and writing about what they enjoy and what makes them feel resistant to picking up the book. Letting students choose their texts whenever possible is important, too. Many students have told me that they would have done a book report, for example, if they could have done it on a book about their favorite athlete or singer. When they were assigned a subject they did not like or understand, they did not do the assignment. Reading a popular book with full attention and enthusiasm is surely a more valuable experience than skimming and pretending to have read a literary book one finds dull.

Students mentioned that some teachers make it easier to get into a book by spending more time discussing the beginning of the book and making sure that every student knows what is going on; Joel longed for such guidance as he struggled with *Cujo*. If the teacher is a good reader and reads aloud some of the book, many students enjoy listening. Those students who are not particularly fluent readers themselves have found that they can let their imaginations move more freely when someone else is doing the reading. All they have to do is listen and let the events take form in their minds. Students are suggesting that they can think about the text better when they do not have to concentrate on the sentence-by-sentence decoding. For them, the act of reading interferes with making meaning from the words.

Several students mentioned that they like it when a teacher who loves the book tells them what parts he or she really admires and why. Then, they can begin to see the book through the teacher's eyes. Students also enjoy a chance to talk about their reading. Wells (1996) found that students thought they learned more when they could talk with one another about new ideas. Alvermann (2000) argues that in a classroom, "discussion is a bargain at any price" (p. 148). Although students' talk about their reading uses class time that could be spent on further reading or more instruction by the teacher, such talk improves comprehension and stimulates thinking about the text. Outside the classroom, many adolescents do share their books and magazines with one another, and recommend readings to friends who share their tastes. The social activity often adds to the reader's pleasure.

It is important to keep communication about reading open and ongoing by means of classroom talk and writing. The more students know about what people read and why they value it, the better equipped they will be to make a place for themselves in the world of reading. The more varieties of reading and texts that teachers are willing to recognize and respect, the more likely students are to find a place in that world, to construct an identity as a reader. I am arguing that students have important purposes for the literacies they practice, and if these purposes are recognized and these literacies acknowledged, high school need not be a place where students learn to dislike and avoid reading. It can become a place where students can learn to use more kinds of literacy, more varieties of texts, and more ways of reading to reach their goals of successful adulthood.

Further Suggestions

If all readers responded to a given text the same way, teaching it would be easier. The stories these students tell about their own reading reveal the differences in their purposes for reading as well as their differing responses to what they find in a text. As students are readers situated in their time, culture, and psychology, so are we who teach them. A first step toward teaching this variety of readers is to analyze our own reading patterns and tastes, paying particular attention to reading that we dislike or think unworthy of class time. Asking someone who enjoys that reading to talk about what it provides for him or her will help us understand what the text-created world is like for the aficionado of that genre. Finding someone who dislikes our favorite kind of reading and trying to help that person understand what it gives us also is a valuable exercise, as is listening carefully to his or her reasons for not liking our favorite texts.

We also need to analyze our expectations of our student readers, both in general and in terms of specific texts they are required to read. It is harder than it sounds to make those expectations clear to the students. This is especially true when the assignment is "Read this" because reading is such a variable process from one person to the next. Joel and Rosa both ran their eyes over various assigned texts but often did not come away with any sense of understanding. Teachers who articulate specific goals for reading a chapter or a passage can provide inexperienced readers with purpose and confidence that the purpose can be fulfilled. This is an important prereading step that applies to all content areas. Communicating with students about how they are responding to a reading during the reading through writing or discussion can provide invaluable information about what to spend class time on. For example, students' discomfort with the ending of *Go Ask Alice* or with the historical realism of *Kindred* can be addressed head-on. Readers are not necessarily going to change their minds about how they feel about these two books, but both examples offer opportunities to talk about ways that readers work with texts, opportunities to talk about the process of reading as well as about the subject matter of the books.

Protherough (1983) points out that "[d]ealing with fiction in schools forces the teacher inevitably into a relationship with students as people" (p. 129). He is speaking as an English teacher, but I would argue that good teaching forces the teacher into a relationship with students as people, whatever the subject. The better teachers can get to know their students, the better they can guide those students in the direction teachers want them to go. Smith and Wilhelm (2002) found that the boys in their study brought up this point about teachers knowing and caring about them many times. Questionnaires, journal entries, autobiographical writing assignments, conferences, and students' comments written on index cards in the last two minutes of class are some of the ways that teachers can get to know their students; responding to these writings is a good way to show their interest. Moje (2000) describes the value of seeing students outside the classroom, whether in a formal setting such as a student concert or less formally at a community event. She has excellent advice for making the most of these encounters, including comparing the teacher's and the student's observations about the event afterward and using those observations to guide classroom teaching. Atwell (1998) incorporates into each class brief conferences with students as well as limited small-group sharing time. Nicholson (1984) describes short, concurrent interviews that take place at the student's desk when students are working independent of the teacher. Instead of simply keeping an eye on students to make sure they look as if they are doing what they are supposed to be doing, the teacher uses this time to find out what sense the student is making of the text (or assignment) while he or she is working with it. In these exchanges, the teacher does more listening than talking, asking just enough to get the student to explain what he or she is doing and what meaning she or he is making of it—or not making of it, as case may be. It is a process, Nicholson says, of "focusing experts' minds on the problems of novice pupils" (p. 526). Cone (1994) tape-records the conversations of reading groups to find out what students are thinking and saying about their books. However it is accomplished, ongoing teacher-student communication about reading is essential.

Some excellent work has been done in an effort to improve students' reading comprehension. Techniques such as reciprocal teaching devised by Palincsar and Brown (1989) explicate the cognitive steps that readers go through in reading: predicting, questioning, clarifying, and summarizing. Reciprocal teaching is a group procedure in which the meaning that is made of the text comes into being through social interaction. Reciprocal teaching provides a setting in which students concentrate on the text, think about it, talk about it, and help each other understand it. The teacher, as expert reader, models the reading comprehension and scaffolds the students' efforts to learn the technique. These all-important principles of guidance through the process of comprehension by modeling reading, thinking, talking, and questioning can be adapted to students of any age. If the students I interviewed had had opportunities for reciprocal teaching, I believe that their confusion and frustration would have been lessened significantly.

Whenever possible, students should have a choice of reading matter, within whatever limitations the teacher's particular personal beliefs or professional situation impose (see Krashen, 1993, for a review of the research supporting the benefits of free voluntary reading). Joel's experience with *Cujo* reminds us that students do not always read what they select, so a system of support for these independent readings is necessary. A reading partner or small group can make the difference between a student reading and not reading (see Daniels, 1994, and Hynds, 1997, for information on how literature circles can work). Students who have already read a book can serve as references and discussion partners for students who are reading a book for the first time. Teachers might set up a collection of books for students to choose from and base the titles on student suggestions as well as teacher's preferences, thereby ensuring that sooner or later everyone will be the resident expert on several books. Reading time in class is important. So is making sure that students have a realistic plan for setting aside time for reading, and following up to ensure that the plan is put into practice. Frank and practical discussions about how to cope with problems such as confusion, impatience, and loss of interest in the text are essential.

Asking students about their preferences for ways of reading (e.g., aloud, silently, in small groups, in class, or at home) will help teachers vary the method according to the needs of readers. It also will help students see that teachers are trying to work with them rather than against them. Students are much more likely to want to cooperate with a teacher they see as caring about them (Bosworth, 1995; Dillon, 1989; Moje, 1996), a point that Rosa and her friend Heather put in terms of their liking the teacher, but affection and respect rarely go only one way. When students participate in the decision making about what is read and how it is read, they are more likely to feel respected and feel some ownership of the reading rather than see it as a burden imposed by an authority figure. Even if the choice of text cannot be shared with students, discussion about the possible ways to read encourages a feeling of community and helps students understand that readers work in different ways, but that whatever the method, they can support one another.

English Class Reading From the Students' Point of View

This work is a study of high school students' reading. Whatever students wanted to say about reading, I wanted to hear. We talked about school reading, leisure reading, boring reading, riveting reading, fiction and nonfiction, as well as movies and television. We talked about interests, choices, goals, anxieties, responsibilities, and assignments. We discussed reading histories, family reading habits, and reading purposes. From this range of reading talk I saw that, although multiple ways to organize the topics were possible, the reading categories that the students themselves made, without stating it in so many words, included free-choice leisure reading on their own time (which not everyone practiced), textbook reading, and fiction assigned in English class. Of the two groups of school texts, fiction in English class generated the most difficulty for most students. Textbooks certainly presented problems, which I discussed as they arose within each case study, but science, mathematics, and social studies teachers rarely expect students to read and understand textbooks on their own without in-class explanation of each point the student is expected to learn. Some teachers use textbooks rarely, or only in class and accompanied by explanatory discussions. One science teacher said that he did not use textbooks except as sources for research reports because he himself dislikes reading and finds it very difficult to understand and remember information he reads in textbooks. So he has created a project-based curriculum that includes students becoming experts in particular areas that they take turns teaching to the rest of the class. Only one of the teachers I spoke to, a social studies teacher working with 12th graders, expected students to take their textbooks home to read and comprehend them independently.

Textbook reading, as it is practiced by the students I interviewed, is fundamentally a different exercise than fiction reading, calling on a different set of expectations of the text and knowledge of a different set of textual conventions (see Rothkopf & Billington, 1979, for a study of textbook reading in action). Textbook reading, if practiced efferently (Rosenblatt, 1978) as it usually is, engages the imagination differently than fiction reading does and calls for comprehension and memory of a different kind of information. More than one student I interviewed said that the word *reading* was associated in his or her mind with novels from English class: large blocks of text uninterrupted by illustrations or the organizing headings and sidebars found in textbooks. According to many students, searching for answers to specific questions about textbook content was not really reading, and it was much easier than what English teachers expected them to do with fiction.

I do believe that secondary students need more instruction in textbook reading, and fortunately there are many resources for teachers to help students with this. (Schoenbach et al., 1999, is an excellent example.) In this section, however, I want to single out fiction assigned in English class as a particularly interesting—and troubling—area of high school students' reading. It is interesting because it arouses such strong passions in individual readers; many readers have written about love affairs with fiction (e.g., Birkerts, 1994; Juhasz, 1994; Rosenthal, 1995; Salwak, 1999; Thomson, 1987). It also is interesting because the people who have chosen to teach it usually do so because of their own love of reading fiction and their desire to help other young people discover the love of reading as someone helped them. Further, it is interesting because it is a vault of cultural wisdom that we, in the United States, have decided that our young people must know. Finally, it is interesting because it is the one art form that is a required part of the core curriculum in high school.

Fiction assigned in English class is troubling, however, because it is a source of conflict between those who believe that it should be taught as a culturally important subject matter (like science, mathematics, and history) and those who believe that it should be experienced as an art form. It is troubling because it generates so much resistance in so many students to particular reading assignments and to reading on a schedule, as well as more general resistance to reading fiction or full-length books. One of the students I interviewed, a young man who plans to become a high school English teacher, said that although he loves to read and wants to read all different kinds of fiction, including the classics, he could not and did not read *The Scarlet Letter* (Hawthorne, 1981). He skimmed it, listened in class, wrote an essay about it, and gained a general sense of it, but he did not read it. He professed admiration for the literary skill with which it was written, but it remained "a bland soap-opera story" that never "caught" him, even though he tried repeatedly to get into it. He came away from the experience convinced that forcing students to read long books they have no interest in is a mistake.

Participants in the debate about what adolescents should be reading in English classes usually come from one of two positions. One side (e.g., Clutter [Clutter & Cope, 1998]; Holbrook, 1984; Prose, 1999) defends the teaching of "high culture" literary texts to adolescents on the grounds that students will never develop either good taste or strong reading skills if they are not assigned works by Charles Dickens, William Shakespeare, and other serious writers. The other side (e.g., Bomer, 1995; Cope [Clutter & Cope, 1998]; Gallo, 2001; Lewis, 1998; Protherough, 1983; Stringer, 1997) defends the teaching of young adult literature, popular genre fiction (such as mysteries and science fiction), and whatever else the students will read, on the grounds that learning to read fiction is a developmental process that requires beginning with the students' current reading levels and progressing at a rate compatible with their acquisition of reading fluency.

The students who participated in this study, like other students in other studies of young people's reading (e.g., Bintz, 1993; Cope, 1997; Evans, 1993; Thomson, 1987; Wilhelm, 1996b), judged required fiction reading harshly. They often used the word *boring* to describe it or complained about the length of books or incomprehensibility of vocabulary or events. When I probed into the specific parts of the text or story that generated these criticisms, I found that the problems usually fell into two large categories: (1) students were in need of more reading instruction tailored to fictional texts, or (2) the stories did not provide the kinds of information or models of characters and events the students were seeking. In Holland's (1975) words, these unsuccessful or boring stories failed to provide an opportunity for the reader to "transform his own fantasies (of a kind that would ordinarily be unconscious) into the conscious social, moral, and intellectual meanings he finds by 'interpreting' the work" (p. 17). Often these two kinds of problems coexisted.

Reading Literature: Art and Angst

The challenge of reading and teaching literature in high school is a topic for another book; however, a discussion of some of the important points is in order because so much dissatisfaction about reading literature was expressed in my interviews with students. Rosenblatt (1978, 1991) points out that literature is often taught and learned in school as if it were an efferent rather than an aesthetic enterprise, that is, as if the reason to read it were to learn characters' names and what the plot involves. But because literature is an art form, it requires multiple readings and time for readers to respond aesthetically, intellectually, emotionally, morally, and spiritually—in other words, with the whole personality—as well as culturally. The concentric circles of response to art end only when responders stop creating them (see Calvino, 1991/1999, for a valuable discussion and demonstration of this point).

Protherough (1983) and Thomson (1987) see learning to read literature as a developmental process in which literary understandings come with maturity. Each researcher describes the stages through which young readers go. Protherough charts the students' development through their understanding of literary themes, such as characters' motivations or how narrative works. Young children have a rudimentary understanding of the same ideas that older students understand in a more sophisticated way. For example, explanations for a character's behavior range from references to "obvious, literal" events in the story "that avoid real explanation" (p. 50) to mature interpretations based on characters' relationships and the "effects of actions on other people" (p. 50). Thomson, however, sees students' responses to literature developing in six stages, each marked by a different quality of understanding. The youngest students care only about the action but later learn to empathize with characters, analogize to real-world experiences, reflect on the significance of events, and so on, until in the sixth stage they are consciously aware of their relationship to the author, recognize textual ideology, and understand the reasons for their own reading of the work.

A developmental conceptualization of students' literary reading is a reminder that young readers are not likely to see an author's wisdom just because it seems to be "there" in the text, as the teacher plainly sees. Making inferences, moving from the literal to the symbolic, and stepping outside the circle of one's own ego and life experience are abilities that take years to develop (see Daiute, 1993, for discussion of connections between developmental and sociocultural theories of learning). The disadvantage of a developmental perspective is that, like all views, it can be misused by a teacher who is looking for a ruler to determine and predict what students should be doing at any particular moment. All teaching requires flexibility and good judgment.

Smith and Wilhelm (2002) build on the work of Vipond and Hunt (1984) to categorize ways of reading short stories that they observed in the young men of their study. They describe seven approaches taken by different readers to different stories: (1) information driven (the literal facts), (2) story driven (getting involved with plot and characters), (3) point driven (ideas, themes, and values), (4) association driven (connection to reader's experience), (5) evaluation driven (thinking the story is good or bad), (6) experience driven (what the reader experiences during reading), and (7) disengaged. Whether the analysis of reading is based on principles of development or orientation, these descriptions of the work that serious fiction requires of readers are enough, in themselves, to explain why reading literature needs careful teaching. To read art well, one must know a great deal about oneself, one's culture, other people, the human race, its history, the world, and relationships between and among all of these. But it is not only what one must know in order to read literature well that makes it extraordinary. One must be in a state of mind and feeling that is open to unmet possibilities of creation and connection, with judgment standing by, watchful but not interfering. One cannot do justice to the "transaction" (Rosenblatt, 1978) between literature and reader in the fact-bound state of mind that the rest of school seems to require. As Britzman (1996) states,

> If education can bear the idea that fiction jeopardizes knowledge, that fiction is curious about its own divisions, differences, wounds—indeed its own otherness—then, I think we might begin to imagine what education can become when what is becoming is the relation, and when the relation refuses to distinguish between education and imagination. (p. xi)

Literature works against the orderly dispensation of knowledge, which is the business of schools. As art, it questions assumptions, challenges authority, and shines light into dark corners. Reading literature is an art itself and needs not only extensive instruction and practice but also instruction and practice in an environment in which education and imagination are not separate. Sumara (1996) sees school life as "anesthetized" and honest literary engagement as an unrecognized antidote to that numbness. He says, "Literary fictions that are meant to provide a space for autobiographical and cultural interpretation are usually stripped of these possibilities in schools and used, instead, as fuel for the curriculum learning machine" (p. 234).

This "curriculum learning machine" does not promote the habit of mind necessary for knowing literature, a habit described by Roth as "requir[ing] silence, some form of isolation, and sustained concentration in the presence of an enigmatic thing" (as cited in

Remnick, 2000, p. 86). So teachers continue to teach literature as if it were just another subject to memorize, and students continue to resent it. Perhaps teachers should give students credit for being bored with these works. Because these young readers are rarely given the time, instruction, or environment for the "sustained concentration" on the "enigmatic thing" (Remnick, 2000), perhaps they are right to find it meaningless. It is invisible as an artistic expression because it was pulled into schools disguised as just another subject. None of the students I spoke with characterized literature as an art form; none saw it as the odd one out among their school subjects. No one, student or teacher, said that literature requires a quality of reader response that is difficult to evoke and maintain in the atmosphere of a school classroom. No one said that entering the worlds of literary creations implicitly challenges the order of school. Yet, such is the case. Literary texts look like other school texts, but they are really alternate lives ready to be lived.

Implications for Teaching Fiction in English Class

Readers do live these alternate lives—but the alternate lives are determined by the interaction between reader and text, so they can and will change from reader to reader and even from one reading to another at a different time by the same reader. Models of transgressive reading provided by, for example, feminist or African American criticism show ways to read that illuminate nontraditional possibilities in texts. We can apply these insights to high school students as readers of fiction. One example of such application occurs in Ricker-Wilson's (1998) account of students reading *To Kill a Mockingbird* (Lee, 1988). Some of Ricker-Wilson's students did not read the book from the intended position in which the author's critiques of racist whites justify her portrayal of African American suffering. Instead, these students identified with the African American characters. They hated the experience of reading about a racist society and vicariously "seeing" African Americans abused. Other students in the class who identified with the white characters of Atticus or Scout did not experience the story as demoralizing, but were pleased with its resolution for these characters. Ricker-Wilson observes that "not only must the teacher address how readers read about someone other than themselves, but how readers read about themselves as marginalized other, even if authorial intent might have been to critique such marginalization" (p. 69).

The five readers in this study evince similar nontraditional readings. When they refuse to become the implied reader (Iser, 1974) of *Kindred*, unwilling or unable psychologically to identify with Dana as she loses control of her life, and unwilling or unable psychologically to travel with her to the U.S. antebellum South, they are revealing not only how they read but also how they feel, think, and imagine. They are revealing what they need and desire as well as what they fear and reject. If teachers are to continue teaching literature, a form of art that interrogates the evil as well as the good in the human soul, they need to be ready to address these various readings and resistances. Teachers need, in fact, to be more than ready for these resistances when they arise. Teachers need to bring them up, to assume that some readers in every class are having the kinds of difficulties with these books that Valisha has with *Kindred*, that Rosa has with *Of Mice and Men*, or that Joel has with *Catcher in the Rye*. The boredom, anxiety, or general discomfort these texts arouse in these readers are interpreted by them as evidence that the book is not a good one and that school reading is not worth doing—in fact, it may be somewhat dangerous, psychologically speaking, as Duke noted when he said that *Go Ask Alice* was "bringin' me down"—and these emotions may, ultimately, persuade some students that reading of any kind is not worth doing. Rather than dismiss the students' experiences with these books as their failure to read or comprehend, educators would do well to recognize that their readings and understandings of the books are based on honest responses. When students do not find a psychological or sociocultural match with a text, teachers can attempt to help them do so. This can begin with helping them understand and articulate what it is about the book that makes them uncomfortable. Identifying the source of discomfort may, in turn, require identification of what stories, characters, or conflicts the reader is most comfortable with. When a reader can describe a kind of "home base" for rewarding reading, he or she is then in a position to look around at other reading experiences and see how they contribute to or threaten the pleasure of the favored texts. Such explorations can help everyone, including the teacher, recognize alternate ways to read particular stories. Once their responses are heard and recognized, students may be open to acknowledging what the writer has accomplished even if they themselves do not love the book. Hearing from other readers who do respond favorably to the story also can help students see why this book is admired enough to be assigned in school. But even if they do not see the value in assigned text, being clear about why a particular text is not enjoyable is valuable in itself. Teachers should be encouraging articulation of ideas, even when those ideas make them uncomfortable because they appear to threaten their control over students' reading.

Teachers also need to give students credit for the reading that they are doing. Rosa's romance novels, Sting's wrestling magazines, and Valisha's Terry McMillan novels all provide critically important experiences and information for these adolescents. If we could spend more time exploring with the students the satisfactions these texts provide, we could encourage their reading and more easily guide them to other reading that also would be engaging and meaningful. We could promote more understanding of what the reading process entails and why we do it. The legitimacy of alternate readings becomes a real part of the English classroom when we encourage everyone to voice genuine opinions, feelings, and reactions. We show our respect for all members of the classroom community when we open the classroom to texts that are, to the students, genuinely meaningful.

One final contribution to the teaching of fiction assigned in English class that these five students make is based on their insistence that they will read if the text is interesting. Popular culture abounds with "texts" of all kinds that interest them. They are finding satisfaction in certain aspects of genre fiction, entertainment, sports, and music that are not commonly included in a school's curriculum but that can provide ways for teachers to show students how canonical texts, to a large extent, deal with the same questions about human existence that popular culture texts do. The questions that these five students are asking about how to be both strong and moral in the adult world are asked by Shakespeare, Steinbeck, Butler, McMillan, romance writers, the writers of professional wrestling scripts, and the writers of television and movie scripts. Duke is asking these questions in his raps, as is Sting. Teachers need to learn how to include big questions and possible answers from all kinds of sources in their efforts to teach students how to read and understand the literary forms of these inquiries. An example of this kind of convergence is described in Hobbs's (1998) article "The Simpsons Meet Mark Twain: Analyzing Popular

Media Texts in the Classroom." Hobbs helps students discover that Twain's project of exposing cultural hypocrisy and greed through humor is very much like that of *The Simpsons*, a cartoon series on television. Another example is Schwartz's (1994) use of a *Far Side* cartoon to stimulate poetry writing. In "Poetry From the Far Side: Risking the Absurd Vulnerability," Schwartz suggests that the work her students do with a popular culture cartoon is more serious than it might look. Smith and Wilhelm (2002) describe other possible big questions around which genuine inquiry can be built, such as "What counts as success?" and "When is disobeying a law justified?" (p. 190). Everything we teach connects with larger fields of knowledge and inquiry. It is a teacher's responsibility to make sure that students see those connections.

A final point in this discussion is that the question of what literature should be read in school needs to be considered carefully. Few students appreciate the high-culture value of reading the classics unless and until a teacher has talked clearly and frankly with them about why the text is valued even though it is difficult to read, and helped them make connections between it and their own lives. Some texts are so difficult for most teenagers to read that a teacher needs an extremely good reason to choose them: *The Scarlet Letter* and *Moby Dick* (Melville, 1981) are two examples of great works that I do not think are appropriate for most high school readers. There are many literary texts that would better serve teachers' goals for their students, including developing an appreciation of what literature can do. It is perfectly appropriate for teachers to tell students about these works—in a book-talk format, perhaps—and offer to provide copies and support if students are interested in reading them. But in assigning texts like these, teachers have been teaching students that reading is boring, a lot of work, and unrewarding. We have been encouraging them to put their creative energies into avoiding reading and faking their knowledge of the text. Further, teachers have been teaching them that classics are boring, onerous, and a waste of time.

The Need for Reading Instruction in High School

Every student in the case studies presented in this book needs reading instruction. It is a mistake to think of learning to read as something that happens exclusively in elementary school; only the first steps of reading are taught or mastered in childhood, and virtually every high school student can benefit from reading instruction (Bintz, 1997; Schoenbach et al., 1999; Wilhelm, Baker, & Dube, 2001). Our current system of hoping that students pick up knowledge of how to make meaning from increasingly sophisticated texts once they have learned the alphabetic code and moved into chapter books is simply not working well enough.

Secondary schools need to teach reading—but English classes are already overloaded with content, especially now that media literacy and multicultural studies have been added to the curriculum. Also, reading is such an important life skill that it should not be tied to one discipline. Consequently, secondary schools need to create separate classes for reading instruction as well as help English teachers see how they can help students read literature more comfortably and profitably.

Schoenbach et al. (1999) describe a program in a San Francisco, California, USA, high school that set up a required course called Academic Literacy for all ninth graders. In this course, which uses an apprenticeship model, the teacher is the master reader for the student apprentices. Although Academic Literacy is a stand-alone course, teachers of other subjects can participate in the program and use the apprenticeship system in their own classrooms. Schoenbach and her fellow researchers do not focus on the problems of teaching literature, but they do describe in detail how students go through steps to develop reading ability in four dimensions: social, cognitive, personal, and knowledge building. In addition, students learn to carry on a metacognitive conversation with themselves and with others about the process of reading in all these dimensions. Pre- and posttesting showed that the students in the program (about 200 ninth graders) raised their reading comprehension scores from a seventh-grade level to a ninth-grade level. They developed confidence in their reading ability and they were able to apply what they learned about reading in Academic Literacy to a wide range of situations, both in and out of school.

An important part of the program is the work that the teachers and researchers do together to teach themselves how to teach adolescents how to read. The basis for this work is "demystifying their own reading processes" (Schoenbach et al., 1999, p. 151) by reading and talking together about reading. Although reading researchers and theorists have long been examining what they do as readers (e.g., Attridge, 1999; Culler, 1980a; Fish, 1980), this is still largely uncharted territory for too many high school teachers. U.S. education does not usually include reading instruction in high school; hence, many secondary teachers do not know how to teach their students to read the texts in their discipline. A teacher's ability to read well does not guarantee that he or she is able to instruct students effectively, especially when the students, as beginners in the discipline, may have blind spots they do not know how to ask about, as happened to Joel when he tried to read his history textbook. English teachers, who often engage in reading easily and almost unconsciously, need to know how to work with students who need explication of every step.

All teachers, not just English teachers, need opportunities to develop an understanding of their own reading processes, as well as those of other readers, in order to clarify for their students what reading involves. Students need consistent and coherent reading support and instruction throughout the school day. Because reading consists of invisible, mental processes, we all need practice in making them visible. Schoenbach et al. (1999) emphasize that being told how reading works is quite different from learning how it works through experience. Teachers, like everyone else, bring their unconscious assumptions as well as conscious beliefs to their work (Bean, 1998; Hamovitch, 1996; Richardson, Anders, Tidwell, & Lloyd, 1992). Teachers must understand that there is no single right way to read or comprehend a text and that the more gaps a text contains, the more creative work a reader can, will, or must do in the process of making meaning of it. Wilhelm (1996b) tells of encouraging a student to visualize the story he was reading. Wilhelm asked him questions that only the reader's imagination could fill in because the author had not specified every detail. Finally, the boy said, "I know what the story says. It's not fair for you to ask me what it doesn't say" (p. 97). If teachers could let students know explicitly about the role of gaps and imagination in reading, so that students could realize that readers do more than decode the letters, these students might be better able to read. They also might be less irritated about it.

Some promising techniques exist for making visible a reader's mental work. Enciso (1992) describes a fascinating procedure, the symbolic representation interview, in which a reader cuts out symbolic shapes to represent a story's characters, narrator, and author as well as the reader and the reader's experiences. The reader retells the story using the cutouts, showing how he or she positions themselves and the other represented figures as the story unfolds. The more freedom the reader has with this process, the more varied are the results. The fifth-grade girl Enciso describes in her case study "created unique representations of such abstract concepts as prediction, an author's relationship with time, and her own awareness of 'being in the book'" (p. 80).

Wilhelm (1996a, 1996b; Wilhelm et al., 2001) and Smith and Wilhelm (2002) describe using this technique. After reading a story and making the cutouts, students used them to tell the story to a partner, the teacher, or a small group, first explaining to the audience what each cutout represented. The students varied, of course, in the extent of their use of cutouts, some including the author while others did not and some using objects or magazine pictures instead of cutouts. The students learned about reading from presenting their stories and listening to others. They learned about their own reading abilities, making their own unconscious processes visible.

Another promising tool for unmasking hidden reading processes is the concept of "the implied reader" (Iser, 1974) and its related concept of "the implied author" (Booth, 1983). These are mental constructs that the reader forms from specific clues and general qualities of the text that imply, for example, that the reader understands the valor of hunting or desires a happy ending even if it is unrealistic. The author, too, presumably constructs an implied reader; Booth (1983) quotes Henry James as saying that "the author make[s] his reader very much as he makes his characters" (p. 49). This idea of interpreting what kind of reader or author is implied by a particular text can be useful in revealing various readings of it. If I feel welcomed by one text and shut out of another, what kind of reader is implied by each? What role do I need to adopt in order to be the implied reader? How do I "read" the implied author of each text? How does thinking about the implied author help me understand that author's purposes and worldview? I may refuse to become the reader implied by a text that offends or distresses me, as perhaps Valisha and Rosa refused to be the reader implied by *Kindred*. Their concepts of the implied reader—and author—of *Kindred* may differ significantly from their teacher's. Sometimes becoming the implied reader does involve pain, a phenomenon of mature reading that adolescents can be explicitly taught and helped to experience productively.

Because all texts, not just literary ones, have implied readers and authors, this concept can be useful in other content areas as well. Authorial interpretation and opinion is an important aspect of history texts; science and math texts, too, are written for certain readers who know certain things and can move, cognitively speaking, in certain ways. When teachers collaborate with students in analyzing the text's expectations of the reader, helping students fill in the inevitable gaps, they are helping students to become better readers as well as better historians, scientists, or mathematicians. In general, teaching students to apply the concept of implied reader and author to all their reading (including movies and magazines) can help them learn to see authors as people who, like readers, have purposes and means. It can help students close the gap between school reading and the personal reading they feel rewarded by.

Thomson (1987) and Wilhelm (1996b) both found that students who examined their reading processes by explaining them to an interviewer were pleased and interested to discover how much they knew about reading and how much they were doing as they read. Schoenbach et al. (1999) also report the satisfaction that readers take in understanding how much they accomplish when they read. I believe that most readers would find similar satisfactions. And although I oppose the practice of adding more and more content to curricula without removing something, I do not see reading instruction as adding to teachers' and students' burdens. On the contrary, we only have to imagine what school life would be like if all students were capable and willing readers to see that not teaching reading—even though we know that many students do not know how to do it and even though we expect them to do it every day—is unprofessional and unproductive.

Primary-grade reading instruction teaches children how to read children's texts; high school students need to be taught to read texts that require more from the reader—more background knowledge, more vocabulary, more experience with rhetorical and structural variations, more gaps for the reader to fill in, more connections to make—in short, more thinking to do. A high school class that focuses on learning to read more demanding texts tells everyone that reading is important, that it can be difficult as well as rewarding, and that it does not happen without knowledge, effort, and practice.

I have argued that talking with students about reading can tell us much that we need to know to make school life better for them and for teachers. Most of what I have discussed in this book comes from my observations and my interpretations of spoken words. But resistance to reading also arises from unrecognized and unspoken sources. None of the students I interviewed said that they needed or wanted to be taught how to read. The teachers are aware that many of the students do not read easily and do not like to read, but they do not know what to do about it. One of them told me that the problem of students' reading comes up in faculty meetings all the time but that none of the teachers has been trained to teach reading, and they would not have room to incorporate it into their overloaded curricula if they had. The fact that reading instruction is so far outside their expertise means that a great deal of work will need to be done to bring about change.

I expect that teachers would resist the idea of a separate reading class because it could mean more work for them—and in the short run, it would. Everyone needs to contribute to making reading processes visible; everyone's consciousness of what reading is needs to be raised. It is a schoolwide community project. In *Becoming a Nation of Readers* (1985), Anderson, Hiebert, Scott, and Wilkinson state without equivocation that "Schools should cultivate an ethos that supports reading" (p. 119), explaining that "[s]chools that are effective in teaching reading are characterized by vigorous leadership, high expectations, emphasis on academic learning, order and discipline, uninterrupted time for learning, and staffs that work together" (p. 119). Teaching reading well is much harder than it looks, especially when students and staff alike are not fully conscious of how much and how varied is the work that readers do.

Teachers might resist a reading class also because they know that many students do not like to read and would complain about more reading. It is discouraging to introduce a change that students resist. But once students begin to see that such a class will help them get along more easily in their print-filled world, they should begin to enjoy some of the increased self-esteem and reading success that Schoenbach et al. (1999) report. Teachers should begin to reap benefits, too, when they understand how to help with reading and students begin to manage reading assignments successfully.

Gere and Gere (1998) describe how the pain of a severe learning disability is confounded by the outward health and beauty of the young woman, Cynthia Gere, who suffers from it. Her mother, Anne Gere, observes that because many people associate disability with deformity, they deny the problem's existence when they cannot see it. Denial is particularly appealing when no cure is possible. If others cannot see the problem and cannot cure it even if it were visible, isn't it simplest to just pretend the problem is not there? Although the Geres' story is much larger than a story of reading disability, it reminded me of the blankness that too many adolescent readers experience in the course of reading at school. It just seems to be the way things are. But blankness should set off warning lights in readers' minds. When readers experience what Joel described as "nothing, really. It's just kinda blank," they are not reading. No schema are activated, no imagining, no connecting, no visualizing, not even feeling is taking place. Duke understands the difference between reading and looking blankly at a page; he says "it's just gonna look like words to me. Like a whole bunch o' words, and I'm like, 'OK, I'm puttin' this up.'" Joel's response is to reread and experience the blankness again; Duke's response is to put the book away. They have not been taught to question, go back to what last made sense and try it again from there, summarize what they have understood so far, identify what textual gaps the reader is supposed to fill, talk to someone about the reading, or seek information about the topic from another source. These strategies need to be taught.

At least as important as teaching readers these strategies for comprehension is exploring the relationship between the reader and text that develops during reading. This relationship begins before reading with the reader's purposes and expectations of what the experience of reading this text will be. Hatt (1976) points out that the first step in reading is deciding to read and the second step is choosing the text to suit whatever purposes the reader has. When schools take away these first two steps and make young people begin at step three, reading, they create an artificial reading situation. School reading is not done for the reader but for a teacher. The five readers in the present study repeatedly emphasized how much they disliked being forced to read an assignment, and I believe that one component of that dislike is having to apply a practice (reading) that could bring pleasure to work that brings little or no personal reward. Choosing one's text is not merely a preference; it may well be a necessary foundation for a successful reading process. Because it is not practical for students to choose all their school texts, it is essential that teachers learn to help students understand their own conscious and unconscious ways of responding to text so that they can then begin to help students formulate useful expectations of the texts teachers believe are beneficial for them to read. Another way to say this is that teachers need to help students accept required reading by making their goals for students' learning from this text explicit, thereby encouraging them to see a purpose in reading the text. Further, teachers need to help students learn to become the implied readers of a variety of texts.

The relationship between text and reader is complicated by the fact that readers may well be unaware of the role that they themselves are playing in this relationship, seeing instead a text that is "interesting" or "boring" or that is "about" whatever they notice first as obvious elements of plot or character. Few students read from what Vipond and Hunt (1984) would call a point-driven orientation; seeing beneath the superficial events of a story (or nonfiction text) takes time, care, thought, guidance, and practice. It also takes a degree of compatibility between the purposes, desires, and fears that a reader brings to a text and opportunities provided by the text to work with those in a satisfying way. Again, the more readers know about the complexities of their reading processes, the better their chances of reading successfully.

Bringing about change will be a long, arduous project. Reordering educators' and students' understanding of reading in high school means reordering our understanding of reading as a whole-person, whole-life practice. It also means reordering our understanding of its role in high school life. The five students in these case studies do use reading in a whole-person, whole-life way, but very little of that reading occurs in or for school. If teachers can heed what students tell them about reading that works for them and reading that does not, teachers can enrich students' lives and their own.

Interview Questions

Interview Questions for Students

Background

1. Code name, age, grade in school
2. Length of time at this school

Reading

1. What comes to your mind when I say *reading?*
2. Can you remember learning how to read?
3. Can you remember someone reading aloud to you?
4. Do you still have times when someone reads aloud to you, in school or out?
5. Do you ever read aloud?
6. a. Walk me through an ordinary school day and tell me where you do any reading.

   b. What are some details about choices you made concerning reading matter, or reading as an activity?
7. Tell me what you do during the Tuesday Sustained Silent Reading periods.
8. What is your favorite kind of reading?
9. What is the worst kind of reading for you?
10. Do you ever get any help with reading?
11. What kind of help would be useful to you?
12. Do you have friends who read more than you do? Less than you do?
13. Do members of your family read at home? At work? What kind of reading?
14. Do you ever read with friends or other people? How does that go?
15. Tell me about reading assignments you get.

16. What happens in your mind when you get a reading assignment?

17. Is there any reading outside school you have to do?

18. Have your ideas or feelings about reading changed as you've grown older?

19. Do you think most people think the same way about reading that you do?

20. How do you think teachers feel about reading?

21. Why should a person read?

School Assignments

1. Do you usually do school assignments?

2. Tell me about a recent assignment.

3. Tell me about a difficult assignment.

4. Walk me through the way you reacted to a difficult assignment, how you dealt with it, and so on.

5. Did you have to do much reading in this assignment?

6. What kind of help was available?

7. Did you use the help?

8. Were you satisfied with your work on this assignment?

Future Plans

1. Do you have a job? Tell me about it.

2. What do you think you'd like to do when you leave high school?

3. How did you get interested in that? Do you know anyone in that job?

4. What kind of preparation do you need for the job?

5. What appeals to you about it?

6. Do your parents have an opinion about your plans for the future?

7. Do you think your future job will involve much reading?

8. Do you see yourself doing much reading in your adult life after you're finished with school?

9. Would you like your children to do a lot of reading?

10. Would you like your children to be good at reading? To enjoy it?

Instruction

1. What do teachers do that helps students become good readers?

2. What do teachers do that helps students get the assigned reading done?

3. Is there anything teachers do that makes it harder to get reading assignments done?

4. Do you see any way to make school reading experiences better for students?

5. Do you think that very many students need to become better readers?

6. Do you think students are learning as much as they need about reading in order to do well in their adult lives?

Wrap-up

1. Is there anything else you would like to say about reading that I didn't ask?

2. Do you have any questions to ask me?

Interview Questions for Parents

Background

1. Student's code name, age, grade in school

2. Does this student have brothers or sisters? How many? Older or younger? Do they all live together?

Reading

1. What do you remember about your child's learning to read? When and where?

2. Did you take part in your child's learning to read?

3. Did the older siblings take part in the child's learning to read? Did anyone else?

4. Did your child read at home when he or she was in elementary school? Middle school?

5. Does he or she read at home now? For school? For pleasure?

6. Does anyone in the family ever read aloud to anyone else?

7. How would you describe your child's attitude toward reading?

8. Have his or her feelings about reading changed as he or she has grown older?

9. Has his or her amount of time spent reading changed as he or she has grown older?

10. How would you describe your own feelings about reading?

11. Does anyone in the family read at home?

12. Does he or she read for information? For work? For school? For pleasure?

Interview Questions for Teachers

Background

1. Name, date

2. How long have you been teaching?

3. How long have you been teaching at this school?

4. Where did you teach before you came here?

5. What grades and subjects do you teach now?

6. What grades and subjects have you taught in the past?

School Policies

1. Do you teach both accelerated and general classes?

2. Do you think that having both accelerated and general classes works well here?

3. Does the school have classes for students who need help with reading?

4. Tell me about who takes those classes, how those classes are selected, and how the classes are taught.

5. How do students feel about taking those classes? How do their parents feel?

6. Tell me about the Tuesday Sustained Silent Reading periods.

Reading

1. What kinds of reading do you assign to your students?

2. What kinds of responses do you get from them?

3. How would you describe the range of your students' reading abilities?

4. Do you see a difference between their reading abilities and their interest in reading?

5. What kind of information did you get in your teacher education classes about teaching reading or helping students with reading assignments?

6. How do you deal with different reading abilities in one class?

7. How do you deal with different reading abilities between classes if you are teaching several sections of the same subject? Is it important to you to keep the sections at the same place in the curriculum?

8. Do you have the freedom to select reading materials for your students?

9. How important do you think being a good reader is for success in school?

10. How important do you think being a good reader is for success in adult life?

11. When you were in high school, what kind of a reader were you? In college?

12. How do you see yourself as a reader now?

13. Do you read both fiction and nonfiction?

14. Do you ever want or need to read something that is difficult or dull?

15. What do you do when you are having trouble reading something?

Summary of Interview Data

Pseudonym	Gender & Ethnicity	Grade	Age	Self-Assessment of Reading Skills	Number of Formal Interviews	Comments
Jack	white male	9	14	can read quickly but dislikes oral reading	1	stopped enjoying reading at age 12
Sam	African American male	9	14	capable but not always interested	1	he and parents focus on good grades
Merry	white female	9	14	experienced, strong reader	1	whole family loves to read
Amber	white female	9	15	reads well when interested	1	reads avidly about romance and relationships
Sting	white male	9	14	capable but dislikes school reading	5	once loved reading, now focused on professional wrestling
Tag	white male	10	15	adequate but slow	1	mother and sister read a lot; father does not
Rocky	white male	10	15	does not feel engaged by most texts	1	reads occasional mystery
Joel	white male	10	15	comprehension ability slipping away	4	read easily and happily until seventh grade

(continued)

Pseudonym	Gender & Ethnicity	Grade	Age	Self-Assessment of Reading Skills	Number of Formal Interviews	Comments
Shelley	African American female	10	15	capable and likes reading aloud	1	deeply bored by school reading
Lannie	African American female	10	16	confident, capable, and experienced	1	enjoys reading in free time
Jamie	African American male	10	15	can read what he needs to	2	dislikes reading but says it is good for him
Joelle	African American female	10	15	confident, experienced reader	1	loves stories about people she relates to
Kristy	white female	10	16	involved, happy reader	1	becomes deeply involved with story
Tina	African American female	10	16	reads well when interested	1	likes reading "about life"
Donley	white male	12	18	adventurous, strong reader	1	mother reads a lot; father does not
Duke	African American male	12	17	capable but prefers auditory learning	3	focused on life outside school
Sonny	white male	12	18	severely handicapped dyslexic	1	reading makes him physically ill
Chip	white male	12	19	adequate but prefers auditory learning	1	likes speeches and horror fiction
Ebony	African American female	12	17	confident, careful reader	1	has always loved to read
Damion	African American male	12	18	adequate when interested	1	likes sports texts but dislikes fiction

(continued)

Pseudonym	Gender & Ethnicity	Grade	Age	Self-Assessment of Reading Skills	Number of Formal Interviews	Comments
Rosa	white female	12	18	fast, strong reader	5	immersed in romance novels
Mitchell	white male	12	18	strong, confident, and experienced	2	wants to be an English teacher
Valisha	African American female	12	18	capable when interested	3	uses reading to learn about adult life
Jerry	African American male	12	18	capable but easily bored	1	enjoyed reading in elementary school
Andrew	white male	12	17	capable, but says he lost vocabulary by reading less in high school	1	has begun to pick up the habit of reading again

References

Alexander, P.A. (1997). Knowledge-seeking and self-schema: A case for the motivational dimensions of exposition. *Educational Psychologist, 32*(2), 83–94.

Allen, J. (1995). *It's never too late: Leading adolescents to lifelong literacy.* Portsmouth, NH: Heinemann.

Alvermann, D.E. (1998). Imagining the possibilities. In D.E. Alvermann, K.A. Hinchman, D.W. Moore, S.F. Phelps, & D.R. Waff (Eds.), *Reconceptualizing the literacies in adolescents' lives* (pp. 353–372). Mahwah, NJ: Erlbaum.

Alvermann, D.E. (1999). Modes of inquiry into studying engaged reading. In J.T. Guthrie & D.E. Alvermann (Eds.), *Engaged reading: Processes, practices, and policy implications* (pp. 134–149). New York: Teachers College Press.

Alvermann, D.E. (2000). Classroom talk about texts: Is it dear, cheap, or a bargain at any price? In B.M. Taylor, M.F. Graves, & P. van den Broek (Eds.), *Reading for meaning: Fostering comprehension in the middle grades* (pp. 136–151). New York: Teachers College Press; Newark, DE: International Reading Association.

Alvermann, D.E., & Hagood, M.C. (2000a). Critical media literacy: Research, theory, and practice in "new times." *The Journal of Educational Research, 93*(3), 193–205.

Alvermann, D.E., & Hagood, M.C. (2000b). Fandom and critical media literacy. *Journal of Adolescent & Adult Literacy, 43,* 436–446.

Anderson, R.C., Hiebert, E.H., Scott, J.A., & Wilkinson, I.A.G. (1985). *Becoming a nation of readers: The report of the Commission on Reading.* Washington, DC: National Institute of Education.

Applebee, A. (1991). Environments for language teaching and learning: Contemporary issues and future directions. In J. Flood, J.M. Jensen, D. Lapp, & J.R. Squire (Eds.), *Handbook of research on teaching the English language arts* (pp. 549–558). New York: Macmillan.

Attridge, D. (1999). Innovation, literature, ethics: Relating to the other. *PMLA, 114,* 20–31.

Atwell, N. (1998). *In the middle: New understandings about writing, reading, and learning* (2nd ed.). Portsmouth, NH: Boynton/Cook.

Ball, M.R. (1990). *Professional wrestling as ritual drama in American popular culture.* Lewiston, NY: Edwin Mellen.

Bandura, A. (1982). Self-efficacy mechanism in human agency. *American Psychologist, 36,* 122–147.

Barbieri, M. (1995). *Sounds from the heart: Learning to listen to girls.* Portsmouth, NH: Heinemann.

Beach, R., & Freedman, K. (1992). Responding as a cultural act: Adolescent responses to magazine ads and short stories. In J. Many & C. Cox (Eds.), *Reader stance and literary understanding: Exploring the theories, research, and practice.* Westport, CT: Ablex.

Bean, T.W. (1998). Teacher literacy histories and adolescent voices: Changing content-area classrooms. In D.E. Alvermann, K.A. Hinchman, D.W. Moore, S.F. Phelps, & D.R. Waff (Eds.), *Reconceptualizing the literacies in adolescents' lives* (pp. 149–170). Mahwah, NJ: Erlbaum.

Bean, T.W., & Moni, K. (2003). Developing students' critical literacy: Exploring identity construction in young adult fiction. *Journal of Adolescent & Adult Literacy, 46*, 638–648.

Beers, K. (2002). *When kids can't read: What teachers can do. A guide for teachers 6–12.* Portsmouth, NH: Boynton/Cook.

Belenky, M.F., Clinchy, B.M., Goldberger, N.R., & Tarule, J.M. (1986). *Women's ways of knowing: The development of self, voice, and mind.* New York: Basic Books.

Bell, J.S. (1993). Finding the commonplaces of literacy. *Curriculum Inquiry, 23*, 131–153.

Berlyne, D.E. (1974). The new experimental aesthetics. In D.E. Berlyne (Ed.), *Studies in the new experimental aesthetics* (pp. 1–25). New York: Wiley.

Bhabba, H.K. (1994). *The location of culture.* New York: Routledge.

Bintz, W.P. (1993). Resistant readers in secondary education: Some insights and implications. *Journal of Reading, 36*, 604–615.

Bintz, W.P. (1997). Exploring reading nightmares of middle and secondary school teachers. *Journal of Adolescent & Adult Literacy, 41*, 12–24.

Birkerts, S. (1994). *The Gutenberg elegies: The fate of reading in an electronic age.* New York: Ballantine.

Bleich, D. (1976). Pedagogical directions in subjective criticism. *College English, 37*(5), 454–467.

Bleich, D. (1978). *Subjective criticism.* Baltimore: The Johns Hopkins University Press.

Bleich, D. (1986a). Gender interests in reading and language. In E.A. Flynn & P.P. Schweickart (Eds.), *Gender and reading: Essays on readers, texts, and contexts* (pp. 234–266). Baltimore: The Johns Hopkins University Press.

Bleich, D. (1986b). Intersubjective reading. *New Literary History, 17*, 401–421.

Bomer, R. (1995). *Time for meaning: Crafting literate lives in middle and high school.* Portsmouth, NH: Heinemann.

Booth, W.C. (1983). *The rhetoric of fiction* (2nd ed.). Chicago: University of Chicago Press.

Bosworth, K. (1995). Caring for others and being cared for: Students talk caring in school. *Phi Delta Kappan, 76*(9), 686–693.

Brandt, D. (1989). Remembering writing, remembering reading. *College Composition and Communication, 45*, 459–479.

Britzman, D.P. (1996). Foreword. In D.J. Sumara, *Private readings in public: Schooling the literary imagination* (ix–xi). New York: Peter Lang.

Bruner, J. (1986). *Actual minds, possible worlds.* Cambridge, MA: Harvard University Press.

Calvino, I. (1999). *Why read the classics?* (M. McLaughlin, Trans.). New York: Pantheon. (Original work published 1991)

Cayton, A., Perry, E.I., & Winkler, A.M. (1998). *America: Pathways to the present.* Englewood Cliffs, NJ: Prentice Hall.

Chall, J.S., Bissex, G.L., Conard, S.S., & Harris-Sharples, S. (1996). *Qualitative assessment of text difficulty: A practical guide for teachers and writers.* Cambridge, MA: Brookline.

Chandler, K. (2000). Rethinking the reading-writing workshop: Tensions and negotiations between a Stephen King reader and her teacher. *Reading Research and Instruction, 39*(2), 135–159.

Christian-Smith, L.K. (1990). *Becoming a woman through romance.* New York: Routledge.

Christian-Smith, L.K. (1993). Sweet dreams: Gender and desire in teen romance novels. In L.K. Christian-Smith (Ed.), *Texts of desire: Essays on fiction, feminity and schooling* (pp. 45–68). London: Falmer.

Clutter, T.J., & Cope, J. (1998). Beyond "Voices of Readers": A dialogue between teachers. *English Journal, 87*(2), 81–87.

Coen, S.J. (1994). *Between author and reader: A psychoanalytic approach to writing and reading.* New York: Columbia University Press.

Cohn, J. (1988). *Romance and the erotics of property: Mass-market fiction for women.* Durham, NC: Duke University Press.

Cone, J.K. (1994). Appearing acts: Creating readers in a high school English class. *Harvard Educational Review, 64*(4), 450–473.

Cook-Gumpertz, J. (1986). *The social construction of literacy.* Cambridge, UK: Cambridge University Press.

Cope, J. (1997). Beyond "Voices of Readers": Students on school's effects on reading. *English Journal, 86*(3), 18–23.

Corcoran, B. (1990). Reading, re-reading, resistance: Versions of reader response. In M. Hayhoe & S. Parker (Eds.), *Reading and response.* Buckingham, UK: Open University Press.

Corcoran, B. (1992). Reader stance: From willed aesthetic to discursive construction. In J. Many & C. Cox (Eds.), *Reader stance and literary understanding: Exploring the theories, research, and practice* (pp. 49–71). Westport, CT: Ablex.

Crawford, M., & Chaffin, R. (1986). The reader's construction of meaning: Cognitive research on gender and comprehension. In E.A. Flynn & P.P. Schweickart (Eds.), *Gender and reading Essays on readers, texts, and contexts* (pp. 3–30). Baltimore: The Johns Hopkins University Press.

Csikszentmihalyi, M., & Larson, R. (1984). *Being adolescent: Conflict and growth in the teenage years.* New York: Basic Books.

Culler, J. (1975). *Structuralist poetics: Structuralism, linguistics, and the study of literature.* Ithaca, NY: Cornell University Press.

Culler, J. (1980a). Literary competence. In J.P. Tompkins (Ed.), *Reader-response criticism: From formalism to post-structuralism* (pp. 101–117). Baltimore: The Johns Hopkins University Press.

Culler, J. (1980b). Prolegomena to a theory of reading. In S.R. Suleiman & I. Crosman (Eds.), *The reader in the text: Essays on audience and interpretation* (pp. 46–66). Princeton, NJ: Princeton University Press.

Daiute, C. (1993). Youth genres and literacy: Links between sociocultural and developmental theories. *Language Arts, 70*(5), 402–416.

Daniels, H. (1994). *Literature circles: Voice and choice in the student-centered classroom.* York, ME: Stenhouse.

DeBlase, G. (2003). Acknowledging agency while accommodating romance: Girls negotiating meaning in literacy transactions. *Journal of Adolescent & Adult Literacy, 48*, 624–635.

Denzin, N.K. (1994). The art and politics of interpretation. In N.K. Denzin & Y.S. Lincoln (Eds.), *Handbook of qualitative research* (pp. 500–515). Thousand Oaks, CA: Sage.

Dillon, D.R. (1989). Showing them that I want them to learn and that I care about who they are: A microethnography of the social organization of a secondary low-track English-reading classroom. *American Educational Research Journal, 26*(2), 227–259.

Eagleton, T. (1983). *Literary theory: An introduction.* Minneapolis: University of Minnesota Press.

Eagleton, T. (1996). *The illusions of postmodernism.* Oxford, UK: Blackwell.

Eckert, P. (1989). *Jocks and burnouts: Social categories and identity in the high school.* New York: Teachers College Press.

Enciso, P. (1992). Creating the story world: A case study of a young reader's engagement strategies and stances. In J. Many & C. Cox (Eds.), *Reader stance and literary understanding: Exploring the theories, research, and practice* (pp. 75–102). Westport, CT: Ablex.

Evans, R. (1993). Learning "schooled literacy": The literate life histories of mainstream student readers and writers. *Discourse Processes, 16*(3), 317–340.

Fetterley, J. (1979). *Resisting reader: A feminist approach to American fiction.* Bloomington: Indiana University Press.

Fish, S. (1980). Literature in the reader: Affective stylistics. In J.P. Tompkins (Ed.), *Reader-response criticism: From formalism to post-structuralism* (pp. 70–100). Baltimore: The Johns Hopkins University Press.

Finders, M.J. (1997). *Just girls: Hidden literacies and life in junior high.* New York: Teachers College Press.

Fleischer, C. (1995). *Composing teacher-research: A prosaic history.* Albany: State University of New York Press.

Fry, D. (1985). *Children talk about books: Seeing themselves as readers.* London: Taylor & Francis.

Gadamer, H.G. (1975). *Truth and method.* New York: Seabury Press.

Gallo, D.R. (2001). How classics create an aliterate society. *English Journal, 90*(3), 33–39.

Gee, J.P. (1989). Literacy, discourse, and linguistics: Introduction. *Journal of Education, 171*(1), 5–17.

Gee, J.P. (1991). A linguistic approach to narrative. *Journal of Narrative and Life History, 1*, 15–39.

Gee, J. (1992). Socio-cultural approaches to literacy (literacies). *Annual Review of Applied Linguistics, 12*, 31–48.

Gere, A.R., & Gere, C.M. (1998). Living with fetal alcohol syndrome/fetal alcohol effect (FAS/FAE). *Michigan Quarterly Review, 37*, 396–408.

Gilligan, C. (1982). *In a different voice: Psychological theory and women's development.* Cambridge, MA: Harvard University Press.

Giroux, H. (1983). *Theory and resistance in education: A pedagogy for the opposition.* Westport, CT: Bergin & Garvey.

Gough, P.B., & Hillinger, M.L. (1980). Learning to read: An unnatural act. *Bulletin of the Orton Society, 30*, 171–176.

Gregory, M. (1997). The many-headed hydra of theory vs. the unifying mission of teaching. *College English, 59*, 42–58.

Hagood, M.C. (2002). Critical literacy for whom? *Reading Research and Instruction, 41*, 247–266.

Hamovitch, B.A. (1996). Socialization without voice: An ideology of hope for at-risk students. *Teachers College Record, 98*(2), 286–306.

Hatt, F. (1976). *The reading process: A framework for analysis and description.* London: Clive Bingley.

Heath, S.B. (1980). The functions and uses of literacy. *Journal of Communication, 30*(1), 123–133.

Heath, S.B. (1983). *Ways with words: Language, life, and work in communities and classrooms.* New York: Cambridge University Press.

Hersch, P. (1998). *A tribe apart: A journey into the heart of American adolescence.* New York: Ballantine.

Hidi, S.E. (1995). A reexamination of the role of attention in learning from text. *Educational Psychology Review, 7*, 323–350.

Hirsch, E.D., Jr. (1987). *Cultural literacy: What every American needs to know.* New York: Vintage.

Hobbs, R. (1998). The Simpsons meet Mark Twain: Analyzing popular media texts in the classroom. *English Journal, 87*(1), 49–51.

Holbrook, D. (1984). [Review of the book *Developing response to fiction*]. *Educational Research, 26*, 149–151.

Holland, N.N. (1975). *5 Readers Reading.* New Haven, CT: Yale University Press.

Holland, N.N. (1980). Unity Identity Text Self. In J.P. Tompkins (Ed.), *Reader-response criticism: From formalism to post-structuralism* (pp. 118–133). Baltimore: The Johns Hopkins University Press.

Hosking, N.J., & Teberg, A.S. (1998). Bridging the gap: Aligning current practice and evolving expectations for middle years literacy programs. *Journal of Adolescent & Adult Literacy, 41*, 332–340.

Howe, K., & Eisenhart, M. (1990). Standards for qualitative (and quantitative) research: A prolegomenon. *Educational Researcher, 19*, 2–9.

Hynds, S. (1997). *On the brink: Negotiating literature and life with adolescents.* New York: Teachers College Press; Newark, DE: International Reading Association.

Iser, W. (1971). Indeterminacy and the reader's response in prose fiction. In J.H. Miller (Ed.), *Aspects of narrative* (pp. 1–45). New York: Columbia University Press.

Iser, W. (1974). *The implied reader: Patterns of communication in prose fiction from Bunyan to Beckett.* Baltimore: The Johns Hopkins University Press.

Iser, W. (1978). *The act of reading: A theory of aesthetic response.* Baltimore: The Johns Hopkins University Press.

Iser, W. (1993). *The fictive and the imaginary: Charting literary anthropology.* Baltimore: The Johns Hopkins University Press.

Iser, W. (2000). Do I write for an audience? *PMLA, 115*, 310–314.

Ivey, G. (1999). Reflections on teaching struggling middle school readers. *Journal of Adolescent & Adult Literacy, 42*, 372–381.

Juhasz, S. (1994). *Reading from the heart: Women, literature, and the search for true love*. New York: Viking.

Junior Achievement. (1996). *Economics student text*. Colorado Springs, CO: Author.

Krashen, S. (1993). *The power of reading: Insights from the research*. Englewood, CO: Libraries Unlimited.

Kutz, E., & Roskelly, H. (1991). *An unquiet pedagogy: Transforming practice in the English classroom*. Portsmouth, NH: Boynton/Cook.

Langer, J.A. (1990). The process of understanding: Reading for literary and informative purposes. *Research in the Teaching of English, 24*(3), 229–260.

Langer, S. (1957). *Problems of art*. New York: Scribner.

LeDoux, J.E. (1994, June). Emotion, memory and the brain. *Scientific American, 270*, 50–57.

Levine, M. (1990). *Keeping a head in school: A student's book about learning abilities and learning disorders*. Cambridge, MA: Educators' Publishing Services.

Lewis, C. (1998). Rock 'n' roll and horror stories: Students, teachers, and popular culture. *Journal of Adolescent & Adult Literacy, 42*, 116–120.

Mahiri, J. (1994). Reading rites and sports: Motivation for adaptive literacy of young African-American males. In B.J. Moss (Ed.), *Literacy across communities* (pp. 121–146). Cresskill, NJ: Hampton Press.

Mazer, S. (1998). *Professional wrestling: Sport and spectacle*. Jackson: University Press of Mississippi.

McNall, S.A. (1981). *Who is in the house? A psychological study of two centuries of women's fiction in America, 1795 to the present*. New York: Elsevier Science.

Menkowitz, R. (1999, September). Editorial. *World of Wrestling, 51 +*.

Millard, E. (1997). *Differently literate: Boys, girls and the schooling of literacy*. London: Falmer.

Miller, P.H. (1989). Theories of adolescent development. In J. Worell & F. Danner (Eds.), *The adolescent as decision maker: Applications to development and education* (pp. 13–46). New York: Academic.

Modleski, T. (1982). *Loving with a vengeance: Mass-produced fantasies for women*. Hamden, CT: Archon Books.

Moffitt, M.A. (1987, May). Understanding the appeal of the romance novel for the adolescent girl: A reader-response approach. (Report No. CS-008-886). Paper presented at the annual meeting of the International Communication Association, Montreal, Quebec, Canada. (ERIC Document Reproduction Service No. ED284190)

Moje, E. (1996). "I teach students, not subjects": Teacher-student relationships as contexts for secondary literacy. *Reading Research Quarterly, 31*, 172–195.

Moje, E.B. (2000). *"All the stories that we have": Adolescents' insights about literacy and learning in secondary schools*. Newark, DE: International Reading Association.

Moje, E.B. (2002). Re-framing adolescent literacy research for new times: Studying youth as a resource. *Reading Research and Instruction, 41*(3), 211–228.

Moje, E.B., Dillon, D.R., & O'Brien, D.G. (2000). Reexamining roles of learner, text, and context in secondary literacy. *Journal of Educational Research, 93*(3), 165–180.

Moniuszko, L.K. (1992). Motivation: Reaching reluctant readers age 14–17. *Journal of Reading, 36,* 32–34.

Morrison, T. (1993). *Playing in the dark: Whiteness and the literary imagination.* New York: Vintage.

Nicholson, T. (1984). The confusing world of high school reading. *Australian Journal of Reading, 7*(3), 115–125.

Oldfather, P. (1995). Commentary: What's needed to maintain and extend motivation for literacy in the middle grades. *Journal of Reading, 38,* 420–422.

Palincsar, A.S., & Brown, A.L. (1989). Classroom dialogues to promote self-regulated comprehension. In J. Brophy (Ed.), *Advances in research on teaching: A research annual, 1989* (pp. 35–72). London: JAI Press.

Phelps, S.F. (1998). Adolescents and their multiple literacies. In D.E. Alvermann, K.A. Hinchman, D.W. Moore, S.F. Phelps, & D.R. Waff (Eds.), *Reconceptualizing the literacies in adolescents' lives* (pp. 353–372). Mahwah, NJ: Erlbaum.

Prose, F. (1999, September). I know why the caged bird cannot read: How American high school students learn to loathe literature. *Harper's Magazine,* 76–80, 82–84.

Protherough, R. (1983). *Developing response to fiction.* Buckingham, UK: Open University Press.

Purcell-Gates, V. (1995). *Other people's words: The cycle of low literacy.* Cambridge, MA: Harvard University Press.

Purves, A.C. (1991). Indeterminate texts, responsive readers, and the idea of difficulty in literature. In A.C. Purves (Ed.), *The idea of difficulty in literature* (pp. 157–170). Albany: State University of New York Press.

Purves, A.C., Rogers, T., & Soter, A.O. (1995). *How porcupines make love III: Readers, texts, cultures in the response-based literature classroom.* White Plains, NY: Longman.

Radway, J. (1991). *Reading the romance: Women, patriarchy, and popular literature.* Chapel Hill, NC: University of North Carolina Press.

Remnick, D. (2000, May 8). Into the clear. *The New Yorker,* 84–89.

Rich, A. (1979). *On lies, secrets, and silence: Selected prose.* New York: W.W. Norton.

Richardson, J.S. (1996). *An English teacher's survival guide: Reaching and teaching adolescents.* New York: Pippin.

Richardson, V., Anders, P., Tidwell, D., & Lloyd, C. (1992). The relationship between teachers' beliefs and practices in reading comprehension instruction. *American Educational Research Journal, 28,* 559–586.

Ricker-Wilson, C. (1998). When the mockingbird becomes an albatross: Reading and resistance in the language arts classroom. *English Journal, 87*(3), 67–72.

Riessman, C.K. (1993). *Narrative analysis.* London: Sage.

Robb, L. (2000). *Teaching reading in middle school: A strategic approach to teaching reading that improves comprehension and thinking.* New York: Scholastic.

Roberts, T.J. (1990). *An aesthetics of junk fiction.* Athens, GA: University of Georgia Press.

Rosenblatt, L.M. (1978). *The reader, the text, the poem: The transactional theory of the literary work.* Carbondale: Southern Illinois University Press.

Rosenblatt, L.M. (1991). Literary theory. In J. Flood, J.M. Jensen, D. Lapp, & J.R. Squire (Eds.), *Handbook of research on teaching the English language arts* (pp. 57–62). New York: Macmillan.

Rosenthal, N. (1995). *Speaking of reading.* Portsmouth, NH: Heinemann.

Rothenberg, S.S., & Watts, S.M. (2000). Students with learning difficulties meet Shakespeare: Using a scaffolded reading experience. In D.W. Moore, D.E. Alvermann, & K.A. Hinchman (Eds.), *Struggling adolescent readers: A collection of teaching strategies* (pp. 148–156). Newark, DE: International Reading Association.

Rothkopf, E.Z., & Billington, M.J. (1979). Goal-guided learning from text: Inferring a descriptive processing model from inspection times and eye movements. *Journal of Educational Psychology, 71*(3), 310–327.

Salwak, D. (Ed.). (1999). *A passion for books.* New York: St. Martin's.

Sarland, C. (1991). *Young people reading: Culture and response.* Buckingham, UK: Open University Press.

Schoenbach, R., Greenleaf, C., Cziko, C., & Hurwitz, L. (1999). *Reading for understanding: A guide to improving reading in middle and high school classrooms.* San Francisco: Jossey-Bass.

Schunk, D.H. (1991). Self-efficacy and academic motivation. *Educational Psychologist, 26,* 207–231.

Schwartz, P.B. (1994). Poetry from the "Far Side": Risking the absurd vulnerability. *English Journal, 83*(18), 72–76.

Schweickart, P.P. (1986). Reading ourselves: Toward a feminist theory of reading. In E.A. Flynn & P.P. Schweickart (Eds.), *Gender and reading: Essays on readers, texts, and contexts* (pp. 31–62). Baltimore: The Johns Hopkins University Press.

Shank, R.C. (1979). Interestingness: Controlling inferences. *Artificial Intelligence, 12,* 273–297.

Slatoff, W.J. (1970). *With respect to readers: Dimensions of literary response.* Ithaca, NY: Cornell University Press.

Smith, M.W. (1992). Submission versus control in literary transactions. In J. Many & C. Cox (Eds.), *Reader stance and literary understanding: Exploring the theories, research, and practice* (pp. 143–161). Westport, CT: Ablex.

Smith, M., & Wilhelm, J.D. (2002). *"Reading don't fix no Chevys": Literacy in the lives of young men.* Portsmouth, NH: Boynton/Cook.

Stanovich, K.E. (1986). Matthew effects in reading: Some consequences of individual differences in the acquisition of literacy. *Reading Research Quarterly, 21,* 360–407.

Sting. (1999, September). *World of Wrestling, 23.*

Street, B.V. (1984). *Literacy in theory and practice.* Cambridge, UK: Cambridge University Press.

Street, B.V. (1986). Literacy practices and literacy myths. (Report No. LPLM 2d.10.86 2563). Sussex, UK: University of Sussex. (ERIC Document Reproduction Service No. ED295474)

Stringer, S.A. (1997). *Conflict and connection: The psychology of young adult literature.* Portsmouth, NH: Boynton/Cook.

Stuckey, J.E. (1990). *The violence of literacy.* Portsmouth, NH: Boynton/Cook.

Sumara, D.J. (1996). *Private readings in public: Schooling the literary imagination.* New York: Peter Lang.

Thomson, J. (1987). *Understanding teenagers' reading: Reading processes and the teaching of literature.* London: Methuen.

Tompkins, J.P. (1980). The reader in history: The changing shape of literary response. In J.P. Tompkins (Ed.), *Reader-response criticism: From formalism to post-structuralism* (pp. 201–232). Baltimore: The Johns Hopkins University Press.

Trites, R. (2000). *Disturbing the universe: Power and repression in adolescent literature.* Iowa City: University of Iowa Press.

Vipond, D., & Hunt, R. (1984). Point-driven understanding: Pragmatic and cognitive dimensions of literary reading. *Poetics, 13,* 261–277.

Vygotsky, L.S. (1980). The genesis of higher mental functions. In J.V. Wertsch (Ed.), *The concept of activity in Soviet psychology* (pp. 144–188). Armonk, NY: M.E. Sharpe.

Wade, S. (1992). How interest affects learning from text. In K.A. Renninger, S. Hidi, & A. Krapp (Eds.), *The role of interest in learning and development* (pp. 255–277). Hillsdale, NJ: Erlbaum.

Walker, E. (1981). *Doors to more mature reading.* Chicago: American Library Association.

Warburton, D.M. (1987). Emotional and motivational determinants of attention and memory. In V. Hamilton, G.H. Bower, & N.H. Frijda (Eds.), *Cognitive perspectives on emotion and motivation* (Vol. 44, pp. 195–219). London: Kluwer Academic/Plenum.

Wells, M.C. (1996). *Literacies lost: When students move from a progressive middle school to a traditional high school.* New York: Teachers College Press.

Whitaker, F. (Director). (1995). *Waiting to exhale* [Motion picture]. United States: Twentieth Century Fox.

Wiggins, G., & McTighe, J. (1998). *Understanding by design.* Alexandria, VA: Association for Supervision and Curriculum Development.

Wilhelm, J.D. (1995). Reading is seeing: Using visual response to improve the literary reading of reluctant readers. *Journal of Reading Behavior, 27*(4), 467–503.

Wilhelm, J.D. (1996a). *Standards in practice, grades 6–8.* Urbana, IL: National Council of Teachers of English.

Wilhelm, J.D. (1996b). *"You gotta be the book": Teaching engaged and reflective reading with adolescents.* New York: Teachers College Press.

Wilhelm, J.D., Baker, T.N., & Dube, J. (2001). *Strategic reading: Guiding students to lifelong literacy, 6–12.* Portsmouth, NH: Boynton/Cook.

Wood, S.S., Bruner, J.S., & Ross, G. (1976). The role of tutoring in problem solving. *Journal of Child Psychology and Psychiatry, 17,* 89–100.

Worthy, J. (1998). "On every page someone gets killed!" Book conversations you don't hear in school. *Journal of Adolescent & Adult Literacy, 41,* 508–517.

Works Discussed By Students

Alcott, L.M. (1868). *Little women; or, Meg, Jo, Beth, and Amy.* Boston: Roberts Brothers.

Anonymous. (1971). *Go ask Alice.* New York: Aladdin.

Butler, O. (1979). *Kindred.* New York: Doubleday.

Clark, M.H. (1977). *A stranger is watching.* New York: Simon & Schuster.

Conrad, J. (1925). The lagoon. In *Tales of unrest* (pp. 187–204). New York: Doubleday.

Crichton, M. (1999). *Jurassic Park.* New York: Ballantine.

Faulkner, W. (1978). A rose for Emily. In R.V. Cassill (Ed.), *The Norton anthology of short fiction* (pp. 479–486). New York: W.W. Norton.

Foley, M. (1999). *Have a nice day! A tale of blood and sweatsocks.* New York: Regan.

Frank, A. (1993). *Anne Frank: The diary of a young girl* (B.M. Mooyart, Trans.). New York: Bantam.

Hawthorne, N. (1981). *The scarlet letter.* New York: Bantam.

Kesey, K. (1989). *One flew over the cuckoo's nest.* New York: New American Library.

King, S. (1994). *Cujo.* New York: New American Library.

Lee, H. (1988). *To kill a mockingbird.* Boston: Little, Brown.

Lessing, D. (1965). No witchcraft for sale. In *African stories* (pp. 67–74). New York: Simon & Schuster.

McCord, J. (1967). *Little dog lost.* In B. Rosmond (Ed.), *Seventeen from seventeen: An anthology of stories* (pp. 215–224). New York: Macmillan.

McMillan, T. (1989). *Disappearing acts.* New York: Viking.

McMillan, T. (1992). *Waiting to exhale.* New York: Viking.

McMillan, T. (1995). *Mama.* New York: Pocket Books.

Melville, H. (1981). *Moby Dick.* New York: Bantam.

Miller, A. (1998). *Death of a salesman.* New York: Penguin.

Poe, E.A. (1978). The fall of the house of Usher. In R.V. Cassill (Ed.), *The Norton anthology of short fiction* (pp. 1126–1140). New York: W.W. Norton.

Salinger, J.D. (1991). *Catcher in the rye.* Boston: Little, Brown.

Shakespeare, W. (1992). *Julius Caesar.* New York: Washington Square Press.

Shakespeare, W. (1992). *Romeo and Juliet.* New York: Washington Square Press.

Shakespeare, W. (1993). *Othello.* New York: Washington Square Press.

Steinbeck, J. (1993). *Of mice and men.* New York: Penguin.

Thomas, R. (1996). *Rats saw God.* New York: Simon Pulse.

Index